Voices of a War
Remembered

Voices of a War Remembered

An Oral History of Canadians in World War Two

Bill McNeil

Doubleday Canada Limited

Canadian Cataloguing in Publication Data

Main entry under title:

Voices of a war remembered

Includes index.
ISBN 0-385-25353-2

1. World War, 1939-1945 – Personal narratives,
Canadian.   2. World War, 1939-1945 – Canada.
I. McNeil, Bill, 1924-

D811.A2V65 1991   940.54'8171   C91-094423-7

Jacket design: Tania Craan
Cover photos courtesy The National Archives of Canada
Printed and bound in the USA

Published in Canada by
Doubleday Canada Limited
105 Bond Street
Toronto, Ontario
M5B 1Y3

Dedicated to the memory of all those
who didn't come home, including my many
friends in The Cape Breton Highlanders.

TABLE OF CONTENTS

Acknowledgements

THERE ARE many people to thank after the production of a book such as this. First, of course, there are all those who told me their stories so willingly and contributed so much of their time in so doing. I was tremendously impressed by their recall of events half a century ago right down to the tiniest detail. I was struck, too, by how most had been able, over the years, to wash away the horror of it all, and mostly remember the happier times. Some reluctantly brought forward the darker side of war in order that the picture I was trying to paint would be more complete.

This book does not pretend to be any kind of an official record. Rather, it is a book of memories; memories of what it was like for some Canadians to have lived through the most terrible war ever to be visited upon mankind. Some of these memories have made me laugh while others have made me cry. Collectively, they have helped me relive what were probably the most important and formative years of my life.

There are others who have helped greatly in this task, if such an enjoyable project can ever be called a task. John Pearce, the Editor-in-Chief of Doubleday Canada, had the idea for such a book in the first place and entrusted me with the responsibility of bringing it off. I thank him for the opportunity.

Jill Lambert of the Doubleday editorial staff took on the massive job of deciding what should stay in the final manuscript. This was not an easy job because each and every memory from each and every person seemed so important. In the end, the elimination was done by a process of reducing duplication and similarity. If the story we were considering seemed too much like any other story we had already selected, one of them had to go. Thank you, Jill, for being the final arbiter and thank you also for being the "compleat" editor. It helped greatly to have someone from the West Coast keep "an eye on the bye from the Bay." In this instance the twain did indeed meet.

More thanks to the staff at Doubleday, especially Christine Harrison for her meticulous copy-edit, and Maggie Reeves for getting the book done on time.

I thank my family: my wife, Eileen, and my offspring; Russell in Nanaimo, Breton and Dawn in Toronto. I can no longer call them "the kids" but nevertheless, there were times when the book kept me from being there at important times in their lives. It helped that they forgave me easily.

To all those others who helped in so many ways, thank you from the bottom of my heart.

Preface

WHEN THE Second World War began, Canada was a relatively small nation of about twelve million people. Yet in terms of its contribution to the Allied war effort, it was a major player indeed. For the majority of Canadians, the war was an "all-or-nothing-at-all" proposition. For a while it seemed as though every man, woman, and child was involved in one way or another. By the end of the war in 1945, 40 out of every 100 Canadian men had entered the armed forces for an approximate total of 735,000 males between the ages of 18 and 45. That's an astounding figure in a country with a population as small as ours was at that time.

The largest percentage was, of course, in the army, around half a million, followed by the air force with 180,000 and the navy with roughly 90,000. In addition, we had nearly 36,000 women in all three services. Yet, when Canada entered the war, its armed forces totalled only slightly better than 10,000!

The rising strength of Canada's armed forces put us third among the United Nations in naval power and fourth in air power. Our country also became the fourth largest supplier of war equipment and one of the chief suppliers of food for the Allies.

Our pre-war merchant navy had a strength of only 1,460 seamen but by war's end this had risen to over 8,000. It was our merchant navy that bore the brunt of the burden of keeping the beleaguered British Isles supplied with food and other necessities without which they could not have survived.

If Canada, as is often said, became a nation during World War One, she truly cemented that nationhood during the Second World War.

Introduction

SOMETIMES it seems like yesterday, and at others it seems a million years ago, but it is half a century since the whole world, at the instigation of one madman, went mad itself.

In the beginning, it was a strange and unusual time of mixed emotions. On the one hand, there was a kind of exultation in Canada because, after a decade of hand-to-mouth existence in a devastating depression, when every new day was just as uneventful as the last, we, the common people, had finally achieved a small measure of importance.

Governments which had seemingly made it their business to ignore the needs and the very existence of ordinary mortals, suddenly found us interesting and useful. Instead of wishing that we'd all just disappear, they found they needed us to fill uniforms which had been lying unused since the last war. They needed us now to fill the factories that hadn't produced anything for a decade. Suddenly, they were ready to welcome us and get us going on the important business of war.

It was pretty heady stuff though, being sought after; we weren't used to that. We were more accustomed to being told in large print that there was nothing for us and that there was no need to apply. Then, as if by magic, the tune changed and there they were, begging us to apply.

For the unemployed it seemed like the opportunity they had been waiting for — a job with three guaranteed meals, a dollar and thirty cents a day, a suit of khaki or blue-coloured clothing and all the glamour a poor boy could ask for.

1

The recruiting offices couldn't keep up with the demand. In they came from the farms and the villages, the towns and the cities, the outports, the mountains and the plains. They came in the mornings before the doors were opened, and they were there at night waiting to be first in line when the offices opened the following day. All that most of them wanted was a job, and a chance to prove that they were men capable of doing that job. For ten whole years before, these ragged youngsters, the cream of our youth, were somehow made to feel guilty and worthless because they couldn't find work in an economy that had no work for them.

They didn't, for the most part, join up to be patriotic or "save their beloved country from the fascist hordes of Hitler." Those feelings did come, but much later when it looked for a while that our side might possibly lose. That first wave of enlistment brought in the worst victims of the Depression, those poor lads who didn't know what it was like to have enough to eat or wear. I know, because many of them were my friends and neighbours. I would have been with them, too, but in September 1939 I was only 15 years old, too young to fool the recruiting officer into thinking I was a mature man of 18. Not that I didn't try many times. I was big for my age, but not very good at lying I guess. One of my friends made it in at 16 and another at 17, but I had no luck at all.

I'll never forget the first time I saw those two friends when they came home in their uniforms. These guys who had never worn anything but patched-up overalls or cast-off hand-me-downs came marching down the sidewalk in our part of town looking for all the world like real soldiers. I couldn't believe my eyes. They marched side by side in perfect unison and they clicked the heels of their boots on the concrete just as if they knew what they were doing. How could they? Neither one had ever worn anything but canvas sneakers on his feet before, summer or winter, and besides, they had only been in the army two goddam days. They couldn't possibly know what they were doing – could they?

We had gone into Sydney from Glace Bay together, just the three of us. We walked into the recruiting office together and we all lied about our ages together. I was just as tall as they were, and, in fact, I had a few pounds on both of them. They were accepted and I wasn't. That's the first time I heard those terrible words directed at me, "Go home son, and come back in a few years time." The recruiting officer told my friends to go into the next room where a doctor was giving medical examinations. He told me to step aside.

I can admit it now, because a lot of years have passed since that blackest of days in 1939, but that was the worst experience of my life until then. I saw those two so-called friends smirk at each other when the officer told me to go home, and worst of all, when they passed in front of me on their way into the next room I could actually hear them laughing out loud.

All the way back home, all alone on that long streetcar ride to Glace Bay, I alternated between crying and wishing those two erstwhile friends would be the first to feel the wrath of Hitler.

I couldn't believe my eyes when I saw them then, two days later, clicking their heels as they marched along that sidewalk in their uniforms. They looked like soldiers, they walked like soldiers, and they had an air about them that stamped them as soldiers. All of a sudden, in a matter of a measly 48 hours, my two raggedy-ass friends had bounded beyond me and had taken on a patina of importance and meaning of which I had always dreamed.

I was crushed and, I can admit it now, devastated and jealous beyond belief. I was so envious, I couldn't bear to meet them face to face. Instead, I hid around the corner of a building and stole furtive peeks, until they marched out of my sight and out of my life forever.

How I regret all of that childish pettiness today. Those moments of glory for my two young friends were about the only ones they ever had. After a few months of basic training, they were shipped off overseas and promptly killed, two of the first casualties from my home town. The sad part of it was, they were not only too young to die, they were too bloody young even to be in the army, just as I had been.

Cape Breton always seemed to be at the bottom of the economic totem pole and when the Depression hit we went down even further. If things were bad elsewhere, they were always that much worse in Cape Breton, or so it seemed. We got rather used to the situation. Our main industries, coal mines and one steel plant, were idle more often than they were working, and the company that operated these two mainstays of Cape Breton displayed little compassion for the workers. Wages, always at starvation level, were constantly being cut to a point below mere subsistence, and when the desperate workers went on strike, the government sent the army in to drive them back to work.

Because of all these factors, Cape Bretoners developed an "us-against-the-world" kind of attitude, a chip-on-the-shoulder bearing that cried out for the rest of the country to "knock it off — if you can." Along with much of the youth of the country we rode the rails across Canada in search of work that wasn't there and we took that attitude with us. Our reputation as wild-and-woolly roughnecks spread across the land and, as people are who have nothing, we were proud of the description.

None were prouder, or acted tougher than the boys of my home town of Glace Bay. They didn't say "boys" though. They called themselves "byes" — "Bay byes". They let everybody know that if Cape Bretoners were tough, "the byes from the Bay" were the toughest of the lot. And that's the attitude they took with them when they swarmed into the army as part of the Cape Breton Highlanders regiment.

Lack of fear, and a desire to be where the battles were raging didn't protect our Cape Breton "byes" from the bombs and the bullets. They died by the hundreds in places like Dieppe and Normandy and Cassino, and their pictures appeared in the home-town Glace Bay *Gazette* and the Sydney *Post Record*. We just couldn't believe it — those of us who were still at home. These were "our boys" — tender of heart and rough of exterior. They were supposed to get rid of Hitler, not get killed themselves.

One of our Cape Breton poets, Margaret Nickerson, put it into words which said it for us all.

Our Cape Breton Highlanders

These are our boys —
The boys who lived next door or down the street,
The boys who whistled on their way to school,
Or else, with laggard feet,
Stopped to toss pebbles in a wayside pool,
Knocked marbles 'gainst a fence or wall.
These are the boys
Whose names were written in school registers
A few short years ago;
Such wide-eyed boys, just five or six or so,
Who, now to manhood grown, have heard the call
And answered with their lives if need be,
So that other little boys of five or six or so
May still be free
To whistle on their way to school,
Or, with reluctant feet,
Stop to toss pebbles in a wayside pool,
Play marbles on the street.

There was great sorrow in Glace Bay over our first casualties, as friends and neighbours rushed to comfort the grieving families. But there was something else. People suddenly realized that this war wasn't just fun and jobs for the unemployed. This was the real thing, just like that other war that was only 20 years in the past.

Our people died in that one too, or they came home blind, crippled, sick, mentally ill, or alcoholic. Many old soldiers would never talk about the horrors of war. If they talked at all, it was about the great times they had had "over there" — about the wine, the women, and the song. Down at the Legion hall they were always singing, and it made us youngsters, listening through an open window wonder, who the hell was this "Madamoiselle from Army-teers," anyway? She must have really been something to have all those old men down at the Legion crying their eyes out over her.

Those old men, those old soldiers from World War One, by the way, were only in their late thirties and early forties when that second abomination came along. Like old fire horses, they were the first out of the gates, lining up at the recruiting offices trying to get back in.

One hopeful in western Canada, with black shoe polish covering up the grey in his hair, was turned down politely and sympathetically by the recruiting officer because of his age. There was no shoe polish in the world that could turn a 76-year-old into new soldier material. But why shouldn't old soldiers like him want to get back into the fray? Their country didn't reward them well for "winning the war" that last time. They came back to a country where those who stayed at home had snapped up all the good jobs while they had to catch as catch can. Then, from 1929 to 1939, they floundered hopelessly about as most others did in the Great Depression, trying to figure out what was so "great" about watching their children starve. The country owed them another free suit of khaki. That, at least, was better than no suit at all, which is what they had after ten years of depression. That's why they wanted to join up again.

The problem was, that when the youngsters saw these veterans rush off to enlist, it gave them the false impression that war must be pretty good if these old codgers, who had already fought in one war couldn't wait to fight in another. They should have made it clear to the young ones that they were just trying to trade off one misery for another, one that at least paid, fed and clothed them. Perhaps if they came straight out and said that, my two friends who sneaked in under-age wouldn't have been so anxious and might still be alive.

After the first flush of enlistments when people joined for jobs, and the war was looking bad from the Allied point of view, there was a different kind of recruit rapping at the door. These were the young men and women who were quitting jobs to join up because they really did want to do something for their country and they wanted to get over there and "kick the hell out of Hitler."

Also we were scared, because we had read in our newspapers and heard on our radios how bad it was for those in the occupied countries, and that maybe it would be just like that for us if the Nazis won. There was a time during the war when even our mightiest leaders from Churchill on down were preparing for the worst and planning what they would do when — not *if* but *when* — Hitler's armies marched in and took over London. Where would they hide the Royal family? Where would they move the key members of the government to make it possible to fight on as a "government in exile"? Canada was a serious possibility, and we were told that Churchill and his war cabinet were set to move here should the need arise.

I was from a coal-mining family and that industry was deemed essential to the war effort. It was therefore very hard for miners to join the services. They would be turned down at the recruiting offices with the words, "You're more valuable to us and the war staying right where you are." However, a lot of them managed, in one way or another, to get by this restriction and they joined the huge number of Canada's youth who sailed off across the ocean to fight.

My twin brothers were among them — one in the army and the other in the air force. I was still only sixteen by this time, in my last year of high school, and still drooling to wear a uniform. A friend of my father who had joined up at the outset of the war came back to town about this time, as the recruiting officer for a unit of the medical corps. I think I was the first through his door telling him I would be willing to do anything. He told me to go home and think about it and he would call me the next day. Well, he didn't do that. Instead, he called my father who raced off in his car to see this man and have my application destroyed. All of this was done while I was in church, of all places, praying that I would be accepted.

On the way home from Sunday morning Mass one of my friends came running up to me all red-faced and out of breath. "Better come fast, Billie," he said, "your mother and father were in an accident with their car down at Table Head and they're hurt pretty bad." By this time the news had spread and everyone was running in the direction of the accident, including me.

When I got there my mother was inside a neighbouring house lying on a chesterfield, her face covered in bloody bandages. I was crying and she reached out to hug me but couldn't quite make it. "Go see your father dear," she said. "They've taken him into the house right across the street."

Well, he was a frightening sight too, although he wasn't as bad as my mother whose head had gone right through the windshield. It turned out that father's arm was almost pulverized and he had other injuries too.

I felt a terrible sense of guilt about all of this after things settled down. If it hadn't been for me trying to join the army, I figured they wouldn't have been out in the car that morning.

Neither of them ever reproached me afterwards nor indeed had they ever told me about their Sunday morning trip to see the recruiting officer. In fact it was the recruiting officer himself who told me all about it. "Don't you see, Bill," he asked, "your two brothers are already gone off and it's important to them that their youngest son not go too? Not yet anyway."

That kept me out of the fray for the next year but I did try again shortly after I graduated from high school. This time it was the navy. Seems I passed all the medicals and other tests okay, but at that particular point in the war they didn't need any new recruits. I didn't like that very much I can tell you, because I had travelled more than 200 miles on the train for that interview, all the way from Glace Bay to Halifax, and it wasn't exactly the news I wanted to hear.

I never did get into the services. I spent one year at university and the rest of the time being "much more valuable on the home front," working in the coal mines and following the war in the newspapers and on radio.

I think the worst part of it all for me was waiting from afar as my friends were dying. The first person in my part of town to die overseas was without a doubt one of the finest young men and certainly one of the most promising that our community produced. Buddy MacDougall was his name and he was all that a mother would want for a son. He was handsome, pleasant with everyone, doing well at university and obviously someone who was going places.

Buddy was one of the first to join the airforce, one of the first to get his wings as a flying officer and one of the first to get his picture in the paper under the caption *Posted Overseas*. He was also the first to have the same picture in the paper less than a month later under a different caption, *Missing in Action* and another one a week after that, *Presumed Dead*.

We were used to sudden death in Glace Bay. Men were frequently getting killed in the mines, but we weren't used to having our young people die on distant shores so that we couldn't mourn at a wake and a funeral. If this was war we didn't like it, but we would certainly have to get used to it. And we did, again and again and again.

Buddy was first, but once started they came after that in a flood. There was Art and Leroy and Billie and Jimmy and Pete. Frank was next and Jack and Joe . . . and all the rest. It was hard when you knew them all, but, frankly, after a while you got used to it.

You also got used to shortages of everything . . . butter, sugar, and even jam. There was a substitute jam that was made from flour, sugar, water and food colouring. Nobody could ever get used to that. The women got used to food rationing though, and they learned to trade coupons with neighbours . . . butter for tea, and meat coupons for sugar. Teetotallers were being courted on the strength of the booze ration they weren't using themselves.

Everything was rationed, even gasoline, and there was no such thing as a new car. Women had to get used to life without their men and raising their children alone for periods of time ranging up to six years.

Just as if we lived in a war zone, we also had to get used to blackouts and air-raid wardens and part-time soldiers on the home front, who were scornfully referred to as "the blueberry squad" by the regular soldiers who accused them of spending all their time picking blueberries.

This is just a bit of what the war was like from my perspective. Other Canadians, of course, remember in their own particular way, which is what this book is all about — the memories of people who remember the Second World War. These are their stories as they told them to me.

The war changed all of us in one way or another. You couldn't go through it at home or abroad without suffering some of its effects.

PART 1
AIR FORCE

An Airman's Letter

AMONG THE personal belongings of a young RAF bomber pilot who had been reported missing was found a letter to his widowed mother with his wish that it be sent to her if he was killed. It had been left open — in compliance with security — and was read by the station commander. The spirit and wording of the letter prompted him to ask the mother if it could be published anonymously. She agreed. On June 18, 1940 the letter appeared in the London *Times*.

Dearest Mother,

Though I feel no premonition at all, events are moving rapidly, and I have instructed that this letter be forwarded to you should I fail to return from one of the raids which we shall shortly be called upon to undertake. You must hope on for a month, but at the end of that time you must accept the fact that I have handed my task over to the extremely capable hands of my comrades of the Royal Air Force, as so many splendid fellows have already done.

First, it will comfort you to know that my role in this war has been of the greatest importance. Our patrols far out over the North Sea have helped to keep the trade routes clear for our convoys and supply ships, and on one occasion our information was instrumental in saving the lives of the men in a crippled lighthouse relief ship. Though it will be difficult for you, you will disappoint me if you do not at least try to accept the facts dispassionately, for I shall have done my duty to the utmost of my ability. No man can do more, and no one calling himself a man could do less.

I have always admired your amazing courage in the face of continual setbacks; in the way you have given me as good an education and background as anyone in the country; and always kept up appearances without losing faith in the future. My death would not mean that your struggle has been in vain. Far from it. It means that your sacrifice has been as great as mine. Those who serve England must expect nothing from her; we debase ourselves if we regard our country as merely a place in which to eat and sleep.

History resounds with illustrious names who have given all, yet their sacrifice has resulted in the British Empire, where there is a measure of peace, justice and freedom for all, and where a higher standard of civilization has evolved, and is still evolving, than anywhere else. But this is not only concerning our own land. Today we are faced with the greatest organized challenge to Christianity and civilization that the world has ever seen, and I count myself lucky and honoured to be the right age and fully trained to throw my weight into the scale. For this I have to thank you. Yet there is more work for you to do. The home front will still have to stand united for years after the war is won. For all that can be said about it, I still maintain that this war is a very good thing; every individual is having the chance to give and dare all for his principle like the martyrs of old. However long the time may be, one thing can never be altered — I shall have lived and died an Englishman. Nothing else matters one jot nor can anything ever change it.

You must not grieve for me, for if you really believe in religion and all that it entails that would be hypocrisy. I have no fear of death; only a queer elation . . . I would have it no other way. The universe is so vast and so ageless that the life of one man can only be justified by the measure of his sacrifice. We are sent to this world to acquire a personality to take with us that can never be taken from us. Those who just eat and sleep, prosper and procreate, are no better than animals if all their lives they are at peace.

I firmly and absolutely believe that evil things are sent into this world to try us; they are sent deliberately by our Creator to test our mettle because He knows what is good for us. The Bible is full of cases where the easy way out has been discarded for moral principles.

I count myself fortunate in that I have seen the whole country and known men of every calling. But with the final test of war I consider my character fully developed. Thus at my early age my earthly mission is already fulfilled and I am prepared to die with just one regret, and one only — that I could not devote myself to making your declining years more happy by being with you; but you will live in peace and freedom and I shall have directly contributed to that, so here again my life will not have been in vain.

Your loving Son,

Within a month after the publication of this letter, the newspaper was inundated with more than 500,000 requests for copies from all over the British Empire. The anonymous young airman had put into words what millions of young men were thinking. It was not a letter that glorified war, but one that accepted the reality and necessity for it at the time. It did not rail at the waste of a life but instead, it put into words the appreciation of a life that, although short, was full indeed. It offered gratitude and comfort to a parent who had done her best.

Note: The anonymity of the writer and his mother was maintained for more than four decades and was only broken when an obituary notice for a Mrs Lillian Rosewarne appeared in the Times *on February 18, 1981. In the obituary it was revealed that she was the mother of the airman (her only child) who had written the letter. His name was Vivian Alan William Noall*

Rosewarne and he was killed with his crew of 36 (B) Squadron during the evacuation at Dunkirk.

Gordon Ritchie
Auteuil Laval, Quebec

I HAD TO leave school in the late thirties to help support our household. For many of us, the services offered the opportunity to get involved in ridding the world of Nazi Germany led by Adolf Hitler. I think the whole country was united in those days as at no other time in our history. We knew what had to be done and we set out to do it. Looking on the services as a job was only part of our story.

I joined the air force in Montreal as an AC2 and I left it when the war was over as a commissioned officer, something I never thought possible when I first joined up.

During my tour of Ops, we in 6 Group RCAF Bomber Command attacked such targets as Berlin, Hamburg, Leipzig, Düsseldorf, Frankfurt, and Essen in Germany, as well as targets in France, Belgium, and Holland, to name just a few.

I often think about the night we shot down a Messerschmitt 410 Nightfighter on a bombing mission to Braunsweig in northwest Germany. Upon return to base, the public relations people for the air force asked me to strike a pose and they had their photographer take pictures. I didn't know at the time what this was all about but those pictures ultimately appeared in the window of the Eaton department store in Montreal, along with the pictures of other servicemen who were at that time serving on active duty. That set of pictures which included me, stayed there for a while and then were replaced by others, and so on until the war was over. Anyway, my uncle went to the store and asked if he could have my picture, since they were no longer using it, as he would like to present it to me on my return. They said they were happy to oblige and I treasure that picture still. It is currently hanging on the wall in the downstairs room.

The Supreme Commander, General Eisenhower, ordered heavy and continuous air attacks against all the enemy's communications for the D-Day invasion, and heavy bombers like ours were directed to attack bridges across the Loire, and in the Paris–Orleans gap. The theory was that any German reserve troops stationed between the Seine and the Loire would be thrown into the battle by the following day, June 7. To stop them bringing in these reinforcements, several heavy bombing attacks were made on some of the key road and rail centres in this area.

I was the rear gunner on 429, a Halifax bomber of the RCAF. On the night of June 7–8, we were detailed to bomb a marshalling yard behind the German lines.

As we crossed the French coast at Dieppe, all hell broke loose as the flak guns opened up on us. The pilot, Squadron Leader W.B. Anderson, caught a large fragment through his side, and he gave us the order to bail out. We were at 18,000 feet at the time, and our plane went into a vertical dive as the pilot slumped over the control column. I had my gun turret slung out on the beam watching out for fighter attacks from below. As I attempted to extricate myself from the turret, I lost one of my flying boots but I did manage to crawl out and pick up my parachute. I squeezed myself through a very narrow opening between the fuselage and the tail wheel, which is a very difficult thing to do at the best of times, but with the plane in a dive and almost certainly headed for eternity, even the impossible can be done.

Once through, I was crawling forward to the escape hatch with my face forced right down on the floor, when I realized that someone was pulling our plane out of the dive. Through my intercom, I found out that it was our flight engineer, Sergeant Gilbert Steere who had pulled the injured pilot from the cockpit and was now flying the plane himself. Along with Flight Sergeant Mangione from Ottawa, I went forward to see if there was any aid we could offer. By this time our navigator, bomb-aimer and wireless operator had already obeyed the order to bail out over France.

The pilot was alive but in very bad shape, so we administered some morphine to ease his pain. During all of this, we had switched

The two gunners of Impatient Virgin, left: *Gordon Ritchie,*
right: *John Mangione. (Courtesy Gordon Ritchie)*

on some lights in the plane to see what we were doing, not realizing
that we had inadvertently also switched on our outside navigational
lights, making us a perfect target.

Our next job was to get rid of our bombs, so we just jettisoned
them near Dieppe and headed for England. This posed another big
problem since at this time there was such a concentration of Allied
shipping in the English Channel, that the standing orders were to
shoot at anything flying overhead. However that was just one more
thing to worry about; we had other problems right where we were.

Our flight engineer, who had taken over flying the aircraft was
sitting in a bucket seat wearing a chest-pack parachute and was
therefore unable to see where he was going. He had to rely solely on
the artificial horizon to keep us somewhat safe and level. In the
meantime, we caught hold of our injured skipper who was just
barely alive, and dragged him to the rear escape hatch. He was a big

man, weighing over 200 pounds, so that was not any easy job. We were over England by this time, but we had no idea where exactly, so we informed several airfields after our *Mayday* call and told them we were about to let our skipper out by parachute. After attaching his D-ring to the snap on the static line, the skipper said, "Okay, let me go," and we slid him through the hatch.

Then it was time for the rest of us to leave because the flight engineer told us we were almost out of petrol. I slid my feed out through the escape hatch into the slipstream, which immediately took my other flying boot and heated slippers, and summoning what courage I could, out I went. What a relief when the 'chute opened and, I have to admit, heavenly to be out of that aircraft with all the noise, blood, and clatter. My next concern was where I was going to land. I estimated we were at 12,000 feet at bail out.

I landed in my stockinged feet on a wire fence before being blown into a field. The first thing I did was reach for a cigarette. I had one of those Victory lighters and with my shaking hand, I flicked the wheel so hard it flew right off the lighter. So there I was, sitting in a field with a cigarette in my mouth and nothing to light it with. I was soon to find out this was nothing at all! compared to my newest problem which I discovered as soon as I turned my head. Right there beside me was a small red and white sign reading *Beware of Mines*. Talk about jumping out of the frying pan into the fire!

No matter what, I decided I had to move out of there so I crawled slowly in a straight line to the edge of the field. I then moved in the direction of our burning Halifax (*LW128–Impatient Virgin*), which had crashed while I was descending. As I approached it across freshly ploughed fields, mud oozed up between my toes and the ammunition from the plane started to explode, with tracers going in all directions.

I made a quick detour and tried several houses without success, because I could not convince those English people that I was a Canadian airman who had just bailed out from a burning aircraft. However, one of them did direct me to the house of a neighbouring farmer who kindly gave me a light for my cigarette. He also drove me to the RAF station Benson in Oxfordshire.

His Majesty George VI presents Gordon Ritchie with the
Distinguished Flying Cross. (Courtesy Gordon Ritchie)

They were expecting me, because the other two crew who had bailed out with me had already arrived. Our skipper wasn't so lucky. An American colonel in a light aircraft had spotted his body earlier that morning and brought him to the mortuary at RAF Benson.

Our bomb-aimer and wireless operator, who had bailed out over France, after a few days of freedom were subsequently taken prisoner by the Germans, and were in the same POW camp until the end of the war. Our navigator made it back to England within six weeks with the help of the French Underground. Squadron Leader W.B. Anderson, DFC, our skipper, is buried in Brockwood Cemetery in Woking, Surrey.

This story is just one incident from "my" war, but I consider it to be the highlight of my tour of operations in which I completed 34 bombing operations, culminating in my being awarded the Distinguished Flying Medal and being invested by King George VI.

I think the most positive benefit I received from my service with the RCAF, was the confidence it gave me in the post-war period and also much later throughout my life. I think often about my colleagues who went through Manning Pool and Gunnery School at Mont Joli where we graduated. Many are buried at Stonefall cemetery near Harrowgate in Yorkshire, a place I never fail to visit on my visits back to the U.K. These friends who never grew old, did not have the opportunity to experience life; they died at the tender ages of 19, 20, and 21.

James Cameron Lovelace
Sydney, Nova Scotia

IT WASN'T always the aircrew who were the only living things aboard those Wellington bombers during their bombing missions. I don't know that anyone has ever mentioned this before but we were always accompanied by plenty of billing and cooing. That's right — billing and cooing — and it came from our good friend Columbus, the homing pigeon. He was our beauty and our connection to the real world. Bluish-grey in colour with a black neck, Columbus tended to be rather fat, or should I say "well-fed" because that's what he was. Also, we thought Columbus was a *he* although nobody ever confirmed that for us.

Columbus was usually a very quiet and well-behaved bird except when we went to pick him up at the dovecote on our station grounds. He'd become very agitated when we came along with our cage and would invite him inside. Actually, the cage was more like a tin box with a pigeon-sized hole at the front which had a sliding cover made of chicken wire. He was agitated because he always seemed anxious to get away from the dovecote and inside that little tin box.

Not all the pigeons were like our bird. When the fellows from the other planes went to pick up their pigeons, they had to deal with raucous and screaming birds that splayed their legs and did all sorts of manoeuvres to keep from going inside that box. In fact many aircrews would sometimes not take their homing pigeons at all because the birds seemed to be so frightened — an emotion that all aircrews knew only too well. Those boys felt it just didn't seem right to subject their poor birds to that kind of thing so they would just head out on their missions without them. But not Columbus! Once inside his "carrier," as we called it, he adapted the stance of an aircrew member and was quite content to settle down in his air-battle station with the rest of us.

What was Columbus's job? Well, it was just to be 'on call' in case we needed him. As the wireless operator, every hour on the hour — or every 15 minutes if in battle — I would write out our latitude and longtitude and the time, on a tiny pad, one inch square and slip it into a message tube attached to Columbus's leg.

We never bothered removing the old messages since each new one would have a new time on it to show that this was the only one that mattered. Another reason we didn't take the old ones out was because we didn't want to bother Columbus too much, what with the excitement of chattering machine-guns and twanging bullets hitting and glancing off the skin of our Wellington. Good old Columbus seemed to have no need of comforting though. When it came time to slip in a new message he would just move his leg up to make my job a bit easier. He would coo just once and take a gentle little nibble at the top of my hand as if to give it a small kiss. Perhaps it was a way of comforting himself. Maybe so, but it sure did comfort *me*.

The thing that comforted me most, however, was the very fact that Columbus was there! If we were ever to ditch, which, thank goodness, we never had to do, Columbus would have been our very first first-class passenger aboard the life raft. It would be my job then to write a quite different message on my small pad, giving not only our location but how many of us were abroad the raft and things like that, and then stuffing the note in the bird's leg and getting him airborne as quickly as possible. According to the rules, our bird would then fly back straight to our station with the information that someone needed if we were ever to be rescued. In a way, Columbus was our protector and our saviour if ever the need should arise to use his services and his talents.

We grew to love that small bird. Whenever we were being fed oxygen I always made sure that Columbus got his share. Whenever we got into our candy and coffee, so did Columbus get his niblets. He was looked upon as a member of the crew just like everyone else, with one small plus in his favour; he was our lifesaver should the need arise. That's what he was all right — up to our last flight when we crashed in flames. Columbus didn't make it out of that.

It bothered me for many years to recall the screeches that Columbus made as the flames engulfed him while the two of us who survived lay helpless in the field and our big Wellington became a bonfire.

Every year on Remembrance Day, with cold arthritic feet and a red and runny nose, I attend the services at the war memorial in Ottawa and think of my former buddies, those other aircrew members who died in the bloom of their youth. I grieve for all of those boys, for that's all they were, and I do remember too, that small bird who somehow became a part of our lives, a beacon of hope whose presence aboard our war-battered aircraft always reminded us that we were not totally alone. Thank you, Columbus.

That's my bird story of the war, but it's not the only "other species" yarn I have. This one, though I am not a superstitious person normally, still leaves me wondering half a century later.

Guy Gibson was one of the most famous aces of the Second World War. It was Guy's squadron that gained fame as "The Dambusters" and their exploits were immortalized in a famous movie of the same name. Guy was a very popular leader and although his exploits had made him a living legend in the RAF, he was apparently a man without a large ego. He treated everyone the same way regardless of their rank and he looked on his whole squadron as a team, and on himself as just another necessary part of that team.

Although he came from the upper reaches of the British class system, and was a product of the most exclusive private schools, he was as much at home with an aircraft mechanic as he was with a

Commodore. It's not much of an exaggeration to say that everyone loved Guy.

Many of our Canadian airmen flew with his squadron at one time or another and when they talked about him it was always with goodwill. I don't think I ever heard any of them utter a bad word about Guy, and of course, just about every story they told had some mention of his big black Labrador dog who was his constant companion.

Now all of this is a lead-in to a strange incident that happened very recently during the summer of 1988. It took place at the air station from which Guy Gibson's squadron flew to bomb those dams. They were holding a memorial to honour the famous Victoria Cross winner and his crew. The local school principal arranged for the whole school to attend the ceremony and, later, to have a group picture taken in front of the Guy Gibson monument at the station.

When the students were all assembled for this historic photograph, a large stray Labrador retriever insisted on putting himself in the picture. The photographer paused as efforts were made to get the dog away, but after some hopeless shooing and skeedaddling, it was finally decided it would be easier to leave the dog where he was. Anyway, the kids liked him and said they'd like to have him in the picture. So be it. When the picture appeared in the local paper the next day, there sat the dog front and centre with his tongue hanging out and what looked like a big happy smile on his face. The accompanying story, written by the principal, asked for information about the dog because the kids wanted to adopt him as their mascot.

One of the readers who happened to have been a guest at the previous day's memorial was none other than Guy Gibson's navigator during those wartime days. The story about the dog intrigued him so he went to the school accompanied by a reporter from the paper.

He told the kids at school that the monument was erected at the very spot where Guy Gibson's plane had always been parked. He said that every evening as the crews were driven out to their aircraft in the crew lorries, Guy and his big black Labrador would be part of the group. The dog would take up a waiting position at the end of

There was still a place for homing pigeons in the Second World War. Here, an RCAF crew man prepares a basket full of pigeons to later be placed aboard various patrolling aircraft. (Courtesy the National Archives of Canada)

the ramp as the Gibson crew prepared to leave on another bombing mission. As Guy and each of his men headed up the ramp to the plane they would pat the dog on the head before heading off to battle. The Labrador was always sitting there waiting in the early dawn as the plane and its crew returned.

One evening as the crew arrived in their lorry to prepare for yet another bombing mission, a rabbit leaped out from the bushes and sped across the tarmac of the airfield. As you would expect from any high-spirited animal, Guy's Labrador was soon in rapid pursuit. At that very moment, another lorry came tearing up to the tarmac and before anyone could even scream a warning Guy's dog was dead under its wheels. It was a very sad and distraught crew who boarded their plane that night.

Before he left, Guy asked the ground crew if they would give his dog a decent burial right at the spot where he was killed at the foot of the ramp.

It was 43 years to the very day that this big, unknown black Labrador insisted on sitting with those kids honouring their hero, Guy Gibson. No one from the community had ever seen that dog before and no one has seen him since. The navigator still insists that this was indeed Guy's dog, back to honour his master. Who am I to argue?

Reg Knight
Huntsville, Ontario

I UNDERSTAND there are something in the order of 100,000 Canadian graves in France, Belgium and Holland. Few, if any, soldiers left Canada for the battlefields of Europe with the belief that they wouldn't return. I know I didn't.

I was married to a very lovely girl ten days before leaving, and I sure didn't want to go but I most emphatically intended to come back, as did all those others whose short time on earth ended thousands of miles from the homes that they longed for. I recall standing on the deck of a ship, the *Louis Pasteur*, at two in the morning on a day in July, 1943. The lights of Halifax were fast disappearing and my thoughts were of my wife of ten days, and how the distance between us was increasing every hour. I was also thinking some very uncharitable and unChristian thoughts about a couple of psychotic megalomaniacs named Adolf Hitler and Benito

Mussolini, but the thought that I wouldn't be back never even occurred to me.

There was lots of time for thinking on that voyage, about many things, even the relatively short life I had led so far in the armed forces. Back in January, of that same year of my embarkation, 1943, I had just finished a general reconnaissance course at the RCAF station in Summerside, Prince Edward Island. A group of us were sitting around a common room, yakking up a storm, and waiting to find out what fate had in store for us — where we would be posted. A flight lieutenant walked in, came up to me and without preamble said, "Knight, where do you want to go, Patricia Bay, British Columbia, or Nassau in the Bahamas?"

I just sat there with my mouth wide open, required to make a decision which would determine my future and whether my life even had much of a future. Since it was winter time in the Maritime Provinces, not a time noted for balmy weather, I pretty well knew what my answer would be. However, I thought it wise to stall a bit before answering so I said, "What's at Pat Bay?"

He replied, "An operational training unit for torpedo bombers."

Now let me tell you something about Second World War torpedo bombers, which were nothing more than skinny little aircraft with a heavy torpedo slung underneath. These planes had to stagger off the ground, fly toward an enemy warship at an altitude of 50 feet, drop the torpedo and then fly up and over the ship through the curtain of gunfire that would follow your attack.

This didn't seem to augur well for a long and happy life with the girl I intended to marry as soon as they gave me some time off. I asked, "What's at Nassau?"

He said, "An operational training unit for long range anti-submarine patrol in four-engined aircraft."

Well, since I always liked to have a comfortable number of engines out there, all working, Nassau seemed like the place for me, not to mention that all that warm weather was pretty appealing. I spent the next four months, from early February to early June, in the Bahamas.

When I had absorbed all the training they could pour into me on this side of the Atlantic, the next step was England, "across the pond," and in the blink of an eye it all happened; fast marriage ceremony, quick leave, sudden embarkation, and a fast crossing safely to the other side.

My job was navigator on a B-17 Flying Fortress which most airmen called simply, "The Fort." Our job was anti-submarine patrol and convoy escort, which could often be very routine. Often but not always.

One night in July, 1944, we were returning from a patrol near the Canary Islands off the northwest coast of Africa, when one engine quit on us. Since there were still three engines left, and a Fort could still fly and land safely with three there wasn't that much to worry about. A short time later there *was* something to worry about; a second engine quit and we started to prepare ourselves, mentally and physically, to ditch the land-based airplane in the water.

Fifteen minutes later a third engine went and we all scrambled to our pre-arranged ditching stations. This looked like "it," because while a Fort could still fly on one engine, it could not maintain altitude. We were coming down at the rate of 100 feet a minute. We were going to crash, no two ways about it.

My navigator's cabin was located in the very nose of the plane which was absolutely no place to be if the plane was going to crash nose first into the water! To get out of there I had to go through a three-foot high doorway, crawl along a small passageway, up a ramp and through a trap-door into the pilot's cabin. Then I had to squeeze through a gun-turret, open a small door, squeeze sideways through a narrow ten-foot long passage in the bomb bay and open another door to get into the wireless operator's cabin, which was the ditching station for everybody except the pilots. It's amazing what one can do in times of stress and emergency; I covered that entire route in 15 seconds flat. Then we took out the plexiglass roof of the cabin so that it wouldn't buckle and trap us inside when we hit.

Now there was nothing left to do but wait. We sat on the floor facing aft, knees up and hands behind our heads. The amazing thing is that there was no panic. I guess the fact that we had practised this procedure many times in aircraft sitting on the ground helped. Not all of us remembered all the details however. One of the wireless operators leaned over and asked me if he correctly remembered the procedure for using the dinghies after a crash landing. "Aren't we supposed to pull the handles to inflate them right now?" he asked. "Not unless you want to swim back ten miles to get them," I replied.

When we hit the water, the bomb bay doors smashed and the ocean came crashing in on us. The first thing to go was the door I had been leaning my back against. I must have been momentarily unconscious, because the next thing I remember I was standing, one foot on top of the radar set and one foot outside the plane on the wing. Now it was time to pull the handles on those dinghies and get away from that plane as fast as possible, which we did. Within ten minutes, our plane had broken in two and both pieces sank to the bottom.

In our dinghy there were just George, the flight engineer and me. We couldn't see the other dinghy and the rest of the crew but then, as we looked about desperately for them, we heard hooting and yelling and great blowing of whistles. It was as dark out as the inside of a whale, so although we couldn't see the other dinghy, we paddled in the direction of the sounds. When we came upon the crew we found they had more than a small problem. Their dinghy had a hole in it and was sinking fast, so very soon there were seven more men in our one good one. These were the old British-type affairs shaped like a large doughnut with a floor. When George and I had it alone we could sit on that floor and lean our backs against the sides, but with nine of us we all had to sit on those sides and fell lucky just to get our feet inside on the floor.

Waves that night were long slow rollers, ten to 12 feet high and about 100 yards from crest to crest. Our little craft would climb up the side of one wave, teeter a bit on top, and then slide down into the trough. It didn't take many of these to produce the expected results on a bunch of landlubbers. We were a horribly sick lot.

Meanwhile our navigator, just before we ditched, had chartered our position perfectly and our wireless operator was able to send off a message just before we crashed so that several aircraft were out

The airplane was utilized greatly in evacuating the wounded
during the Second World War. Here, a Canadian soldier on a
stretcher is being carefully placed aboard a Douglas Dakota
during the D-Day operations in Normandy, June 6, 1944.
(Courtesy the National Archives of Canada)

searching the area almost immediately. The squadron commander spotted us about 4 A.M. and just after daylight an air-sea rescue plane dropped us a lifeboat. What a beautiful sight it was: that big lifeboat floating down toward us on three parachutes. It didn't take long for us to scramble inside it. About six hours later we were picked up by a Portuguese merchant liner and taken to the Island of San Miguel where we were interned overnight but released the next day after the intervention of the British Consul.

How often I think about all of that and think how differently it could have turned out. First of all, it was comparatively calm that evening. I've flown over the Atlantic on many missions where the weather was such that to ditch would have been certain death.

Secondly, our rescue planes knew pretty well where to look for us and they found us in about four hours on a moonless night in the middle of the Atlantic. Thirdly, the Portuguese ship that picked us up just happened to be coming our way and didn't even have to alter course to get us. A fourth point in our favour and the most important one, was that our aircraft stayed right side up when it hit. Very often they flip over on their backs, and when that happens those inside become disoriented. The result is that when you're underwater, your instinct is to head for where you think the surface is, but when the plane is on its back, the surface is the floor and you have to have the presence of mind and enough air in your lungs, to dive down first, then out and then up. That night, all factors were on our side, and while some might say we were lucky, I think we had Divine intervention. We did a lot of praying that night.

It's over 45 years now since that terrible conflict ended and I returned to reunite with the lovely woman I had married just ten days before I left. The 45 years we've been together seem a lot shorter in many ways than the two long years we were parted by war.

Kitty Hawker
Don Mills, Ontario

THE EVENT which propelled me into the war was the attack on Dieppe in 1942. I had been waiting for the Red Cross to send me overseas with their unit, and I was busy drilling two nights a week with them, but the profound effect that Dieppe had on my city of Windsor, Ontario was extraordinary. Our own homegrown regiment, the Essex Scottish, had been in the raid, and very few of those men came out of it. Most were either killed or captured. On the streets of Windsor people were openly crying. I simply couldn't wait any longer to get into the fight.

I had heard that the RCAF were recruiting women for very secret work, and that it was difficult to get in because the standards were so high. This made me more determined than ever, and in September, 1942, one month after Dieppe, I set off for Ottawa and my new life.

There were mixed reactions to my signing up. My parents were very proud but my sister was upset, because she was going to be married as soon as her airman got leave, and she wanted me to be there. Some of my mother's friends were horrified, because there were many false stories going around about the "looseness" of women in the services. Mother's answer to this was, "Water seeks its own level," and said there would be hundreds of girls of the same calibre as her daughter joining up.

The train ride to Ottawa and the Number One Manning Depot was quite unreal, and when we were met at the train station, herded into buses and urged to sing, "I've got sixpence," we were all left wondering what we had got ourselves into. Everything was strange and new, almost like being put down on another planet, but with the issuance of the uniforms and the hesitant overtures of friendship among all the girls, we soon melded into a cohesive group. When I think now of girls among that group in 1942 who are still my friends, it seems incredible.

After basic training, during which time we almost despaired of ever learning how to march properly and become a "smart squad," I went on to take a trade course in Filter Ops. Yes, the "secret" work we were going to learn was radar. Radar stations on Canada's coasts fed information into a Filter Room, where the track of the aircraft was identified, and if they proved to be "unfriendly," fighter planes would then be sent up to take a look.

Course finished, we were then sent off to Halifax on a train ride never to be forgotten. We sat up all night in an old wooden car filled with soldiers and sailors with their shoes off, who were squirming around trying to find a comfortable position in which to sleep. The smell of that closed-in old railway car is with me still. Also with me, I might add is the more pleasant memory of our arrival on New Year's Eve, 1942 in Halifax. There was a kiosk in the station, which was connected to the Nova Scotian Hotel, and it was manned by volunteers working for the A.N.A. (Army, Navy, Airforce). One of these nice women took one look at the three of us bedraggled souls and said briskly, "Here. These are the keys to my suite upstairs in the hotel. Have a nice bath and a rest." What a welcome! I shall never forget it. This was, as I later learned, typical of the women of Halifax. My father was born a Haligonian and had talked so much about the city that I was excited just to be there, and especially in the hustle and bustle of wartime.

A bit later, refreshed and smartened up, we reported in and found that we were to work in the Filter Room in the basement of Eastern Air Command Headquarters, directly next door to the Naval Ops room, so if we didn't know what was going on with the war, we had only ourselves to blame.

Very quickly our lives fell into a routine of shifts. We learned the positions of all aircraft in the area, identified them, and watched them give cover to the convoys leaving for Ireland. We kept track of them as far as we could, and then the airwomen of Britain's WAAF would pick them up and guide them into Ireland.

Also, we were always keenly aware of the ships that were in Halifax harbour, what ships would be in the next convoy, and always, always, aware of the wolf packs of German subs that were waiting for them. Many of our ships never did reach the other side, and this proved to be very hard on those of us who had boyfriends on these ships; friends with whom we may have danced the night before they left.

In May, 1943, we found that we were to be sent to St. John's, Newfoundland. Five Canso aircraft were ready to fly us there. This was because of the Conference at Argentia between Churchill and Roosevelt. As well as 50 destroyers, Britain was to get an Operations Room on the American base — Fort Pepperell in St. John's. So, as a result, we were to be 200 Canadian girls working on a base with 5,000 American GIs!! In the deal, as it was worked out, Canada had to supply the airwomen.

Leaves were cancelled at once. My sister's wedding was coming up and, of course, I wouldn't be able to attend. What a mess! In addition to all that, I had never been up in an airplane so that flight, in the old Canso, would be my first.

By this time, I was a corporal and in charge of my group. Up to this point in the war, we had not yet been issued with slacks, but even so the airforce insisted we wear parachutes. With our skirts, I can assure you that we looked and felt pretty ludicrous as we laboured like gorillas, with the straps between our legs, lugging our kit bags out on the tarmac and onto the plane. The things we had to do for our country!!!

To be in St. John's during the war was a rare opportunity, because just about every navy in the free world was there, and one felt very close to all the action. Because we airwomen were allowed to wear civvies when on leave (the WRENS were not) we often went aboard these ships when they were in harbour and made many friends among the sailors and officers who were on the North Atlantic run. We did all of this quite secretly, you must understand, because it was very much against regulations. Only once did I run into an RCAF Women's Division officer who might have turned me in, but she didn't. The crime was that airwomen of my status, sergeant at that time, were not supposed to be going out with officers.

Several of us had our own special doryman who would take us out on special occasions to a beautiful spot called Freshwater Bay, and he would just leave us there to enjoy our day off, swimming and picnicking. He wouldn't come back to pick us up until hours later.

I left St. John's several times during the two years I was there, as I had become a "lofty" sergeant. Every once in a while I had to deliver new recruits who would be gathered up along the route of the "The Newfie Bullet" (the famous narrow-gauge railway) and I would take them to a recruiting officer on the mainland at Sydney, Cape Breton. On one occasion, the ferry before ours had been torpedoed by Nazi U-boats and greater precautions were put into effect. We had to cross by daylight instead of after dark, and every single one of the girls got deathly seasick in her bunk below. The only reason I didn't, was that I stayed upright in the fresh air on deck. Every once in a while I would go below to check that they were still alive, which they were, but not by their own choice.

After I delivered my charges to Sydney, I was allowed a 48-hour pass to go to Halifax, and later I boarded the *Lady Nelson* for the return trip to St. John's. On board were several Newfoundland boys who had joined the British navy and were now going home on leave.

A memory that will live with me forever is the look on their faces as the ship neared the shore and turned into St. John's harbour. Their love for their rocky homeland was so clearly etched in their faces that it just brought tears to my eyes. How they cherished that moment of return, to what was then Britain's oldest colony, after their dangerous time in the treacherous waters of the wartime North Atlantic‼

It would not be true to say we were not having a good time in the services, but the real purpose of our being where we were was never, ever, out of our minds. Off-duty was one thing, on-duty was another.

I remember one day when we were having lunch at a restaurant overlooking a small bay on the Avalon Peninsula, when we saw three of our Fairmile planes circling and dropping depth charges in the bay just outside our window. Before long, we saw the telltale oil slick appear on the surface and we heard the cheers of all those assembled as the German sub came to the surface. Reminders like this of how close to the war we really were were always at hand.

Another time, as Churchill and Roosevelt were meeting at the Quebec Conference, an unidentified aircraft suddenly appeared on our screens, and it was obviously headed in the direction where the conference was taking place. That, as you can imagine, caused quite a stir as all hands were called to action stations and all fighter planes at the base were despatched in pursuit. The outcome of that, however, was that it was just one of our own planes and the poor pilot was left to provide an explanation of why he was off course.

As D-Day neared, we were all well aware that invasion forces were being built up. That much was almost common knowledge. My board was solid with B-17s refuelling at Gander before heading "over there." The big invasion at Normandy finally did come, and it marked the beginning of the end for Hitler's Europe. This affected my life and, I imagine, those of thousands of others in the services in a way that the average person might never think about. Since it was fairly obvious that the war was moving inevitably towards its end, those in authority decided that it was time to make the first moves towards dismantling the huge war-machine they had built up. The first step was to declare an end to promotions for those of us who had been following career goals for the past five or six years. In my case, I was one of 12 girls from all across Canada who had been chosen for the next Officer's Training Course in Ottawa, along with another advanced radar course to be taken before advancing to OTC. Naturally, I had been excited and thrilled about all of this, but alas, it was not to be.

I hadn't even finished saying my goodbyes to all my good friends in dear old Newfie, when word came through that OTC for the twelve of us had been cancelled, and we were all to go back to our stations and pick up where we left off, as sergeants. Disappointing? That's a mild description. Some of the girls had already ordered their new officer's uniforms, which they had to cancel. Fortunately I hadn't done that. But what it meant really, was that we had reached the only top we would ever reach in a profession that we had come to know so well. The war would soon be over and we would all have to start thinking about new roles in civilian life.

In May of the next year, 1945, we were brought back to Halifax, which meant we were there as the war abruptly came to an end. The V-E Day parade in Halifax was great, something you'd not forget in a thousand lifetimes. Halifax had endured a lot in two world wars, and was ready for much rejoicing at the end of this one. There was, of course, the infamous Riot as spirits got out of hand, but one has to remember that it was a long war and the joy of victory drove some of our servicemen to the point of distraction. In our case, we were all confined to our Gorsebrook barracks and we were driven to our points of duty in paddy wagons.

They kept us on in Halifax until September, 1945, and we spent most of our time endlessly discussing what we would do with the rest of our lives. The government was offering us a chance at an education that most of us would never have dreamed of in those Depression pre-war years, so all of my group grabbed for the brass ring. Some chose McGill and others in our group chose the University of Toronto. One phase of our life was over and another was about to begin.

Our group has always maintained contact with each other over the years, and it's such a joy to me to see what a fine bunch of women all of them have always been, right to this day. I'm sure that the airforce experience had a lot to do with that, moulding and shaping us at a very impressionable time in our lives. We were given a difficult job to do and we were trusted at times with great war secrets. Though we were young and inexperienced, we gained a confidence in ourselves which, I am proud to say, has stayed with us.

Frank Cauley
Orleans, Ontario

I GUESS you could call this a story that involves a whole lot of luck and a whole lot of chewing gum. It was chewing gum that saved our bacon, you might say.

I had just finished a tour with the RAF Bomber Command and I was supposed to be going home for a month's leave but they needed Coastal Command navigators, so they promised me a month's holiday in Blackpool, if I would join a crew that was going to be flying out of Northern Ireland. They said that if I did that for them they would whisk me home immediately after so that I could take my discharge and get a job before anyone else. This was in March, 1944. It sounded pretty good to me, so I picked up a crew and we headed over to RCAF 422 Squadron in Northern Ireland where we took over a big four-engine Sunderland flying boat. We were assigned to submarine patrol which wasn't too exciting at that point in the war, but there were still some subs around if you could find them.

We took off about 11:00 in the morning on our patrol. You go out about 500 miles and start examining the water below you for anything that moves. Up to this point in the war, the RCAF hadn't been too successful in finding subs and in fact they had never had a confirmed sub kill. You can imagine the excitement of our whole 11-man crew when we spotted this German sub right up on the surface of the water. It was a beautiful sunny day and the crew of the sub were right out there on the conning tower sunning themselves and having a swim. We couldn't believe our eyes really because we

A bomber on submarine patrol. (Courtesy Frank Cauley)

were flying low and they should have easily picked us up on their radar. Somebody on their team goofed. The first thing I did was to break radio silence and give the base operator our position, saying that we had sighted a sub and we were attacking.

The crew on the deck of the sub saw us as we went in for the kill. We couldn't weave or anything like that, because we had six depth charges on board and with a load like that you don't fool around. As we were heading for them they recovered enough from their surprise to get their surface gun going at us and we caught one of their shells. That punched a big hole in our fuselage beneath the waterline and a whole lot of smaller shrapnel holes around it. However we got them good; our depth charges were right on the mark and it wasn't too long before the destroyed sub went to the bottom. All of this was photographed and we were able to get a fantastic record of everything as it happened. In fact, the picture of the sub going down became one of the great pictures of the war and Churchill had a

A depth charge hits its target. (Courtesy Frank Cauley)

The destroyed submarine goes down. (Courtesy Frank Cauley)

The crew of the German submarine in a dinghy. (Courtesy Frank Cauley)

copy of it in his library until the war ended. Eleven members of their crew died in that action, but a goodly number survived and were able to climb into their rescue dinghy and were picked up later by one of our surface vessels. They were a defiant bunch though, and kept shaking their fists at us and giving us the Hitler salute as we flew over to survey the scene. They spent the rest of the war in a prisoner-of-war camp. A week or so later when they took us to see these fellows, we were really surprised at what a scruffy-looking lot they were. Hitler was scraping the bottom of the barrel for his crews at that point in the war; all the good ones were gone.

But we had our own problems what with that big hole in the bow of our Sunderland and all those small holes around it. We knew that when we got back to base and tried to land her on the water, she'd go down like a brick. We radioed the base and told them of our predicament, and they said that they would send out surface craft to pick up the survivors and the rest. Strangely enough, the big hole wasn't the biggest problem. We had an emergency kit on board that covered situations like that, so the engineer was able to make a big patch and bolt it over that hole, much as you would with one of those Meccano sets we used to have as kids. The little holes were the biggest problem.

Our engineer, Ted Higgins, came up with the solution when he said half-jokingly, "Maybe we can patch them with chewing gum." Well, anything is worth a shot so we decided to try. We each had five sticks of Spearmint as part of our normal rations, so we all started to chew them up a stick at a time. Then, as fast as we chewed, Ted could come around and collect it from us and he'd cover up these small holes. Of course, none of us knew if this was going to hold, so when we got back to base we told them to have an emergency crew standing by. But, by the time we got there, the cold air had solidified the gum, and when we landed on the water we just coasted in to the dock as normal as you please. Everybody at the base was gathered to meet us or save us, whatever the case may be, because this was, after all, the first confirmed submarine kill and they didn't want to lose us now. The chewing gum saved us and there was a great celebration at the base that day.

A funny little follow-up to all of that is that both the Skipper and I were "only" warrant officers, non-commissioned, and the brass decided that this would never do, especially when the story hit the papers. They felt it just wouldn't be proper if the public should think that a couple of ordinary enlisted Canadians became in such responsible positions. So in no time at all, the two enlisted Canadians became commissioned officers and all was right and proper in the British perspective.

There were other rewards too; our captain received the Distinguished Flying Cross and the rest of us, the other ten crew members, were mentioned in dispatches.

The company that makes the gum sent each of us a complimentary 24-pack of Spearmint, but there wasn't any desire in any of us to ever have to see that gum in the same way again — once is enough.

Bob Loughlan
Thunder Bay, Ontario

THE TWENTY months from September, 1939 to April, 1941 were the slowest-paced months in the history of this particular man. This was the period from the start of the Second World War to my eighteenth birthday, an event which would allow me to get down to serious business with a recruiting officer.

For a sixteen-year-old it was a cruel wait. I had to stand by and watch many of my contemporaries who happened to be a couple of years older, sign up, leave for training, come back home for embarkation, leave in uniform, depart for overseas after having their pictures in the paper, and receive good wishes from everyone. I could only dream and curse the fact that I was born two years too late. Like most of my peers caught in a similar position, I was certain that the war would be over before I would get my chance to show them all how a fight should be won.

However, reality determines the outcome of most situations, so I spent the next two years working in a local aircraft factory and planning what I should do just in case there *was* a war to win when I finally became old enough to join.

When one of my slightly older chums came back from a tour of duty overseas wearing his beautiful air force uniform with the wings up on the left breast, *Canada* on the shoulder patches and a stripe or two on the cuffs of his jacket, my resolve to break away and get into the battle strengthened, especially since that same chum was also sporting under his golden wings a blue and white Distinguished Flying Cross ribbon. It was then I started to think seriously about which branch of the services would be for me.

When I thought about the army all I could come up with were visions of the trench fighting of World War One; going over the top, running across no man's land into the steady drumming of enemy machine guns, lying wounded in a wet, muddy shell-hole and mixing it up with fixed bayonets, one on one with the enemy. Somehow all of that didn't seem to be very attractive. Laying down your life for your country, it seemed to me, is an honourable thing to do, but only if you can't use a bit of friendly persuasion to get the enemy to lay down *his* life for *his* country. After careful consideration I ruled out the army as a career choice.

The navy didn't fare much better in my boyish and romantic way of thinking. The common image of the boys in navy blue in those days was that of a poor sailor trying to swim through diesel oil burning on the surface of the North Sea, while in the background you would see his ship burning and sinking. In addition, he would be trying to help a buddy make it to a life-raft that kept drifting farther from his reach. One of the two would always have a leg blown off or a hand that was burned down to the bone. (We did see a lot of war movies back in those days.)

The air force, my remaining alternative, brought forth images of a beleaguered pilot in a damaged aircraft trying to coax a few more miles out of his dying machine so it would make it to the landing strip. He would always lose the argument and the plane would go into a long dive ending with a big crash and a gigantic ball of flame.

The three choices weren't especially attractive. I could die in the mud of a Flanders-type field, in a flaming puddle of diesel oil in northern waters or in the flaming crash of an aircraft. Which was better?

I chose the latter because, in my boyish and romantic mind, if one is going to die, isn't it better to get it over quickly and completely in the flaming holocaust of a plane crash? So that settled it; when the time came for me to face the recruiting officer it would be the RCAF for me.

For the next two years while working in the war factory, I devoured everything that was written in the newspapers or broadcast on the radio about the war. The best thing about the movies would be the Movietone News that brought you — in those pre-TV days — live film from the Front. It was hard, though, to separate fact from fantasy and propaganda. Censorship was tight and we didn't know what was true and what was false.

Returning heroes who had been wounded in battle and sent home helped to fill in some of the blanks but even with them we couldn't decide which of their stories were true.

Then there were the rumours. One story that made the rounds was that one of our crowd from high school who had joined the air force had suffered a nervous breakdown because on the 11 bombing missions he had made and returned from safely, he had lost 11 tail gunners, and it was more than he could stand to watch their bodies being pulled from the aircraft.

Another of my high school classmates was hit by enemy fire over the English Channel but he was able to nurse his Spitfire the last few miles and land beautifully. While the ground crew cheered he taxied up to the hangar, cut the motor and died.

Other friends had been in aircrews that just disappeared without a trace. Others who were first reported missing turned up on prisoner-of-war lists many months later.

The effects of this on families back home was horrendous. Some of the relatives would hear first-hand accounts of how a family hero had crashed straight into the ground at speeds of up to 400 miles an hour in a dying fighter bomber and yet they refused to believe he had died. The hope would go on that he had somehow survived and was in a prisoner-of-war camp somewhere. For some, these hopes persisted many years after the war ended.

Eventually my own time came to get into the battle and get shipped overseas as a pilot. It was all I expected, with many chills and thrills and brushes with death, but as in all human experiences, thrills come in varying degrees of intensity. Compare the quiet thrill of finally breaking through the cloud cover and finding that you are right over the airport that you had been searching for for hours in a dense grey fog, to the tumultuous thrill of bailing out in the darkness, pulling the D-ring, and feeling the shock of your parachute taking hold of the air and knowing only then that you are going to make it after all.

I think, though, that it's the humour of war that you remember best of all. The mind seems to have a way of censoring things that we don't especially want to remember. One of my favourites occurred at a small elementary flying school that was located on a farm in the flat country of the English Midlands. It was where would-be pilots got their first taste of that wonderful bliss and sheer terror that are part of the process of learning to fly.

The airfield on this farm was in the form of a square, with the hangars, mess hall, barracks and offices grouped together on one side of the field. In the dead centre of this field was the farmhouse of the previous owner. It was just a simple cottage really, surrounded by a complete hedge of lilac bushes grown so high that they very nearly hid the building completely.

Our training aircraft was a deHavilland Tiger Moth, a light and beautiful little yellow biplane, where the instructor and his pupil were seated in separate cockpits in tandem.

By this time the war had advanced to the stage where the need for elementary training no longer existed, so that this particular airfield was now being used for pilots who already had a great deal of experience, but had to wait for postings to other operational units which would train them for service in the Pacific. In the meantime, because of their experience and skills, they were being used to fly navigators around the country practicing map reading in poor weather.

This is where the "hero" of this story comes in — a tall, ungainly Englishman who had already served a tour of duty on fighters and was now awaiting the time to go on a course where he would learn to fly the new Lincoln heavy bombers. "Spider," as he was nicknamed

— being skinny and all arms and legs — compensated for his unusual appearance by taking undue pride in his luxuriant moustache which he constantly groomed.

On the day in question, Spider had taken a Tiger Moth for a solo check. The wind was such, that he had landed behind the farmhouse out of sight of the hangars and offices. Much to his chagrin, he overshot slightly and the airplane, lacking brakes, rolled right into the lilac hedge which surrounded the farmhouse. There was no damage done but his propeller tangled in the lilac branches and stalled his motor. It was no big thing but it wasn't something you'd want any of your colleagues to see.

Climbing out of the aircraft, Spider walked over to the edge of the lilac hedge and peeked around in the direction of the hangars. Good; there was no activity whatsoever. If he played his cards right, he could get out of this with no one having witnessed his landing.

He pulled the little Tiger Moth out of the lilacs and pointed it across the field. His plan was to take off, join the circuit and then just land again as though nothing had happened. Of course, being alone, he had to swing the propeller himself to start the engine before running around quickly to jump in the cockpit. This would normally present no problem. However, this time there *was* a problem; he had left the throttle full on and when Spider gave the propeller a mighty heave, the motor roared to life at full power and lunged forward. Spider, taken totally by surprise, leaped off to one side and grabbed the handlehold at the starboard wingtip.

The plane was moving now at a pretty good pace and the only thing holding it back was Spider determinedly holding on to the wingtip. The Moth, desperately wanting to take off, was moving in circles around poor old Spider who was just as desperately trying to keep it tied to the ground. Needless to say, they were making quite a little ruckus between them, enough to attract the attention of those back at the hangar. One of the young mechanics there ran full speed across the field, jumped into the centre of this wild situation and when the opportunity came, flung himself into the empty cockpit and cut the switches to the motor.

The airplane came to a complete stop and so did Spider who was by now so dizzy and exhausted, he just collapsed to the ground in a flurry of elbows, arms, legs and knees. As he lay there in a heap, the only thing left to cover his total humiliation was that magnificent moustache which was gently waving in the breeze.

Poor Spider. His innocent little attempt at cover-up turned into an incident that will never be forgotten.

I don't know what became of Spider, or for that matter most of those people one came in contact with for brief periods of time during the wartime years. I guess all of us were, in fact, just ships that passed in the night. Those were years full of experiences and incidents of many kinds; chilling, thrilling, frightening and ordinary . . . most to be forgotten . . . some to be remembered. In the latter category, for anyone who has ever had to use one to save his life, will be the invisible parachute — or the "chair of air" as we used to call it. My first experience of this kind took place one wild night in 1944, along with three other companions.

It was January 21, and our Anson 367 was in the air humming along nicely for our return trip from the base at Saint John, New Brunswick to our home base at Dartmouth, Nova Scotia. It was just another routine trip really; we had been called upon to deliver a small parcel of medical supplies to the Saint John RCAF base and then home again. Old 367 was a good, stable aircraft that had seen service in the Battle of Britain and was now being used on Canada's Eastern Air Command for routine trips such as the one we were on. It had reliable motors, a sturdy frame of aluminium tubing and the whole thing was covered with good, strong camouflaged fabric. The undercarriage was the kind that had to be wound down by hand whenever it was needed. There was one door on the starboard side just after the wing.

As pilot, I felt very comfortable that night as I set my course to intercept a leg of the radio range that would take us home "on the beam" without having to do a lot of navigation. To get back to Dartmouth air base at Eastern Passage just across the harbour from Halifax, was relatively easy anyway, as it was hard to miss Bedford Basin where all the Atlantic convoys were assembled. A person could always see the lights on the masts of the ships in the basin and the lights of the city itself. By just following the north shore of the basin and the harbour until you reached the red lights on the smokestack of the sugar factory, you could then make a sharp turn to the left and find yourself right over the airport. Nothing to it.

As the evening progressed, weather conditions worsened. The visibility went to zero as we ran into a thick fog bank that rolled in suddenly from the Atlantic. In a matter of minutes all ceiling and visibility in every active airport in the province was wiped out — with the exception of the one at Sydney, far to the northeast on Cape Breton Island.

Despite the most heroic efforts of our operator Kenny, radio reception on our aircraft had deteriorated badly. He had managed to get us on the frequency that would allow us some chance of getting home but the thunderclouds along the storm front were kicking up so much static it was sheer torture to try to listen. If you did latch on to a beam and try to follow it on your earphones, a piercing burst of this static would erupt and make you feel as though your head had been blown off.

For an hour or so, the two of us who were doing the piloting fought the situation without any due alarm. We hung onto the right-hand edge of the beam with the knowledge that eventually this would take us over "the cone of silence" marker which would lead us to the airport. However, at the very moment when we were expecting to hit this marker, there was a deafening burst of static in our headsets which continued long enough to make us miss the spot completely, meaning we would have to start our procedures all over again.

The next try brought us down over the airport but in such a way that we were in no position to land; there was nothing for us to do but shoot back up into the thick, black fog. By this time it was obvious to all of us on board that we weren't going to make it in the conventional manner. We set our course then for a spot over the ocean so that we would be able to fly low enough to be able to see the water. So positioned, we started following the shoreline which would eventually lead us to the airport. The problem here was that the bottom of the fog was not a consistently level sheet. It varied up and down a couple of hundred feet, which made it very risky to be flying at a low level towards obstructions that were known to be there, but which we couldn't always see. It was a game of Blind Man's Bluff with life or death as the prize.

The four of us agreed that we should make one more attempt to do it on the radio range. This time we were able to navigate to a spot where we could actually see the lights of the ships in Bedford Basin, but the fog base kept forcing us to go down lower and lower until at one point we found we were no higher than the tops of the masts of the ships we were passing. We found ourselves swerving in and out to avoid crashing into masts.

We followed the shoreline in this fashion until, out of the gloom, we could see the red lights on the smokestack of the sugar factory. Once again we made the familiar left turn to the airport. But once again, we were too low to land and too low to manoeuvre safely.

Meanwhile, the control tower was going crazy trying to make contact with us. When he finally made it to us through the static to ask how much fuel we had left, I replied, "Twenty minutes only."

"Good," said the voice from the tower, "Go to Sydney then."

"Thank you for that good advice," I answered. "You and I both know that Sydney is an hour away. We are going to bail out. Over and out!!!"

Having finally come to this decision I must confess that I experienced a great feeling of relief. I climbed old Anson 367 up to five thousand feet and headed north to where I knew we'd be over land and not ocean. I asked Marcel, my co-pilot, to go back and make sure that the other two on board were properly harnessed and instructed in the use of the parachute. He found that Kenny, the radio operator, needed no instruction having long ago decided that if he was going to be up in the air doing a job, it might be a good idea if he also knew how to get down.

Such wasn't the case with Oscar who wasn't part of the crew but a hitch-hiking hospital orderly who had asked me in Saint John if he could ride with us back to Halifax so that he could visit his parents on his 48-hour pass. That was just a few hours ago. Now here was this poor guy who had never even been up in an airplane before being told to jump out, and not only to jump, but to jump first! After a few attempts at stalling for ". . . a final cigarette . . ." Marcel had to put his foot against Oscar's back and administer the final shove before he disappeared into the darkness.

Now it was Kenny's turn. He told Marcel to hold the door wide open so that he could dive out head first and not hit his head on the tail of the plane. He backed up as far as he could and took a couple of running steps towards the open door but at the last split second, spread his arms out at the opening, grabbed on and held himself back.

"Oh what the hell," he said, "I think it's just as safe to slide out slowly." And that's what he did.

By this time, Marcel and I were beginning to realize that this bailing out business was serious stuff. We had seen too, that if it took one man to hold the door for the other man to jump, then the last man would be caught inside with nobody to hold the door. This was a situation that called for a fast solution, so Marcel grabbed hold of the fire-axe from its clip and chopped a big hole in the wall of the cabin over the wing. After that he came back to the cockpit, shook hands with me and said, "See you down below tomorrow."

Then he too was gone and I was alone steering the aircraft and trimming the controls so that when I left, it would keep on course straight and level as long as possible before crashing.

I felt a variety of emotions: relief brought about from the stress of trying to guide the plane into the airport, concern about the safety of the others, excitement brought on by the high drama of the event I was caught up in, determination to do everything right, and a slight concern, but no actual fear, about the jump that I still had to make from the aircraft.

Remembering the drill from my classes, I picked up my parachute chest pack and clipped it to the rings of my body harness in such a way that I would be able to use my right hand to pull the D-ring to open the 'chute while I was in the air and falling. That done, I climbed out feet first through the hole that Marcel had smashed through with his axe, held on briefly to the jagged sides and let go.

Falling rapidly through the air, I could see the red and green running lights of old Anson 367 disappear into the night. I could feel myself still falling but in such a way that I was in a seated position, quite comfortable really, supported only by the stream of air that appeared to be supporting me from below. This was "the chair of air" that I had heard others talk about!! Well, there was no time to sit around enjoying such luxury. The time had arrived to pull the D-ring that would open the 'chute and float me safely down to earth.

I reached inside the pack with my right hand as planned and discovered to my horror that the ring was not there. After a few moments of panic during which I relived every story I had ever heard of men whose parachutes failed to open. I located the D-ring on the *left* side. How it got there after my careful packing procedures I don't know . . . and at that moment I didn't care. I just grabbed it gratefully and pulled. I experienced such tremendous relief when I felt the impact of the opening of the canopy above me that I actually screamed aloud, "Thank you, God!"

Next thing I knew, I was dangling upside down, feet caught in the upper branches of a spruce tree. Once again I remembered my classroom lessons of what to do in emergency situations. I reached out and felt for the trunk of the tree, grabbed hold of it firmly, hit the release plate of my parachute harness, and hoped that everything worked the way it should. It did and in short order I was free of the parachute and harness and able to regain an upright position so that I could lower myself to the ground. It wasn't exactly ground though; I had landed in a swamp covered by about two feet of snow.

After some sloshy walking around for something like an hour, I heard a man's cough some distance away. I did some pretty loud shouting and whistling and eventually attracted the attention of the man who turned out to be a lumberjack on his way back to camp. Somewhat surprised to find a stranger wandering around in a swamp in a bulky flying suit, he quickly overcame the shock and guided me out to the highway and the home of a country doctor who examined me, found me fit and prepared me a breakfast of bacon and eggs.

I used his phone, and was able to locate the others of my party, all of whom were safe, and also to find out that old Anson 367 was now a pile of rubble in a farmer's field.

When we finally got back to the station in Dartmouth and reported in to our Group Captain, his only comment was, "I'm happy that there were enough parachutes packed on board." We didn't say it to him but we were kind of glad about that too.

Looking back on the whole war experience after almost 50 years, it was something that most of us wouldn't have wanted to miss. But the ultimate thrill after four-and-a-half years was striding through that last gate of that last air force station with my Discharge Certificate firmly clutched in my hand and knowing that now my real life was about to begin.

Les Alexander
Flin Flon, Manitoba

THE BRITISH Commonwealth Air Training Plan, according to many war historians, was Canada's greatest single contribution to the Allied victory in the Second World War. The contract for this was signed on December 19, 1939, a mere four months after the outbreak of war, and was announced to the public one week later. The BCATP was a co-operative effort between Canada, Australia, New Zealand and the United Kingdom to establish a training program for pilots at a point in the war when they were most desperately needed.

When the war started, Hitler and Goering knew that their superiority in planes and crews could swamp the Allies. The Allies knew that too and they knew they had to move fast or else. Before 1939 was over, the master plan was in place and in no time at all, it seemed, young men and women from all over the commonwealth were flocking to this country to "get their wings" in the more than 100 schools and depots that showed them how to fly. I am proud to say that I was one of those young men.

It was an absolutely stupendous effort brought about in a very short time and, indeed, what Canada had achieved was looked upon with something akin to awe by the other allied powers. Franklin Delano Roosevelt, the President who brought America into the war, called the BCATP "the aerodrome of democracy."

The BCATP did a great job, but one of the things that should be made clear is that it wasn't just the RCAF that was involved here in Canada. The Plan involved not only service personnel like me but it also included a very large number of civilians who worked their heads off with the same kind of dedication. Something in the order of 60 percent of those working for the plan were civilians, and at least one-third of these were women who have never been given proper recognition for the work they did. This was because they were given all the dirty jobs to do, the no glory but very important jobs. As a pilot, I always felt safe flying the aircraft that the civilians serviced; they seemed to be very careful in their attention to the details of their work.

We were trained as precision crews and our task was to fly at night to bomb a specific target, or if that one turned out to be impossible, some alternate target. Our flights had a duration of three hours with only 15 minutes allotted for the actual dropping of bombs. I made 500 of these training flights and never had one iota of trouble with any of those machines — not even an uncalled-for flutter of an engine. I have always attributed this to those women who did much of the servicing.

As far as I was concerned, my time was easy, all of it spent sitting on a foam rubber cushion so that whenever we landed back at base, I always felt sorry for those girls who were there to replace our gas and oil and whatever else had to be done, in weather that was often cold and wet. Sure, the pilots and the air crews did a great job but it's time now to give credit to those on the ground without whom we couldn't have kept those planes aloft.

Let's also remember the "parachute ladies" who did their work, not only at Portage, Manitoba, where I was trained, but at other centres all across the country. It was their job to properly pack parachutes and maintain them. Only a flier can fully appreciate how important it was to have confidence in the pack that might some day save your life. Every 'chute had to be done perfectly and it had to be inspected and hung every 30 days. The harness had to be cleaned and repaired continuously. By the way, these parachutes cost about $350 each and the harnesses were $84. That was as a lot of money during the war years — enough to buy a new car if you could find one, which you couldn't, of course.

Under the Plan, air crews were given training as close as possible to the actual conditions they would encounter when they went overseas. Everyone who took part in training them was as dedicated as if it actually were the real thing. I take my hat off to them all, especially those women who have never been given any credit. Because of their caring, many of us have been given many extra years of life. When our planes and equipment were called on to do a job, they were ready to perform.

Jack M. Peaker
Guelph, Ontario

I COULDN'T get into the services because of a disabled arm, but that didn't stop me from wanting to be there. I partially solved that problem through my active imagination; I lived my service life through a relative who was very much involved. Reading about his exploits in the newspapers made me feel very close to what was going on.

This relative was my uncle, Air Chief Marshal Lloyd S. Breadner, who was one of the key Canadian military men of the war. He was involved in all of the high-level planning and often had meetings with Churchill. He was married to my mother's sister, and would often come to our Ottawa home where he would engage in long conversations with my father about the war and how it was progressing.

Listening to these conversations made me feel very important and very much on the inside. He would talk about the British Commonwealth Air Training Plan and the number of new flying schools that were opening all over the country at that time and the number of fliers from all of the Allied nations who were being

Taken on the roof of the Citadel, Quebec City, during the Quebec Conference, 1944. **Left to right:** *Prime Minister Mackenzie King, Chief-of-Staff Air Chief Marshal L.S. Breadner, Lady Churchill, Chief-of-Naval-Staff Admiral Nelles, Chief-of-Army-Staff Field Marshal K. Stewart, (Photographer unknown)*

trained in Canada. My dad was very interested in all of this because he had spent four years in World War One and he followed closely everything that was happening in this new one.

Just listening to them gave me an insight on the war that my friends couldn't possibly have, and I think I probably knew as much about the Air Training scheme as anyone around, even though I was just a bystander. That was an intriguing part of my life and it kind of made up for the disappointment I felt at not being able to wear a uniform.

Uncle Lloyd had a fascinating career and played a very important role in Canada's conduct of the war. He was, of course, Chief of the Air Staff throughout the whole of the Second World War.

As we moved out of the early stages of the war and had more and more RCAF servicemen stationed overseas, Uncle Lloyd moved his offices out of Ottawa and was headquartered on Downing Street, London, and his daughter, who was in the WAAFs, acted as his secretary. His son Don, who was 19 at the time, was also in the air force and all ready to embark for overseas. Don was flying a Mosquito in his last training exercise at Debert, Nova Scotia, when his plane crashed and he and his navigator were both killed.

When Don's body was taken back to Ottawa for the funeral, Billy Bishop stood in for my uncle who couldn't get back from overseas to be with the family. That took place at a very bad time in the war and things were very hectic in the air over Britain. It was very hard on my uncle not to be at the funeral. I was there of course. Don had not only been a good friend, just six months older than I, but he was also a close cousin.

Uncle Lloyd, being headquartered on Downing Street, came into almost daily contact with Winston Churchill, and in fact he accompanied him to the Quebec Conference between Roosevelt and Churchill. As you can imagine, our family was very proud of our Uncle Lloyd.

My own working career in Ottawa during the war included being in charge of the files for next-of-kin for the armed forces. I was also involved in other duties with the Defence Department.

You might say, too, that I have the war to thank for the lady I married. She came to Canada towards the end of the war after having been through the Blitz and all the other horrors of wartime Britain including once spending hours crouched under the dining room table while outside the bombs were tearing the city to pieces.

Prior to meeting my future wife, though, one of the good things that I remember about the war years in Ottawa, is that it was a perfect place for a bachelor. There were 20 females there for every male and dates were no problem, although getting gasoline for my 1935 Packard Straight Eight was. That was a problem for anybody with a car at that time. Gas was strictly rationed and the penalties were harsh for anybody caught getting more than they were supposed to have. A lot of people solved the problem by just putting their cars up on blocks until the war was over.

John McQuisten
Don Mills, Ontario

THROUGHOUT EUROPE in late 1944, the Allies were on the offensive and we were driving the Nazis out of France, Belgium and the Netherlands. Aerial bombardment played a major role in the success of the operations and I was part of that, being a bomber pilot with Number 415 Squadron of the RCAF.

The period between September, 1944 and March, 1945 was the busiest time of the war for me because that's when this cleanup operation was at its height. I kept a sort of diary while all of this was going on so that I can just turn a page and certain incidents come flowing back as if they had happened yesterday. I also have a copy of the squadron diary and, of course, my own flying log book. In addition to that, my father kept all the letters I wrote home. With all of that, it isn't difficult to bring those days back again.

The thing I remember most is a word that maybe a lot of Canadians are not familiar with — unless they've spent a lot of time in Britain during the war — and that word is Tannoy. To explain, let me state first of all that the English have a habit of attaching the name of the manufacturer to devices that they use. For instance you'll never hear them speak of a vacuum cleaner. It's always referred to as a Hoover. Well, Tannoy is the name of the company which is the pre-eminent manufacturer of public address systems so that they will never say that they heard it on the public address system — they heard it on "the Tannoy."

When we were summoned to our flights with the words "Tannoy calling, Tannoy calling," it for ever more guaranteed that when you heard those words you would picture yourself scrambling to get out to the field and on board your aircraft. If you were being called to the mess you would hear those same words first "Tannoy calling, Tannoy calling." Every message that came over the system was always preceded by those words and I often thought, "Could there ever be a better commercial for a product?"

The plane I flew was a four-engine bomber, a Halifax 3 or a Halifax 7. Most people, I guess, are more familiar with the Lancaster 25; more of those were flown, but Canadians mainly flew Halifax bombers, although the two planes were rather similar. The Lancaster carried a bigger bomb load but aside from that they were very much the same. It's rather strange to report that there is not one Halifax bomber left in the world today as far as anybody knows. There are rumours that there are a few in India but nobody yet has confirmed that. A couple of Lancasters are still flying because of the loving care given to their restoration by groups who care, but not one Halifax is flying today — that's unfortunate.

Our mission between September, 1944 and March, 1945 was to sweep up, or complete unfinished business. When France was being cleared out of enemy occupation the Canadian First Army was given the left wing to clear the Channel ports. The Germans decided to defend them to the death to deny us use of these facilities. Until Antwerp was captured, supply lines were very tenuous and that greatly slowed down the Allied advance. The Germans were well dug in.

Then somebody had the bright idea that if you bombed the thing into rubble it would help the army take it. That was a good theory but it was only that — theory. Cassino was the battle that proved that this theory wasn't quite true. The enemy just buried themselves down in the rubble and came up to do battle when necessary, using the rubble as fortifications. So that theory was then modified.

What they did after that was have the army get close to the enemy — to within about 1,500 yards. This seemed like a pretty long distance but it really wasn't, because they had very accurate bombing in those days. We would be well-prepared for these bombing runs. The army would display coloured panels for our guidance, we would do timed runs from the lighthouse, for example, and from a low level we would fly in and saturate the German defences. Then the Canadian army would move right in. This proved a very successful plan. From the reports that came in afterwards, it was established that Canadian casualties were few. I have talked with many soldiers who were involved, and they all vouch that this system was very successful. I found it very satisfying.

When we dropped those bombs we never had the feeling we were killing human beings. In fact, we hoped we weren't. We were just dropping bombs on military targets trying to destroy the enemy's capability to wage a war against us. Also, the very fact that we were being shot at ourselves while doing this was foremost in our minds. The truth is, it wasn't hard to push a button and not have to look the enemy in the eye. It makes it much easier to kill. That applies to any military man. You don't have to be a bad person to do it.

One of the phrases we would hear a lot was "press on," and that was drummed into all of us. People would go to a target all the way and back, with an engine out, and always in the back of their minds driving them forward was "press on."

I remember one run we made over Germany in daylight, after we had long-range fighter planes available to us. I guess I made 16 daylights out of 36 trips. We went to Cologne one day — I think I bombed that place five times — but on this particular day there was a double raid planned. The early raid hit the west bank and we were to hit the east bank later on in the day. The problem was that cloud covered the east bank and the Master Bomber gave us the code to bomb any built-up area.

Before we got to Cologne, we flew over a large building with two tall smoke stacks. I didn't know what it was — perhaps an institution of some kind. Eight hundred bombers bombed this one building; they obliterated it. Then my plane came over the target and my bomb-aimer said to me, "Shall I do it too?" I said, "No. It's just a waste of time. There's nothing left. Anyway we came to bomb Cologne so let's just press on and do it."

So, we flew over Cologne all by ourselves, which seems kind of stupid as I think about it now, but it seemed like a good idea then. Oddly enough, there wasn't a lot of flak which indicated to us that the earlier raid must have been effective. Anyway, we bombed Cologne all by ourselves. All the other planes had dropped their bombs on that big building.

When we got back, we found out that the building was a place called Haversak, which was the main generating station for the area's industries. The tactical air force had been trying to knock it out for years but hadn't been able to, because of all the flak that constantly surrounded it. Of course, our squadron was flying so high their flak couldn't come near us. It might have taken 800 bombers to wipe it out but everyone figured afterwards that it was worth it.

Donald E. Watson
Etobicoke, Ontario

I WAS EIGHTEEN in the late summer of 1940, as carefree as one could possibly be in wartime Britain in the city of London. We were getting used to the air raids by this time and life just seemed to go on. I had a job at the time and on this particular afternoon I was sauntering down a sunlit road on my way to the bank to deposit the day's cheques for my employer. I was in a pretty good mood as I swung along, thinking about my imminent callup for the Royal Air Force. It should come very, very soon, I thought. I had been waiting for months now and each day made me more impatient than ever to join my friends who were already in uniform serving their "King and Country" in the fight against Hitler and his gang.

It was one of those ideal English summer afternoons. The sky was dotted with cotton-batten clouds sailing across an azure background. I paused to look at a baby in a carriage in the garden across the road. It was chuckling and gurgling in obvious contentment, and for a moment, one could hardly imagine that this little scene was taking place in a country that was under siege by a vicious enemy.

The peace of the moment was suddenly shattered by the sound of a menacing-looking black plane that appeared from out behind one of those deceptively beautiful white clouds. As the aircraft moved in my direction, I could spot the swastika on its fuselage and I realized it was a German Heinkel about to make a sneak bombing run.

As I stood glued to my position on the sidewalk, a half-dozen bombs left the plane. At first they tumbled crazily from the bomb racks, and then they began their deadly, straight descent earthward. I could see I was directly in the path of the deadly load so I flung myself down behind the nearest big tree and held my breath waiting for the explosions.

I didn't have long to wait. Seconds later, the whole world seemed to be filled with ear-splitting sound and the air around me was filled with clouds of dust, the fearful racket of bomb fragments and rubble falling from the nearby houses. I stayed put, praying that this shower of shrapnel would not find my hiding place.

Out of the corner of my eye, I saw something white, something that looked like a bundle of rags, come flying through the air and land at the curbside near where I was cowering. I didn't dare move, even to see what it was.

Then, almost as suddenly as it came, the plane sped off, its mission accomplished. I sat up and looked around at the devastated landscape which only a few moments before had been such a vision of peace and contentment. Garden walls were piles of rubble and every house on the street lay in ruins. And then I noticed again that small, white bundle that landed near my feet during the raid. The bundle was no longer white and I noticed that it was almost sliced in two, both parts drenched in what looked like blood.

Tentatively, and with a mounting dread, I made my way over to examine it. As I peeled back the layers of cloth, I realized that what was inside was the remains of that tiny, happy baby which only minutes before caused me to stop in this spot in the first place. As I stood there, the air was suddenly and chillingly pierced by the terrible shrieking of a woman who was tearing across the road in my direction. The anguished cries of that young mother still haunt me and will continue to do so until the day I die.

That was the day I found out what war was all about. It wasn't the dreams of glory and the glamour of the uniform that I had been imagining in my desire to become part of it. It wasn't the blaring of the military bands and the mouthing of patriotic platitudes by politicians. War is the cesspool that condones the most hideous of human crimes — including the wholesale and indiscriminate maiming and slaughtering of the innocent.

When my time came to wear the uniform I entered the service with no thoughts of glory. All I wanted was revenge for the death of one baby.

"National Selective Service"

WHEN THE war first started, Canada was just starting to pull itself out of a ten-year period of depression. More than a million men, women, and children were on relief and close to half a million Canadian workers were unemployed — this out of a population of 12 million. The outbreak of war soon made a big dent in these numbers as the men rushed to volunteer for the armed forces and other work. Employment opportunities for both men and women started to emerge as a result of the money the government was spending on war materials and war construction.

The fall of France in 1940 had a great impact on the thinking of the Allied powers. Pre-war theories about the invincibility of the Maginot Line suddenly changed to a realization of the power held by the forces of Hitler. Where Canada's role had been blueprinted as a supplier of food and ammunition, it was now realized that Canada would also have to make a heavy manpower contribution to the Allied forces.

In June, 1940, the National Resources Mobilization Act was passed requiring all Canadians to put their persons and property at the disposal of the state. National Registration required every person over the age of 16 to sign up for National Service. At the same time, voluntary recruiting for overseas serve was supplemented by compulsory military service for duty in Canada. In October of that year, the first group of men was "called up" for limited periods of military training. Later the "limited" was dropped, and those who were called up were required to serve for the duration of the war.

In 1941, a national employment service came into being to administer manpower policy, followed in 1942 by a National Selective Service designed to use efficiently the people of Canada for the varied purposes of the war.

Under all of these new regulations every industry, whether engaged in war work or otherwise, was given a priority as to its right to the use of the labour force. Under the new regulations those industries engaged in producing war materials would get a *very high* priority and would have first call on available manpower. The other classifications came down the ladder from there: *high, low,* or *no,* priority, the latter classification going to an industry that was perceived to be making things that were of no consequence to the war effort. Ammunition factories, naturally were rated *very high*, while factories producing private automobiles or silk stockings ended up with a *no*. Canadian men soon learned how to patch up the old family buggy themselves and women learned the art of painting their legs.

Under NSS regulations all employers and employees had to use the government employment offices, and no employee could quit or be discharged without giving or receiving seven days' notice. Employers were not allowed to conduct interviews, and the workers themselves couldn't look for work or accept work unless they first obtained a permit from the local employment office. These permits were restricted as to duration, locality, industry and occupation and were even restricted to specified employers. Employers were not allowed to advertise for workers and they had to requisition all of their workers from the employment office. The result of all this was that there was very little turnover in the labour market for the duration of the war. Most people stayed in their jobs and with the companies that first employed them.

War employment reached its peak by October 1, 1943, when more than 13 percent of Canada's total population aged 14 and over — 1,166,000 people — were engaged, directly or indirectly, in war work. Add to this number the nearly 800,000 in the armed forces and you come up with almost 2,000,000 out of our 12,000,000 people who were directly occupied with the business of winning the Second World War. To borrow the title of a popular National Film Board series being seen in theatres during the war, *Carry on Canada*!

John Grimshaw

NUMBER ONE Manning Pool in Toronto! There was a certain war-inspired romantic sound to that name for the thousands of adventure-seeking youngsters who joined the services either for patriotism or fun. The manning pool was the next step after seeing the recruiting officer and it was here that the raw recruits received their indoctrination and learned the facts of service life.

There were manning pools, or manning depots, all across the country and because of the swiftness with which Canada went to war, we had to use whatever buildings were already at hand — warehouses, empty factories and things like that.

I was just another youngster, one of many thousands, who had been anxiously awaiting his eighteenth birthday so I could get into the action with the air force.

It all seems so long ago now, but after all these years I can still smell the scent of the equine occupants of the place mixed with the body odours of several thousand newly enlisted and slightly bewildered new members of the Royal Canadian Air Force. The RCAF's Number One Manning Depot was the recently vacated home of the Royal Winter Fair — the Coliseum building of Toronto's Canadian National Exhibition. The horses were gone but their smell still hung heavily in the air.

This is where I found myself in December, 1941, Aircraftsman Second Class, Grimshaw, J.R., #148511, after having sworn allegiance to King George VI to defend the British Empire and Dominions beyond the seas from those Nazis and their nasty Allies. I was just one more of those slightly bewildered, raw recruits full of romantic illusions about war.

But disillusionment set in quickly. (The lingering smell of horse manure didn't help.) "What," I thought, "is this 18-year-old innocent doing in a reeking den of iniquity?" The question seemed especially pertinent as I stood in a long line waiting for "Shortarm Inspection" from a no-nonsense medical team. The Medical Officer — already we had learned to call him the M.O. — matter of factly moved down the line of naked and embarrassed youngsters checking our private parts to determine if we had become infected by some unmentionable disease. Silently I wondered who had coined the name "Shortarm" for such an inspection.

Just two years earlier on September 3, 1939, I passed a newspaper box and glanced at the bold, black headline of a special edition of the *Toronto Telegram*, **WAR DECLARED—POLAND INVADED**.

On that sunny summer day the headlines meant little. After all, they were referring to something in a far-off land. Here in Canada we were peaceful, snug and safe; my immediate problems were high school and the Depression.

One week later, Canada threw its hat in the ring and issued its own declaration of war. After one short week of neutrality we were in it up to our necks and I realized that even as a sixteen-year-old this was now my problem too.

Two years later, I was one of the many thousands of young men who decided to enlist and get into the excitement. It was a release from the boredom and the sameness, a chance to see the world and, corny as it may sound, a chance to serve and fight for one's country against a common enemy. Also, to be brutally frank, it was a good idea to join up if one didn't want to be called a draft dodger.

But we had fun, too — even at manning pool. Every new batch of recruits that came marching in was greeted by raucous shouts, jeers and the inevitable question, "Anyone from the West?" And when some poor soul answered in the affirmative, the cry came back loud and clear, "F--- the West."

The same abuse was suffered by those from other parts of the country too.

In those days, just before the United States entered the war, there were RCAF volunteers from that country who would proudly display right under the RCAF insignia the letters U.S.A. and the American eagle. We Canadians delighted in calling it an albatross.

It was around that time too, that the white flashes worn in their caps by air crew trainees became the subject of some nasty rumours instigated by those who weren't entitled to wear them. They told stories, particularly to all those nice Toronto girls, that airmen who wore white flashes had venereal disease and that it would be a good idea to stay well away from them.

While we were stationed at manning pool for basic training and indoctrination, one of the things we had to do was check in and out by punch clock, much the same as factory workers. Each of us had our own timecard and woe to the unfortunate who was negligent about using it. It was up on the carpet for him and then, after an embarrassing dressing-down, he would end up on potato-peeling detail or some other menial task.

Manning pool was also the place where one learned to queue for everything — haircuts, meals, sheets, blankets, pay, toilet, showers and shaves. Everything — including the ubiquitous Shortarm Inspection, ID cards and mail. There was also the rumour that this was the place where the food we ate in the mess hall got its heavy lacing of saltpetre, which was supposed to keep young airmen's active hormones under control. Judging by what I saw while I was there, I don't think it worked.

Inside that vast CNE Coliseum building was one area called the "bull-pen." It was here that we did the rest of our living in a sea of double bunk beds made of metal. This was our "home away from home" until we received our posting to some training school or other. At night this cavernous room was bathed in an eerie blue light and it was filled with the night noises created by a thousand sleeping bodies. The only other sounds were those which came from those unlucky souls on night guard duty making their rounds. Occasionally, if one were awake and listening, you could hear the soft sniffles of some lonely youngster who couldn't get used to being away from home.

For despite the huge numbers of people crowded into this colossus of a building, it was, for some, the loneliest spot in the world. Most had never been away from home before and now here they were, facing a world where everyone and everything was foreign to them. All of one's possessions were crammed into a blue issue kit bag stencilled in white with the owner's name and number and it didn't take us long to realize that that's all we were now — a name and a number. Any individuality we may have had was being stifled by military discipline. This is where we recruits came in the door clothed in the "civvies" of the world we left — the zoot suits and the duck-tail haircuts of the early forties — and we re-emerged from military stores looking exactly like everybody else on the parade ground with the same standard uniform and the same standard haircut. As we used to say at that time, the barber gave you a choice of two styles — short and shorter.

Route marches were held daily and these usually consisted of a brisk march along Toronto's Lakeshore Road to a coffee and doughnut shop several miles away where we were allowed to take a break and listen to juke box records of Big Band music. All too soon we would be formed up again and marched back to the Coliseum. If the weather was bad we did our parading indoors, around and around the arena.

Everything we learned, including staying awake on guard duty, was new to us. We learned to challenge the N.C.O. (Non-Commissioned Officer) with a "Who goes there?" We learned that everybody else in those first few weeks was homesick too. It was just that some were better at hiding it than others. Our officers knew, though, and they saw to it that we were kept busy all the time with seemingly endless and meaningless chores. Meaningless they may have been to us, but they did have the desired effect of making us forget what we were crying about.

There were brass buttons and belt buckles to be polished, shoes to be shined, uniforms to be pressed and more subtle things, like learning how to keep out of the way of corporals and sergeants. Perhaps most important of all, we learned that we should never, ever, volunteer for anything.

And so it went, day after day, and week after week, until one magical day we were declared trained, ready and fit to face the next stage in the transformation of civilian to serviceman.

It was on now to skills training and then, one hoped, to that next step, about which we had all dreamed, that of crossing the ocean and getting our own personal crack at Hitler.

My time did come, and an exciting time it was too, as part of the

At Fano on the Italian front, an RCAF Vickers Supermarine Spitfire 417, City of Windsor Squadron. (Courtesy the National Archives of Canada)

RCAF contingent in the RAF Transport Command and in Bomber Reconnaissance Squadrons in both the Atlantic and Pacific Commands. That was my world from 1941 to 1946.

Don Shade
Arnprior, Ontario

I WONDER how many people remember the Elsan? Perhaps I should say, how many people who used one can ever forget?

The Elsan was the portable metal toilet used in bomber aircraft and it was something that was hated by air crew and ground crew alike; the air crew because they had to use it, and the ground crew because they had to empty it. It was a horror.

The name Elsan is something of a mystery but I've heard it said, and this seems to make sense, that the "El" and the "san" in military parlance stood for "lavatory-sanitary." However, it was anything but sanitary, believe me, a veteran user of the Elsan.

While we were flying in rough air, this devil's convenience often shared its contents with the floor of the aircraft, the walls, the ceiling and, sometimes, a bit remained in the container itself.

It doesn't take much imagination to picture what it was like, trying to combat fear and airsickness, struggling to remove enough flying clothing in cramped quarters, and at the same time trying to use the cursed Elsan. If it wasn't an invention of the devil, it certainly must have been one foisted on us by the enemy.

When seated in frigid cold amid the cacophony of roaring engines and whistling air, away from the war for what should have been one of life's peaceful moments, the occupant had a chance to fully ponder the miserable condition of his life.

This loathsome creation invariably overflowed on long trips and in turbulence was always prone to bathe the nether regions of the user.

There are those today who may decry the inconvenience of the long-gone outdoor "biffy" but in comparison to the Elsan, the outhouse is heaven on earth.

I have yet to come across one of these torture chambers in a museum, and I think it is a mistake that at least one is not included. It is one of the true reminders to me that war is hell.

Ann Farrell
Toronto, Ontario

I WAS MUCH too young when the war started to get into any branch of the services — I was only fifteen — but that didn't stop me from trying at all the recruiting stations. It took a while but they finally accepted me as a volunteer in the women's branch of the air force in 1941, although I didn't start my actual service until 1942 when I was 18.

Things were a bit different in Canada than they were in England where I lived at the time. We didn't go away to war. We were already there, right in the centre of it. In London, during the battle of Britain, the Luftwaffe was trying to bomb us out of existence every night so I think that all Britons felt an urgency to do something to ensure their own survival. So, to do my bit, I joined the air force. I wanted to join the navy, but they wouldn't have me. My father was Dutch, although he had been a British subject for 20 years or more, and the navy turned me down because I didn't have two British-born parents, if you please, so I went for air force and I told them I wanted to be a radar operator. This was before many women were being conscripted.

One of the things you had to have before getting into radar was a certificate of matriculation, which I did have, but even that didn't get me in. They gave me a pretty minor test which I passed but they were full up with radar operators at the time so they took me into the air force in a general category. I didn't really care because I just wanted to get in. There followed a period of what we called "square bashing," which simply means basic training and endless drills and marching. This was in Gloucestershire in what was called the Women's Auxilliary Air Force — the WAAF. I was categorized as an Aircraft Woman, 2nd Class (ACW2). They didn't have women in the regular air force in those days as they would have now. I ended six weeks of square bashing more than a little entertained, I can tell you. Nearly all of us were middle-class girls and some had never been away from home before. I'd been to boarding school but some of the others had never spent a night away from their parents and the home hearth.

I remember the first morning in the air force. The place was full of crying girls who were so lonesome for their mothers. Some of them had never put out their own clothes before and they were completely baffled as to what they had to do. Every little thing that came up would start them crying again. It was hilarious in a way, if it hadn't been so tragic for them.

I was a little better off then they were because of the boarding school experience but not that much. I remember when I was first told to black-lead the stove — they had one of those Quebec heaters in the middle of the hut — I didn't know what they were talking about. Black-lead is black polish. I was a city girl and had never even seen one of those stoves, let alone polish it. But there were some girls from the working-class area of Glasgow who thought that this was a huge joke, that someone didn't know about black-leading. So they initiated me into this new skill.

Most girls were middle-class but not all, and you must remember that the English were very class conscious in those days. We had one kid whose mother put her out into street-walking at the age of 13. Things like that were happening even then. That, of course, was during the Depression years and then, as now, people will do any-thing rather than starve. She was a very pretty girl who had a full head of blonde hair which seemed to stand almost a foot above her head. She used to sit on her bed cross-legged, absolutely starkers, with her little air force hat on top of this pile of blonde hair and regale us with her stories from the street. Of course, this was the first time that this mostly middle-class crowd of girls found out what really happens on the street. Youngsters at that time were not so street smart as early as they are now. It was highly entertaining for us to be educated into the ways of the world in such a way.

After basic training I was temporarily posted to Uxbridge, just outside London, as a clerk working on war records. I found that rather depressing, as I was dealing with the records of people my own age who had been killed, and those who had been taken as prisoners-of-war. I remember handling the files on Douglas Bader, the airman who later became famous as "The Legless Ace of the Second World War" and I found it completely incredible the way this man just absolutely refused to give up.

After that, I was posted to the Air Ministry in London and for the first time I got close to something that was almost radar, the thing I wanted to learn when I joined up. I worked at what was called The Radar Board. Three services were there running radar for the whole war and the chairmen of that board were none other than Sir Robert Watson Watt and Sir Edward Appleton who were acknowl-edged to be the inventors of radar. We were located in a very beautiful home at 143 Piccadilly which was next to where the Queen

Mother and King George VI had lived when they were Duke and Duchess of York. It was a very splendid place to work and the boardroom looked like the Palace of Versailles, with silk wall coverings, and mirrors and gilt everywhere. I was really living in high society on that posting. We were dealing with the most secret of documents and records.

There's something I have to tell you about that happened to me while I was there. One day I was called into the boardroom to deliver a document to one of these high-faluting people who were there with their gold braid and what not, and I was to give this piece of paper to the man who was at the head of the table. When I got up there, and stood beside him the elastic on my panties broke and they slid down around my ankles. All I could think to do was kick them under his chair and flee. I was only a kid of 18 at the time and I was extremely embarrassed. One of the men I worked for, a Lieutenant Commander Whittaker who was an absolute dear, saw this, I think, because there was a twinkle in his eyes that I saw as I departed. There's a small bit more to the story: the panties were returned to me in a Top Secret envelope on my desk. Not even my name was on the envelope.

That was an exciting place to work because of the nature of the work and the kind of people who would be in and out of there. You never knew who you would see. I remember once bumping into Lord Gort, a member of Churchill's wartime cabinet and another time as I was coming through the park just outside our building located down with kit bags and all sorts of other baggage, I practically ran into Princess Mary. When I realized who she was I said to myself, "Good Lord, I'll have to salute her." As I was trying to get this kit bag over from my right shoulder to my left shoulder, I got myself into a terrible mess and couldn't even move my arms, much less salute her. I don't think she realized what was going on. In fact I don't think she paid any attention to me at all.

After my half year at the Air Ministry, I went on to Cranwell in Lincolnshire, where they trained radar operators. The men there had very good quarters but all the women were put in these little huts that had already been condemned as not suitable for human occupation. If you had a bed near the centre of the hut where the heater was, the steam would rise off your bedding. It was a far cry from the luxury of Piccadilly but we had a good time anyway. For people as young as I was at that time, those who had no worries about their children back home, you could have a good time any- where. If you weren't in the middle of an air raid, you could have fun doing anything.

We were all at an age where if we had been at home, we would have been a lot more restricted than we were in the services. In fact, the services were very paternal with us. For instance, the women were issued sanitary towels once a month. You had to go to the M.O.'s office and get them so if you didn't turn up for a couple of months someone would come round and check, just to make sure you weren't in the family way.

If they found out a WAAF was going out with a married man, they would usually post her to some place else in the hopes of breaking up the affair. Of course you had very restrictive hours. You had to be in at 10:30 and you had only one midnight pass a week and one sleeping- off-the-base pass a month. Naturally, we broke all these rules as often as we could but at the same time, we knew the rules were there for our protection.

They were awfully protective about girls who got pregnant too. The girl would go off to one of these special places that they had for pregnant service girls and the air force would arrange to have their mail continue coming to their old address. There it would be picked up quietly by a courier and delivered to where she was waiting out her pregnancy. This way, there was no chance that her parents would know anything. They took care of all the other matters too, including the adoption of the child, if that's what the girl wanted. When it was all over, the girl would usually come back to her station and as far as anyone else knew she had just been away on some temporary assignment at another post. It proved that the brass were at least trying to do the right thing and that there was a heart beating in there somewhere.

I eventually did learn radar, and it was late 1943 before I actually got down to my first radar station at a place called Trelanvean in

RCAF team member Corporal David Dumphries is seen here twisting the propeller for Captain Tom Thompson who is getting ready to take off from Ortona Beach in Italy in February 1943. (Courtesy the National Archives of Canada)

This RCAF Supermarine Spitfire, City of Toronto Squadron, was destroyed on the ground during a Luftwaffe attack on Allied airfield Eindhoven in the Netherlands on New Year's Day, 1945. (Courtesy the National Archives of Canada)

South Cornwall, about 30 or 40 miles from Land's End. The station was part of a long chain of stations which had tall towers and they were spread out over many miles along the coast. They were known as Chain Home and they were designed in such a way to track enemy planes, or hostiles as they were called, as they crossed the coast en route to inland targets. I would often spot hostiles on my screen. If we happened to miss them, which didn't happen very often, we could be sure that one of the other stations along this chain would see them. After a while, though, the enemy discovered that they could escape detection by our radar stations by dropping clouds of little aluminium strips which would jam the radar and we would see nothing but a snowstorm effect on our screens.

In many ways it's a wonderful thing that happens to people in wartime. There's that feeling that we're all in this together and I remember when it was all over there were great celebrations everywhere and people were piling onto trains to take part in the big one in London. For some reason I couldn't bring myself to do it — to party it up while there were still so many of our people fighting and getting killed in the Far East. What I found comforting to do instead was to go to Canterbury and spend some time there taking the famed Pilgrim's Walk. There was nobody there but me that day and it gave me the most wonderful feeling. I thought deeply about all the things that had happened during those long years of the war and the meaning of it all. I felt very refreshed and somehow cleansed.

I was horrified when those atomic bombs were dropped on Japan, killing and maiming so many people. I vowed then that I would never take part in a war again and I meant it. I've been a pacifist ever since and I continue to participate in peace demonstrations and peace walks.

Many of the soldiers who volunteered to go overseas found there was very little difference between Canada and wartime Britain. This was because the jobs they found themselves engaged in were no different than the ones they were doing back home, inside or outside the armed forces. Some who had worked in the war industries of this country and grew weary of the monotony of the production lines joined the services to get in on the action before it was all over. However, a lot of them found themselves posted to quiet parts of Britain doing necessary but boring tasks which, they were assured, were just as important as being in the front lines.

Perhaps that was true, but for the battle-ready youngsters who had come to Britain "to finish off Hitler," tightening bolts and doing maintenance work on trucks and airplanes didn't seem to match their dreams of destroying Nazi strongholds. But of course when you are in a country at war, you could never tell when all of that might change. One lazy afternoon could suddenly erupt into a nightmare that would stay with you the rest of your life.

Mel McIlveen
Winnipeg, Manitoba

I WAS IN the Motor Transport Section at Linton-on-Ouse, part of the 6 Group Headquarters station. This was in the early part of 1945 and although nobody knew that the war would be over in a matter of a few months, there was optimism that it couldn't last much longer. Most of the news reports were good and it looked to us like the Germans were beaten and it would only be a matter of time. It was our job in the M.T. Section to keep the machinery of war operating and to be truthful about it, my job wasn't that much different than working in a garage or a factory back home. I went to work in the morning, did a full day's work, and came "home" again in the evening. We didn't do battle but we tried to fix up the things that were damaged in battle or were just plain worn out. Up to this point in the war I had never seen an injured soldier or, as they say, never even heard a shot fired in anger. I had accepted that situation as my lot and didn't worry too much about it anymore. The folks back home were happy that I wasn't involved in the thick of it so I suppose I should have been happy at least about that. Perhaps it was because I was so young that I had this nagging feeling inside that I should be doing more than fixing machinery.

I was working late that night, later than usual, but I didn't really care because this bombsight that had been giving me trouble all day was finally fixed to my satisfaction and I wanted to see it installed in the aircraft before I headed off to supper. By the time I finished and fastened its computer and the sighting mechanism into position and levelled the whole assembly, it was just past 6:00 and I was the last person left in the hangar. I realized that I was late for afternoon tea — as the Brits referred to the evening meal — but I shrugged and thought I could catch the last part of it anyway.

I hurried across the tarmac and decided to cut through the M.T. Section on my way to the Mess hall. It was a quiet evening, still bright and sunny, for we were on double daylight saving time, and the only activity I could see was that of a large crane being manoeuvred towards its parking space by a lone airman on the operator's saddle.

As I continued across the outdoor lot I suddenly experienced a great rush of air, somewhat like a wind gust, except that it was coming right down on top of my head. I looked up and to my horror there was a Lancaster bomber coming in almost silently. All four engines were off and the propellers were just windmilling on their own due to the forward thrust of the plane. It was an eerie sight and as I watched it crabbing sideways as it lost altitude, I knew it was going to crash. I remember being thankful that the pilot must have realized he was going to crash and had had the good sense to shut everything down.

The Lancaster smashed into the crane that the airman had been moving into a parking space the minute before and then it just bellyflopped onto the tarmac right in front of me. The wings seemed to have taken the shock of the landing and at first glance the fuselage appeared to be undamaged. I started to run towards the wreck but the ammunition in the gun turrets began to explode, making a sound like the staccato burst of a hundred machine-guns. My first thought then was for the crew and I remember thinking that they must have all bailed out because there was no movement and no sounds of human voices coming from the wrecked plane.

The entry door was clearly visible and undamaged so I ran towards it but stopped because I realized that if there was an unexploded blockbuster bomb aboard, which was certainly possible, I would be in a very bad position. By this time airmen were running towards the crash site from everywhere and one of them, an armourer, who had seen me stop in my advance towards the plane said, "Don't worry. There were no bombs loaded at all today on any of our aircraft. This one's empty."

We tried to make our way once again towards the entry door but were forced back by a new series of explosions from the area of the undercarriage where the fuel tanks were situated. "What's wrong with the crew?" I thought, "Why don't they get out? Where are they?"

Suddenly, the entry door was pushed open from inside the plane and a figure appeared. "Help me! Please help me!" said the apparition before falling back inside again. It was one of the Lanc's gunners and it was obvious that he was badly hurt and had used up every bit of his strength just getting to that entry door and flinging it open. My companion and I reached in through the open doorway, pulled him forward and between us we managed to lift him to the outside. Fearing more explosions, we lifted him up again and carried him a good safe distance from the wreck.

Crisis situations bring out a lot of unknown qualities in people and I found within myself a lot of courage I didn't know I had. Despite the explosions from the gun turrets and from the undercarriage, my companion and I ran back to the open door to see if anyone else was coming out, but by now the inside of the aircraft was ablaze and the din of the exploding ammunition and the explosions of the fuel tanks kept both of us from getting any closer. The worst of the fires seemed to be coming from the magnesium steel of the undercarriage. The white hot flames drove us and everyone else back and shortly, the fuselage itself was no longer recognizable.

Meanwhile, someone from the hospital had come with a stretcher and the one man we had managed to extricate from the wreck was taken away in an ambulance. We heard later though that he was seriously injured and that there was no chance he would live.

By now, the firemen from the station were on the scene, but they too found it impossible to cope with the intense heat that was now threatening to destroy the whole transport section. Then someone shouted, "There was a man on the crane that was hit and he's over there lying on the ground in flames." All our efforts then turned from the burning plane to the burning man on the ground. We pulled desperately at the wreckage of the crane and pulled off our tunics to try and smother the flames that were threatening to consume the man's body. We finally succeeded in pulling him free and putting out the fire to his clothing, but by this time he was terribly burned and we were told that his chances of making it were practically nil.

Meantime the fire from the area of the plane continued to spread and eventually a squad from the National Fire Service had to be called in. When it was finally cool enough to approach the wreckage of the Lanc, we still had the most horrible sight of all to face. All six remaining members of the crew were hunched together in death in the remains of the cockpit. Why they couldn't get out we don't know; perhaps they were dead when the plane crashed. There was no way of knowing as there was nothing left for the stretcher bearers but skeletons, and the plane itself was only a mass of burned and twisted steel.

I've had many nightmares about those boys. I guess it's only one incident from a war full of horrors, but this one was different — this one happened to me.

Herb Deavy
Navan, Ontario

FEBRUARY 25, 1941, was a big day for me. It was my eighteenth birthday. It meant I was now officially old enough to join the services, something I'd been looking forward to for a long time.

I didn't waste any time. I marched right down to the recruiting office and I did it — that very day. I joined the RCAF. I may have been just an eighteen-year-old raw recruit but it was the most exciting thing that had ever happened to me. All I could think about was the adventure that lay ahead in our job to save democracy from a madman and me being there smack in the centre of it. This was exciting business but it was also very serious.

Herb Deavy at Uplands, Ottawa, during the summer of 1942.
(Courtesy Herb Deavy)

It was great, too, to be involved with aircraft, something that had fascinated me from the time I could crawl. Now I would learn something about those planes, how they got up in the sky in the first place and how they managed to stay there.

After I made my career goals known, I was assigned to be trained as a "fitter," an Aero engine mechanic, a course that was ideally suited to my ambitions. After the preliminary indoctrination at the manning depot in Toronto, I was sent to the school for fitters which was located in St. Thomas, Ontario. After a few months there and another short posting at Aylmer, Ontario, it was on to No. 2 S.F.T.S. at Uplands in Ottawa.

I arrived just a few days after Winston Churchill had visited the station on one of his wartime trips to Canada. Why couldn't they have posted me there sooner so that I could have seen the greatest of wartime leaders in person? We all admired this man, and to think that I had missed seeing him by a matter of about 48 hours. Swallowing my disappointment, I plunged into learning the business of servicing aircraft and keeping them in top condition.

Part of our learning equipment was a real airplane called a Harvard Trainer. I know a lot of former air force men will downgrade the Harvard, but I always found it extremely reliable and efficient.

I remember once after I had just changed a variable pitch propeller that had been leaking oil and had to sign a "work completed" form the test pilot called me in afterwards and said, "Okay, Deavy, let's see how good a job you did. Get yourself a parachute and we'll see if your prop stays on."

Well, we climbed into that Harvard and took off and believe me, he turned that plane inside out with every manoeuvre and loop and spin that he knew. The propeller stayed on and I knew then that I was being taught the most important lesson I would ever learn: work on every plane as if your own life depended on it.

Not all our maintenance men did the same thing, though. For example, when an aircraft that had been flying during the day came in, there were certain checks that had to be performed before it went out again that night on a mission. Some men would say, "If it flew today, it will fly tonight," and never check the aircraft at all. This always disturbed me because although you can always replace an aircraft, you can never replace the man or the crew who flew it.

I was never in Bomber Command although I often longed to be. I can still remember the sound of those huge Lancaster and Halifax heavy bombers straining with their huge loads of bombs as they tried to gain altitude before getting into formation for their nightly raids. Then in the morning light, they would come straggling home, many with two of their engines out and huge gaping holes in the fuselage. Gazing upwards as they prepared to land, I would always wonder how many members of their seven-man crews had survived. Sir Winston Churchill mentions in his memoirs, that on one raid on Nuremberg, 795 aircraft were despatched and 94 did not return. I remember that raid, and I could only imagine the courage of the air crews involved and mourn the loss of those who didn't survive.

Something that was absolutely taboo for everybody at the base was taking pictures of the aircraft, and as much as I wanted to, I always obeyed this restriction — except on one occasion. Most people may not remember this, but a lot of women pilots were used to ferry aircraft from one base to another during the war. They did a good job too, and I know that a lot of them wanted to go on real missions but never did. On this particular day, I saw this tiny, little woman jump down from the controls of this huge Stirling bomber. She looked so small and the plane looked so big that I just couldn't resist getting a snapshot. Well, no sooner had I snapped the camera, than I felt the huge hand of a military policeman take me by the shoulder and march me off to the headquarters of the Commanding Officer. I was in deep trouble and I knew it. However, lady luck was with me; the C.O. was a Canadian and instead of landing in the slammer, I was let off with a reprimand and had my film confiscated.

Air crew and ground crew didn't mix much but on one occasion I was fortunate enough to meet one of our famous and legendary fighter pilots, "Buzz" Buerling. That was a thrill because these air aces were just as renowned to those of us serving overseas as they were to people at home who read about their exploits in the newspapers.

Speaking of air aces, another one was Spitfire pilot "Bus" Kennedy who earned a DFC and Bar. He served in Malta and Europe and has 12 enemy aircraft to his credit. On one occasion after being shot down, the French Underground saved him and ferreted him back to England where he immediately went back into action. Imagine my surprise when, after the war, I discovered he was living in Cumberland, Ontario, next door to the small town of Navan where I live! He became my family doctor and remained so until just a few years ago when he retired.

Those of us who served, in whatever capacity, have many memories of those unusual and impressionable times of our youth. I was one of the lucky ones who had the opportunity to serve and return home safely. Each November 11, I stand in front of our cenotaph and remember all the others who weren't so lucky — especially the two who were schoolmates of mine. When the piper plays the Lament, I cannot help shedding a few tears. At the Legion afterwards, over a wee dram or two, we also remember some of the good times. We don't want to forget everything about that war and why we were over there in the first place, and we especially don't want to forget those friends we made. After half a century, I still keep in touch with one of them from Lachute, Quebec. We don't see much of each other, but we do communicate.

How did it end for me? Well, after being repatriated for medical reasons and spending some time at the Old Christie Street Military Hospital in Toronto, as well as various other hospitals, I was finally discharged.

I gained much from that experience, not the least of which was the discipline and the comradeship that has helped me through many rough patches in civilian life, but God forbid that we should ever have another conflict like that one.

PART 2
NURSING

A casualty in war falls into one of four categories: dead or presumed dead, wounded, missing, prisoner-of-war or interned. In the Second World War when 759,000 young people donned uniforms to save democracy, 103,000 were listed as casualties, 38,000 died and another 3,000 went missing and were presumed dead. Fifty-three thousand were wounded and another 9,000 suffered the misery of confinement in prison camps.

It is impossible to measure the amount of suffering associated with just one casualty of war for there is not only the victim to be considered. It has been said that those who suffer most are those who wait at home. Multiplied by those at home, that 103,000 figure of total Canadian casualties is very large indeed. Canada paid dearly in human terms for her participation in the Second World War.

Kay Poulton
Moose Jaw, Saskatchewan

I GUESS I wanted to be a nursing sister right from the time I was a child. That may have had something to do with the fact that here in western Canada we were always made aware that the first Nursing Sisters of the military took part in the Riel Rebellion in 1885, the year my mother was born and that some of the great battles of the Rebellion happened not very far from where we lived in Moose Jaw, Saskatchewan. We heard a lot about that in school.

As I grew up, I had two heroes, both of them nurses, Edith Cavell and Florence Nightingale. Also, there was a hospital unit set up in

North Battleford, Saskatchewan, not far from my home, which took care of the wounded at the Battle of Cut Knife during the Rebellion. All of these things had a bearing on my own decision to become a nurse but I think it was an aunt of mine who had more to do with it than anything else. She had trained in the U.S. and then came up to Canada to nurse her brother who was very ill. She stayed on in Saskatchewan to continue her nursing career and became a greatly admired woman, not only by me but by everyone who knew her. So, with Edith Cavell, Florence Nightingale and this aunt of mine, it was kind of in the cards that I should follow the nursing profession.

When I finished high school I was only 17, too young to get into a hospital in Moose Jaw where you had to be 19, but a friend wrote to me and said that I should come to Saskatoon because the hospitals there didn't ask for your birth certificate. I followed this up and just for good measure I told them that I was a year older than I actually was. They let me in at the hospital there and I stayed on until I graduated. After that, because I was still too young to get into the army, I went down to Ottawa to work.

I was 21 by this time and the war had started, but the army was getting so many applications from young nurses that they changed the age limit to 25 from 21. Again, I was on the outside looking in.

While I was in Ottawa, I heard about a woman who was recruiting nurses to go to Bermuda, so I went to see her and within three weeks I was on a boat for Bermuda. The only connection I had to the military on this job was that at the time a lot of boats were being sunk in the Battle of the Atlantic and we were getting a lot of these shipwreck survivors in our hospitals. There were also a lot of military people in Bermuda at that time. The Americans had both an army and a navy base there. That was before Pearl Harbour, of course, but we would see all these American military men all the time as they went out on patrols. Although the U.S. wasn't in the war yet, they would tell the Brits where all the enemy ships were located. Not many people realize that the Americans were really that active before their own hostilities got started.

I stayed in Bermuda a year and put my name down again to join the military. I still wasn't old enough at 23, but I figured it was worth a try anyway. I didn't make it in until later when they were making all the preparations for D-Day. They lowered the age to 23 and finally I realized my ambition and was in uniform.

I was called up on Valentine's Day, 1944 and was sent to a base hospital in London, Ontario. Our patients were all service men who were sick with various illnesses from measles to diphtheria, and all sorts of other contagious diseases, but it wasn't until I got a contingent in from the Italian campaign, that I got my first taste of the horror of war.

These were the first wounded that I saw and it was rather earth shattering for me. There were these young boys with their arms and legs off and all sorts of other horrible injuries. I felt so sorry for them, and the thing that impressed me was how wonderful they were as patients. They were all in good physical condition when they were wounded so that they responded well to treatment and they were so appreciative of whatever you could do for them. The experience there made me even more anxious than ever to get overseas where I could possibly be of more help.

After five months I got my wish and right after D-Day I was posted to a unit hospital near Gatwick airport in England. They used to fly our wounded right into Gatwick from the battlefields of Normandy, up to 300 at a time. They got them to us very quickly following their being wounded; some of them would still be under the anaesthetic that had been given to them at the scene of battle.

Any soldiers that the field medical officers diagnosed as requiring more than three months of recovery were shipped immediately to the field hospitals in Britain so that most of our patients were those who were quite badly wounded. Despite this, we had few deaths in our hospital, and we were proud of that record. We had a group of dedicated doctors and nurses who worked like dogs and of course by this time, we had the new wonder drug penicillin.

When penicillin first came to our hospital, I remember we had a soldier who was suffering from what was called cellulitis. It was a strep infection in the tissues of his legs and he was terribly ill, and lay unconscious in an oxygen tent. Then right at that very time, we received our first bottle of penicillin shipped over from Connaught

Laboratories in Toronto. Once the drug was injected into him he came around quite dramatically and appeared to be recovered almost overnight. However, we ran out of penicillin and before long he was at death's door again. Thankfully, another supply came in and we were able to save his life. Penicillin saved a lot of lives and it truly was a wonder drug.

I often think of those poor boys coming in wounded from the field. They were so brave and uncomplaining. Two of the bravest I recall were French-Canadian boys from two different Quebec regiments, the Maisonneuve and the Chaudière. One of these lads had been on the operating table for 17 hours. He had an eye out, shrapnel wounds to his arms, legs and all over his body. They operated and took out his spleen, part of his liver and I don't know how many feet of intestines but he survived it all. I never heard him utter one word of complaint of any kind during the whole ordeal except for the day he went for his glass eye. He came back and said to me, "Sister, my new eye doesn't match." I told him not to worry about that and that he'd get a new one when he got back to Canada.

It wasn't all sad, though. I often think about four patients from the Hamilton Light Infantry, all of them sergeants, who were well enough to go on Christmas leave with 48-hour passes. They went up to London but while there, decided they wanted to come back to the hospital to spend Christmas. About 2:00 on Christmas morning they arrived with a little bit too much to drink under their belts. I eventually got them into their beds and later, when I went back to check on them, one of them had a huge enamel basin at the foot of his bed with a pillow case next to it. I asked him what the basin was for and this man, who lisped pretty heavily, said, "Juth in cathe Thanta Clawth ith givin' way liquids."

When we went on our leaves, three or four of us would go together and head out to explore London or Scotland for a week or so. The leaves were always welcome and really very much needed. We would always wear our uniforms and because we were clad in navy blue, some people thought we were police women or air raid wardens or something like that. They never seemed to notice the *Canada* flashes on our shoulders.

We had a club that we could go to in London and we also had a rest place up in Buckinghamshire, at the Maitland estate. It was lovely to go there as this Maitland family, who had donated the use of the property for nursing sisters, treated us like royalty. We would have breakfast in bed and all that sort of thing. Quite a change from what we were used to in the service.

It was while we were up there that I saw my first jet aircraft. It was a deHavilland, I think. It was amazing to see a plane flying without propellers. This was all pretty secret stuff, too, I might add.

I stayed at the Gatwick unit hospital until the end of the war. VE-Day was an especially wonderful time for me. Not only was the war over, but my fiancé, Ron, who had been working in Italy on the army newspaper, *The Maple Leaf,* arrived in Gatwick on leave. We planned to get married but found we couldn't right away because I was an officer and he was a sergeant. This meant he had to go back to Brussels to get the necessary permission. Eventually we were married on August 4. We had been childhood sweethearts in Moose Jaw and it was just by circumstance that we were within commuting distance of each other during the war. We were on our honeymoon when V-J Day came.

The whole thing was an experience I wouldn't trade for anything in the world. The friends I made at that time are still my friends and even though we're scattered all over the country, we all try to keep in touch with each other.

Louise Jamieson
Toronto, Ontario

WHEN THE BRITISH government asked Canada for 300 nurses to go to South Africa to staff five hospitals the British had built there, they started recruiting from the civilian nurses first. I was a nursing sister in the military at the time so I asked for a transfer in order to join the group going to South Africa. This was in 1942.

There were four of us military nurses and the rest of the South African Corps were all civilians. We were nursing sisters in Cana-

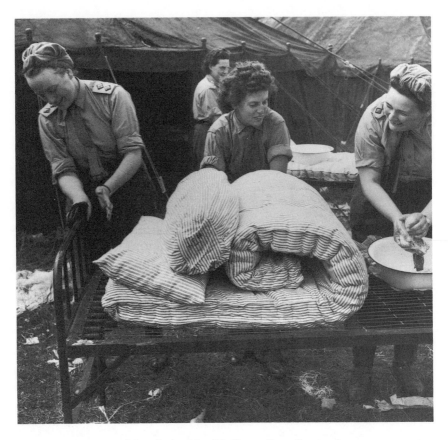

*Nursing sisters washing beds, No. 10 Canadian General
Hospital, R.C.A.M.C., near Bayeux, France, August 2, 1944.
Left to right: Thelma Finlayson, Joyce Chapman, Ida
Rothwell. (Photo by Lieutenant G.K. Bell / DND / Public
Archives of Canada)*

dian uniforms but paid by the South African government on a one-
year contract. I was sent to the hospital at Baragwanath outside
Johannesburg because Miss Gladys Sharpe who had been in the
military at Camp Borden when I was there was asked to go as Chief
Matron.

The hospital had a thousand beds and we had mostly British troops along with some Greeks and Poles. Half the hospital turned out to be a tuberculosis facility, the main reason being that the British didn't X-ray their troops before accepting them into the army. All of these troops came from the fighting in the Middle East and the Far East, and were called Long-Term casualties who arrived on hospital ships.

I was 25 at the time, and anxious for new adventures so South Africa seemed to fill the bill for me. Most of us felt the same way, especially the four of us who came from Camp Borden, where we were totally surrounded by a military environment. We were more than anxious to get involved with the war.

I found the atmosphere in the army to be excellent. The women were treated with the utmost respect by the men and that proved to be even more so when we left Canada where most of the troops we dealt with were British. They seemed to treat "those Canadian girls" with an extra amount of consideration.

I spent about a year-and-a-half in South Africa, part of which time was at a native hospital. I think that was just to give us a different kind of experience. I found it very interesting working with all those black patients at that hospital which was in their homeland away out in the country.

The most memorable part of that experience was being able to observe first hand how badly the Afrikaaners treated the black people. This was brought home to me one day while I was at work in the operating room. I had two black boys helping me, and during a break they came over and one of them said, "Sister, can you get a book for us on magic?"

I said, "What on earth would you want that for?"

"We want to learn these tricks," he said, "so that we can go back and perform them for our own native people and earn money so that we can buy tickets and come to Canada to live."

They said that the Canadian nurses treated them so well that Canada must therefore be a good place for black people. They didn't know anything about Canada aside from what they had seen of four nurses who had come from there.

There were many white South Africans who felt that their country should never have been in the war and they blamed Field Marshal Smuts, their Prime Minister, for the fact that they were in it. One group, I think they were called the Ossawa Drandwa, were very overt in their anti-British attitude. They would push British personnel off the sidewalks and all sorts of other things. One of them slapped one of the British nurses hard across the face for no other reason than that she was British.

After my contracted time there, I stayed on for another six months and in early 1944 accompanied two South African units who were going up to Italy to fight. We left from Durban on a hospital ship, up through the Indian Ocean and then up farther to the beginning of the Suez Canal where all of us had to get off the ship. The reason was that it cost money, so much per person, to go through the canal and somebody thought that this was much too expensive a journey for the government to pay.

So, we went by train to Cairo where we had to wait around for a couple of weeks while somebody figured out how they were going to get us the rest of the way.

We were billeted in an old schoolhouse which was pretty primitive to say the least. Then we went by train to Alexandria where we met our same hospital ship as it emerged from the canal! This took us into Taranto on the east coast of Italy, from which we were sent hither and yon to relieve some of the overworked nursing sisters in the English hospital units.

We then formed a casualty-clearing unit and were sent off to Florence to the site of one of the big battles. We were there for three months and very much in the middle of all that fierce fighting. The casualty load was extremely high, as this was one of the decisive battles of the whole Italian campaign.

In addition to fighting the Allied troops the Italians were also engaged in fighting among themselves — the Fascists and the Partisans — and they were killing one another.

That winter we went back to a place called Orvieto. There wasn't much fighting in the winter months but after a few months we moved on to Bologna, stationed in a tent hospital where the patients

Some of the heaviest fighting of the war took place on the Italian front and it was here that Canadian troops played a major role. Here, a member of the Seaforth Highlanders searches German prisoners for hidden weapons on Italy's Moro River front in December, 1943. (Courtesy the National Archives of Canada)

were mostly German prisoners-of-war. I must say though that I had a hard time of it the first time I came up against German prisoners.

I didn't feel kindly disposed to the Germans because, for one thing, I had already lost my brother in the airforce and I had to learn to overcome my own personal feelings. I remember one German who wasn't especially sick who was able to be up and around. He came over to where I was and said, "Get me a basin of water." There was no "please" or "thank you," just an order. So I just looked him in the eye and said, "Get it yourself." That made me feel a bit better anyway.

It was while we were in Bologna, that the Italian Partisans captured and executed Mussolini and his mistress and strung them up in the square in Milan. That all happened very close to where we were stationed.

We then moved to Milan to a large hospital treating British troops who were coming through on their way home. A lot of them were sick with malaria and typhoid. I was there right through the end of the war, and in October, 1945 I came back to Canada.

It was difficult to adjust back into the mainstream of civilian life after being away so long. There were so many changes — changes in family being foremost I suppose. Aside from the brother who had been killed in the air force, my grandparents and my mother had died, and anyway I think it takes a long time to adjust — deciding what you're going to do with your future and that sort of thing. In the end I decided to go to university under the veteran's education scheme.

I got my B.A. and also took Nursing Education both of which served me well in the years that followed.

For me, the time in the services was a wonderful, valuable experience. I think it makes a person stronger and teaches how to stand up to any situation, but once is enough. I wouldn't want to do it again.

Kay Christie
Toronto, Ontario

I WAS JUST as impatient to go overseas as any of the men. I was a registered nurse who joined the forces as a nursing sister with the rank of lieutenant and the usual two officer's pips on the shoulders of my uniform. We didn't join to be in Canada. We wanted to be "over there," where the action was.

After a number of hospital units sailed to England in 1940 there weren't any more major moves from our area for some time so that, in mid-October, 1941, on being informed that I was slated for duty in a semi-tropical climate and that I had only five minutes to make up my mind, I threw aside my usual caution and immediately accepted this new posting.

Kay Christie on duty at Chorley Park Hospital, 1945. With her are Sergeant Moore, a patient who lost a leg in Italy, and Jean Dickenson, a soprano who was visiting the troops. (Courtesy Kay Christie)

One week later to the day, on October 19, 1941, I was on board a train to Vancouver, final destination unknown. So great was the alleged secrecy surrounding this whole operation that when a second nursing sister, May Waters, joined me on the train at Winnipeg, neither of us knew for sure that we were both on the same exercise. However, by a cat-and-mouse kind of discreet questioning of each other, we assumed that we must be. As it turned out we were.

On October 27 we sailed, along with 1875 other troops, all of them male, on board the troopship *Awatea*, while another 100 men travelled in the escort ship, *Prince Robert*, an armed merchant cruiser. The troops were mainly from the Royal Rifles of Canada from Quebec, and the Winnipeg Grenadiers, including four medical officers and two dental officers. Two women and 1975 men!

Six days later, following a stop in Honolulu, we were officially informed for the first time that our destination was Hong Kong. The three-week journey across the Pacific was no pleasure cruise. Our 54-bed hospital on board ship was filled with patients all the way.

On November 16 we docked in Kowloon and two days later we were on duty in the British Military Hospital, which was located between Magazine Gap, where the ammunition was stored, and the China Command Headquarters — not exactly an ideal place to be during hostilities.

Three weeks after our arrival came the Japanese sneak attack on Pearl Harbour and simultaneously, Kai Tak airport in Hong Kong. The three small planes that were there and the air-raid warning system were totally destroyed and within a few days, as the shelling from the mainland began, there were several direct hits on our three-storey hospital. We had to immediately evacuate the top two floors and crowd all the patients and equipment into the ground floor area.

After ten days of aerial and shelling attacks from the mainland, the Japanese troops crossed the harbour to the island and, with their superior numbers, began to overcome the various areas. Word reached us in the large British Military Hospital, also known as the Bowen Road Hospital, of the atrocities committed by the Japanese as the small auxiliary hospitals were overrun, and we knew that our fate could be the same. At night in the darkened corridors whenever footsteps were heard, we would wonder, "Is it our turn?"

On Christmas morning, at a brief service, the padre relayed a message to us, allegedly from Winston Churchill, to the effect that the eyes of the world were upon us and not to worry because things were going well. Then we went to the shelters to sleep. During the afternoon, we heard a British army officer talking about surrender, and shortly after that, a message was sent to us to report at once to the Matron's office where we were informed officially of the surrender of Hong Kong.

Things proceeded as usual in the hospital that night. The next day several Japanese officers arrived at the hospital to speak to the Commanding Officer.

The hospital building and the immediate environs were declared "Prisoner-of-War Camp A" which earned for May Waters and me the dubious honour of becoming the first and only Canadian nursing sisters to be prisoners-of-war. Within a few days, a barbed wire fence went up to remind all of us that we were indeed prisoners. Shortly after that, electrified wire was added just to be sure that nobody tried to escape.

Before long the food shortage was felt and the medical supplies dwindled and could never be replenished. We fully realized that we were no longer free people. That, along with the fact that Hong Kong had surrendered, gave us a feeling of guilt and degradation which the Japanese never allowed us to forget throughout the time of our incarceration.

No longer able to give total nursing care to our "boys," we tried to compensate by spending a lot of time listening to problems and confessions and offering encouragement to the seriously wounded, the sick and the dying.

As well as taking over our residence buildings, our Japanese captors had also set up a guardhouse right outside the dormitories where the nurses and volunteers slept. Over the ensuing months we had ample opportunity to witness the various methods of torture they used on captives.

Kay Christie, October 19, 1945. (Courtesy Kay Christie)

We were guarded constantly throughout the hospital building by the soldiers who were never without their bayonets. They strolled through the wards and our dormitories at any hour, frequently making horrible slurping noises as they ran their fingers up the blade of the weapons.

In one hospital the Japanese soldiers lined up all the females, many of whom were just young girls. These women were mostly British, who had been employed as secretaries or teachers and so on, or they were wives of British businessmen or army officers. They were such a wonderful group who worked so hard at their volunteer duties in the hospital.

As one of the soldiers stood in the doorway with a machine gun, the others took the younger girls, laid them on the floor and raped them while the mothers could do nothing but stand by helplessly and watch.

At one of the other auxiliary hospitals at Stanley Peninsula on Christmas morning where the fighting was bitter, the wounded were on mattresses on the floor. One British nursing sister and six VADs were sent there to look after them. Well, the Japs just roared in there in all their fury, although you might argue that there was some just cause. This was a hospital with a Red Cross on it, supposedly immune from fighting of any kind; but there in the doorway stood our O.C., the Medical Officer, with a gun in his hand. Medical people were not supposed to be armed. So the soldiers slashed him with their bayonets and gave the same treatment to his assistant who was also armed.

At another auxiliary hospital, on Christmas morning, Japanese troops burst in and began bayonetting the patients on the floor. I remember one of these young fellows, a young Canadian lad of about 17 who tried to escape and those soldiers went after him, constantly sticking their bayonets in his arm. This went on until he just played dead and they finally stopped sticking him. His arm had to be amputated when he was returned to the British Military Hospital.

By this time they had killed a lot of the other patients, so they dragged their bodies into a smaller room and took the mattresses and tossed them on top of these corpses.

Then they went after the nursing sister and the volunteers. They stripped them, they slapped their faces with their Red Cross arm bands and started raping them on top of the mattresses that had the corpses underneath. This went on and on. Then for some reason, which the four girls who survived could never figure out, they took three of the volunteers and, after raping them, cut their heads off and piled their naked bodies outside. One of the patients in the hospital at the time was a British officer whose wife happened to be one of these volunteers. He recognized her screams and he went stark-staring mad, completely out of his mind.

I find all of this very hard to talk about even today, almost 50 years later. The nursing sister who was involved in that was a friend of mine, a Scottish girl named Molly, who was a bit older than most of us. I'll never forget the look in her eyes when she and the other three who survived were brought back to the British Military Hospital.

After eight months there, during which time we learned to cope with hunger, deprivation and overcrowding, the Japanese moved us to a civilian internment camp on Stanley Peninsula on the south side of the island. With no warning at all and with no reasons given to us, all female personnel were moved from the service hospitals still operating, loaded onto trucks like cattle and taken away. This of course left these hospitals without nursing care of any kind.

We became part of the 2,400 men, women and children who were herded into all manner of buildings where privacy and the basic comforts of life were conspicuous by their absence. According to the Japanese authorities, we service nurses were being shown "preferential" treatment, which meant only three in one room and luxuries like one three-piece bathroom to serve all 83 of us. If you didn't live within a few doors of this "luxury," your chances of ever getting there for a bath were practically nil.

However we did learn the art of "scrounging" and making do. On another floor that was less crowded, we found two primitive cold-water showers that were sometimes vacant and which sometimes even had water.

One of my proudest possessions was a hot plate made from a five-pound jam pail with the help of a former electrician in return for a few precious cigarettes. I was lucky in that I didn't smoke, and I could use for bartering the few cigarettes sold to us by the Japanese — which were apparently awful. Since our rations were meagre, all of us learned to skimp and save and trade, even crusts of bread.

The ration lorry drove through the camp each afternoon and just threw the supplies for each block to the ground. There was no refrigeration, so whatever small thing we got, meat or fish or whatever, had to be in a stew form to make it go round. The next morning we got the rest made into a thin soup. Each person's daily ration amounted to three-quarters of an ounce of meat or fish; four tablespoons of greens, also known as weeds; eight ounces of rice; and four ounces of flour which was often unfit to eat. Since we were fortunate enough to have a baker in our block who would turn the flour into bread, we accepted the "unknowns" in the flour as extra protein.

Life dragged on like this until the middle of 1943 when we learned that the Canadian government had negotiated to have all Canadian civilian internees from the Far East repatriated, along with the group of American civilians remaining in other parts of the Far East. This was arranged by their government in an operation that was to be carried out under the auspices of the International Red Cross.

As far as the Japanese were concerned, May Waters and I were Canadian civilian refugees and we were thus included in the group who left Stanley Camp on September 23, 1943, on the first leg of a ten-week journey home. The first four weeks of this trip was on a dreadful Japanese ship called the *Teia Maru* where the conditions were even worse than at the internment camp. Built for 400 cabin passengers, there were 1,530 of us on board.

After our arrival in Goa, four weeks later, the Swedish–American liner *Gripsholm* arrived with 1,530 Japanese internees from the U.S. who were to be exchanged for us. Several days later, the Japanese internees were put on board our ship and we went aboard the *Gripsholm* which was like a touch of heaven, clean and well-loaded with good food, such a contrast to what the Japanese had forced us to endure.

During the next six weeks on board I gained 20 of the pounds I had lost in captivity and I actually learned to enjoy myself again. Because of wartime restrictions, we had to take a much longer and more circuitous route home, but there were several interesting stops, including one at Port Elizabeth, South Africa, where the civic officials and residents were most hospitable. At Rio de Janeiro, we were able to see some of that city, even including a night club.

Exactly ten weeks after leaving Hong Kong we disembarked at New York, where it was a pleasure to note that the armed guards, this time, were *American*. They escorted the Canadians to a bus which took us to a special train for an overnight trip to Montreal. At the old Bonaventure station next morning we said our goodbyes and our group dispersed, fanning out to homes spread all across the country. We were back in Canada where we belonged and every one of us had a brand new appreciation for a way of life we had previously taken for granted.

When the Second World War broke out, Canada was almost totally unprepared. In most areas we were like babes in the woods, forgetting most of the lessons that we had learned just 20 years before.

Our first boys to enlist were dressed like raggle-taggle soldiers, wearing bits of uniforms salvaged from the scrap pile of the first "war to end all wars." We had old-fashioned guns and very little else, except the spirit to face the conflict ahead.

On the home front, we knew little or nothing about civil defence and nobody was thinking much about it, forgetting that if you fire a shot at somebody in anger they might well fire back at you. There were however, a few people with foresight and not all of them were in government positions.

A young Toronto housewife, Kay Gilmour, had the feeling all through the thirties, through the time of Hitler's rise in power, that a war was inevitable, and that if it did come we should be prepared to look after the wounded.

Kay Gilmour
Toronto, Ontario

I HAD NO doubt at all that war was coming, and it wasn't just because Hitler was creating such a storm in Europe. For me it went back a lot farther than that, to the time when I was a young schoolgirl in France and saw these great fortifications being built, which I found out was the Maginot Line. On another occasion, on a school holiday, we were taken to Italy and the Fascists were everywhere and there

Repatriated Canadians — government officials and missionaries — from Japan and occupied China arrive at Bonaventure Station, Montreal, August 26, 1942. (Courtesy the National Archives of Canada)

was such an atmosphere of "getting ready" and all-round preparation, that it was scary. This was ten years before the Hitler rumblings of the thirties. This made such an impression on a 14-year-old, one of tension and fear, that I was absolutely positive that it wouldn't be long before we had another war.

My mother had been in the Boer War, one of the few Canadian

women who went, and I guess out of all of this I got the impression that our side just wasn't going to be ready if it happened. I resolved then and there that I would start preaching the gospel of readiness, which I did all through the thirties to such an extent that I think most people thought I was quite wacky.

I had never done a full three-year course of nurse's training because I got married when I was very young. What I did have was a lot of very professional nurse's training in fits and starts between having babies and things like that but nothing formal on paper. Then, because I thought that there was going to be a war, I decided I should be getting something more specialized and official.

Accordingly I went back and asked at Women's College Hospital in Toronto if I could go and do some very special operating-room work. They graciously allowed me to do that and so that's what I did from 1937 to 1939.

After this training, I set up my own training centre in our house. Our large living room and dining room were turned into a hospital ward and we arranged for a number of doctors to come and lecture our volunteers. While all of this was going on I was able to choose certain volunteers who I thought would make good officers later on. Now this was all taking place in early 1939, quite some time before the war started.

By the time the war started we were well underway with the training program at St. John Ambulance. When my husband went overseas in 1940 I officially joined the Brigade which is the full-time uniformed branch of St. John. At the height of our activities during the war we had 12,000 members of the Brigade in uniform but we didn't have any of them overseas until 1940, although a great many of our men had joined the Army Medical Corps. They did brilliantly, were decorated and mentioned in despatches and so on.

On the other hand there was nothing much going on in the women's part of the Brigade and there was nothing much going on in civil defence. It was a bit of a farce at that stage. I was asked to go and speak to a large group who were going to be running a large centre if Toronto was ever bombed and I realized that this group really didn't have much idea of what they would have to do. For

*A chapter of the Women's Volunteer Reserve, Montreal, June
27, 1940. (Courtesy the* Montreal Gazette)

example, there had been no thought given to the obvious necessity
of setting up a morgue or to the problem of emergency feeding.

That's when I thought I should go to Ottawa and see if there were
any better plans there and if not, I'd better get over to London to see
how they were handling the situation. So I went up to see Dr.
Manion who was the Minister of Health at the time. He asked me if I
would be willing to make the trip to London and, if so, he would
arrange the exit permits which were needed to leave the country

during wartime. He said he would like a report from me after I returned.

Word somehow got around that I was going to go, so I soon heard from all the provinces that they too would like to get copies of my report on my return. It took about ten days to arrange everything but I soon departed for England on a little French freighter from Montreal.

Once in London, I went to the St. John Headquarters and met with Lady Louis Mountbatten who was head of the English units. I asked her where I should go to get first-hand experience in all aspects of what to do during a bombing raid. She told me that most of the action at the moment was taking place on the east coast and that the Luftwaffe were particularly concentrating on Canterbury.

I boarded a train heading there and sitting right opposite me was a charming woman who smiled and nodded and offered me her newspaper after a bit. The train stopped about three miles before Canterbury and the train guard told us there was a big raid going on and that the train would have to stay there. So this delightful lady leaned across to me and said, "I'm Frances Temple. My husband is the Archbishop of Canterbury and I know they'll be sending a car out for me. Would you like to come along?" Sure enough, along came a big black limousine and the two of us scrambled out of the train, down through the ditch and into the car. She said, "Where are you staying in Canterbury?" and I said that I hadn't made any arrangements at all but I would be going to see the St. John Ambulance people when I got there. "My dear," she said, "You must come and stay with me." Under the circumstances I could see no reason to decline her offer.

Another day I was in the office of Vincent Massey, Canada's High Commissioner to Britain. I told him that I was going down to Plymouth, to inspect what had been described to me as their really terrific civil defence system. Of course, poor Plymouth had been flattened by the bombings. So Mr. Massey said, "Well, if you're going to Plymouth, you must stay with the Astors." I had a lovely letter the next day from Lady Astor inviting me to come, which I did. They were perfect darlings and since Lord Astor knew everybody I had an entrée to everything.

That's the way the whole thing went for me while I was there. I was so lucky. I had seen all I wanted to see under the most extreme of wartime conditions, so that before I left for home I was able to draw up a very complete report on what we would have to do here in Canada if the country was ever to be attacked. I had seen it all, from the feeding and casualty care, to the morgue set-ups, emergency housing, food stockpiling and everything else you could imagine.

Once back in Canada, with my report submitted, I was asked to take over all the women's activities in St. John Ambulance as Chief Superintendent. The first thing we did was find a lot of the former volunteers and put them through an extensive training period. I went back over to London and Mrs. Massey volunteered to give us her office in Canadian Military Headquarters, which we used for almost a year before we got one of our own. Then our people started coming overseas in batches of 10, 20, 30, and sometimes 40. We only had a little over 300 in all but they did some of the most amazing jobs.

We were all volunteers. The headquarters staff wasn't paid anything at all. Not a nickel. Members working in Civil Defence in the hospitals got a pound a week, which was enough to pay for some stamps and a bus ticket and things like that. That's all they got in addition to their board and lodging and their uniforms.

Our girls didn't get any rewards, as did all the regular veterans, but we did come away with a lot of satisfaction for the part we played.

PART 3
HOME FRONT

War Savings parade, Toronto, February 1, 1941. (Photo by Alexandra Studio, Public Archives of Canada)

A very important part of Canada's war effort was the voluntary home front contribution given freely and willingly by the civilian population. All over the country individuals and groups gave of their time and energy, performing innumerable tasks like providing recreation and comforts for the armed services, running canteens for the war workers, soldiers, sailors, and airmen, collecting salvage materials and many other jobs.

Three days after Canada's official announcement of war, the government passed what was known as the War Charities Act to supervise the raising and spending of the funds which would be needed for such services. In the remaining months of 1939, two hundred registrations of war charities funds were granted and before the war ended, almost four thousand such charities were registered.

A large proportion of the money was at first raised through voluntary contributions to national organizations but the government felt that these money-raising campaigns were interfering with their own Victory Loan drives. In March, 1941 the voluntary system of giving was replaced by another system whereby the government gave direct grants to certain organizations that were involved in a larger way. The beneficiaries under this new way of doing things were the Salvation Army Red Shield War Services Fund, the YMCA and the YWCA War Services Funds, the Navy League of Canada, the Canadian Legion War Services Incorporated, and the Knights of Columbus Canadian Army Huts Fund.

The Canadian Red Cross was allowed to continue making its own national appeals. Its volunteer workers in Canada packed and shipped thirteen-and-a-half million food parcels during the war and operated blood donor clinics that collected close to two million individual donations. The work was done entirely by voluntary workers including the doctors and nurses.

Besides all of this, the National Women's War Work Committee of the Red Cross throughout the country made and distributed millions of articles of clothing, mostly for overseas, packed prisoner-of-war parcels, operated canteens and engaged in many other forms of voluntary service. There was also a trained Red Cross corps of full-time voluntary women workers numbering more than 6,000. Five hundred of these women were serving overseas when the war ended. They assisted in the work of the Canadian Army Medical Corps, drove ambulances, visited the sick and the wounded in hospitals, and taught handicrafts.

Citizens' committees in every province were organized to co-ordinate all services for the armed forces. These services included setting up urban recreational centres and canteens, arranging concert parties at camps and stations, collecting, sorting and shipping magazines to the forces, providing home hospitality, setting up information centres, and issuing permits for war charity organizations.

Zone magazine collection and forwarding depots were established in ten cities across the country, and by the end of the war, 150,000 magazines were being sent out to our troops every month.

Civil Defence was another area that operated on a volunteer basis and by war's end it was estimated that across Canada more than 225,000 volunteers were enrolled, 45,000 of whom were women. These volunteers included doctors, nurses, stretcher-bearers, rescue squad members, firemen, public utilities experts, drivers, helpers, messengers, police, wardens, clerks and telegraphers.

More than 1,800 voluntary committees across the country took on the immense job of collecting war salvage materials for essential production. Besides iron and steel, these committees put on drives to collect waste paper, rags, rubber, fats and bones, glass, and anything else that was deemed valuable. Over 300,000 tons of valuable waste material was added to the war effort in this way, and all by volunteer effort.

Nobody was left out of the campaigns. A complementary phase of the loan drives was the introduction of war savings stamps and certificates in which even the children had an opportunity to invest. One could buy a stamp for

25 cents and when you had four dollars' worth of stamps you turned them in for a certificate that had a face value of five dollars, if you kept them for seven-and-a-half years.

The biggest thing, though, was that we who contributed on the home front felt that we were helping our troops who were paying the greatest price of all.

Pauline McGibbon
Former Lieutenant-Governor of Ontario
Toronto, Ontario

IN SEPTEMBER, 1939, my husband Don and I were living in Sarnia, Ontario. He was working with Imperial Oil and I was involved with various voluntary organizations, particularly the IODE, Imperial Order Daughters of the Empire. With the declaration of war, the Red Cross immediately took over a store on the main street of town where they started teaching volunteers how to make hospital supplies. I got involved in this right away and learned how to roll bandages, a skill I later taught to others.

The IODE then cooperated with the Red Cross in making these hospital supplies but this came to be seen as a duplication of effort, so the IODE withdrew in favour of the Red Cross and turned its attention to other volunteer war work like sewing and knitting for the troops on active service. Everything we needed to get going was donated, including the furniture, the sewing machines and even the large tables we used for cutting out material for pyjamas and other articles of clothing. The public was so very good to us that almost immediately we were in operation. Directions came from National Headquarters and the chapters across Canada were anxious and willing to carry these orders out. The result of all this early activity was that the IODE, as far as I know, was the first organization to send relief to Britain in the form of new clothing and bedding.

At the very beginning of the war, the National President and War

Bless 'em all – the long and the short and the tall. Service personnel were always among the first in line to buy Victory Bonds. Left to right: *Service personnel Moorhouse, Robinson, Louks, Paterson, and Shuttleworth. (Courtesy Elmer Eadie)*

Service Convenor made a trip to Ottawa to consult with the authorities on how the 30,000 members of the Order could best serve the country. One of the things they were asked to do was to supply a library service for men and women in the armed forces in co-operation with the Canadian Legion. This was done, but later on, as the Legion became involved with so many other things, the IODE took over the service by itself, doing a terrific job of supplying books for ships, hospitals and army camps. It kept up for a year after the war as a service for the returning veterans, and it was all done by volunteers.

We were also raising money for specific projects in connection with the war. In one month, in 1940, 100,000 dollars — the equivalent of at least a million today — was raised to purchase a Bolingbroke Bomber which was presented to the Canadian government. Later, we raised 300,000 which was sent to the British Ministry for Air. Another 50,000 was used to send a fighter plane to Australia. All of this money was raised by just one chapter.

In October, 1940 Don's company moved him to Toronto, but it wasn't entirely unexpected because he had been spending a lot of time there anyway because of his job. About six months before, I had become the Head of the IODE for Sarnia, and by virtue of that, I became a member of the provincial executive. This was all rather fortunate, because it meant that when we moved to Toronto I had already met the women who were at the head of the municipal chapter and I felt right at home. They asked me to come to head-quarters, which was in the old Timothy Eaton home, and get further acquainted.

I will never forget that first visit. First of all, I was shown around the offices and the old stables where the books and comforts were packed before being sent off to the different services. Then, out of the blue, I was asked if I could type some envelopes for them. Well, I had never typed in my life but I thought that any nincompoop with an ounce of common sense could manage to use a typewriter so I said, "Yes." I soon found out how wrong I was, as my wastebasket filled up with spoiled envelopes. I was so mad with myself that I went home and called Shaw's Business School and told them that I just wanted to learn enough typing to be able to do envelopes for a voluntary organization.

Needless to say, they were waiting for me with some curiosity when I arrived for the first of my eight lessons. I did advance a bit beyond envelopes, though. I rented a typewriter with blank keys and eventually became good enough that by the time I was made Secretary of the IODE Municipal Chapter, I was typing minutes, stencils, letters, and everything else.

After this, as the war progressed, it wasn't long before Headquarters realized it needed a telephone switchboard. I learned to run that and eventually I was in charge of the voluntary operators. I soon found that my volunteer job was keeping me at National

Headquarters five days a week but along with this, on the provincial
scene, I had returned to the Provincial Executive as Film Convenor.
Before the war, the IODE had always supported British films, but
with the coming of the war, support for our own National Film
Board was added, especially for the "Carry On Canada" series.

All of us took our volunteer war jobs very seriously and most
often we paid any expenses incurred out of our own pockets.

I honestly believe that the IODE had an important part to play in
the opening up of movie viewing policy in Canada and that was due
to something that happened during the war. Barb Osler, who was
our National Film Convenor, and I, went to see the people at the
Lord's Day Alliance to try and persuade them that some theatres in
designated parts of the country should be open on Sunday afternoons for men and women in uniform. I think it was because such an
organization as the IODE was in favour of this form of entertainment
that certain theatres in Toronto, Edmonton, Halifax, Prince
Rupert and Victoria were given permission to show movies on
Sunday and allow free admission to service personnel until the end
of the war. That was a real breakthrough. We were also actively
involved in an advisory capacity with the Ontario Board of Film
Censors so that when they were faced with a very controversial film
we would be invited to attend a special screening to offer our
opinions. My role was to attend these screenings as a representative
of Canadian women.

When Russia became our ally during the War, Russian films
started to be admitted to Canada and I was asked to attend a
screening along with my husband, Don. In our report later I remember saying that anyone who saw that film would never want to
live in a country with such dreary conditions.

I've really only touched on the work of the IODE during the
Second World War and the many projects which were undertaken,
mostly at the request of the government. We had a Polish Relief
program, for example, an Adoption of Ships program, a National
Cigarette Fund, and many other things. We also co-operated with
the Consumers Branch of the Wartime Prices and Trade Board in
the distribution of their literature.

In dollars and cents, the value of the work of the organization during the war has been placed in the millions, but in human terms, it would be impossible to measure the amount of good work and comfort given voluntarily by its members across the country. The IODE, with good reason, is proud of the role it played in the Second World War.

Dorothy B. Inglis
Toronto, Ontario

WHEN CANADIANS were called upon to go to war in 1939, the call was taken seriously by the whole population, not just those who rushed to join the colours. I was working for the Ontario Civil Service at the time, and as soon as war broke out, all the women there held a meeting to decide what we could do. Out of that meeting came a hastily formed organization called the Queen's Park War Service Guild.

The Red Cross supplied us with wool and the whole lot of us set to work with our needles making socks for men of the services. Throughout the war, we made literally thousands and thousands of pairs of socks. Anytime there was a spare moment in the office the knitting needles would be out. We knit before work, during work, during our lunch hours, after work and at home. For those of us who were unable to join the forces or take jobs in the war industries, it made us feel as if we were really doing something useful.

In addition to the socks, the girls in our office also had a quilt project. The government gave us a room on the top floor of our old building and allowed us to set up a quilting frame there so that during our lunch hours, if we weren't knitting, we would be there working on a quilt. Four or five of us at a time would take our bag lunches with us and quilt away our lunch hour. All of the material was donated. One firm that made shirts gave us a whole pile of their sample materials. The pieces were all the same size so I would take them home with me and stitch them together to form the tops for the finished quilts. It was always a proud day for us when we had one

During the Second World War, thousands of women joined all branches of the forces and were assigned non-combat roles which freed men for the more dangerous front line duties. This is a group from the air force women's division handling stores at the flying training school at St. Hubert, Quebec. (Courtesy the National Archives of Canada)

finished and ready to be packaged up and sent over to England for those people who spent many of their nights shivering in an air raid shelter.

In a way, I think most Canadians realized in the months leading up to September, 1939, that there'd be a war and we were ready for it when it came. We had all been aware of the gathering storm clouds in Europe and, through our newspapers, radios and newsreels, we had come to realize that this funny, little Charlie Chaplin-like character in Germany was not so funny after all. We had seen him take over one country after another, and we had watched the long lines of homeless refugees on the screens of our motion picture theatres, as they straggled along the roads of Europe looking for some place to lay down their pitiful possessions. Even though we had just suffered through a decade of poverty and want ourselves, and had seen people in bread lines in our own country, we hadn't seen anything like the horror that was going on in Europe.

In the newsreels at the movie theatres we came to know the face of Hitler, and we heard his voice as he screamed in a language we did not understand, but we recognized him as a crazy man who sent innocent people off to concentration camps and camps of forced labour. We saw pictures of his storm troopers burning books and terrorizing and beating the Jews. Jews who were, in fact, more German than he was. We called him the Viennese paper-hanger; the Austrian Corporal. We could see that this was a man full of hatred, leading a movement of thugs who beat up and murdered all those who didn't follow his line. We viewed Hitler right from the beginning as the monster he later proved to be, and we were terrified at the thought that he could eventually win the war. I think that this fear, more than patriotism, forced us into participating in any way we could.

All of us, of all ages, accepted that we must do something, no matter how little. There were bottle drives, scrap metal drives, used-paper drives and drives to save anything and everything that could lessen civilian needs for material that could be better used for war. The automobile companies stopped making cars and trucks for civilian use and we drove the old ones into the ground — that is when we drove them at all. Gasoline for civilian use was severely rationed, so that those who had cars strove to use as little as possible.

Everybody was doing something. The bakeries even stopped slicing bread, because this was an unnecessary and needless use of energy and manpower. A penny saved was a penny earned and "waste not, want not" became our national philosophy.

Across the country in every hamlet, town, village and city, women's groups formed on their own, to do things for the war effort, or "the common cause," as it was often called. They sewed and they knitted; they scrounged old clothing and fixed it up; they ran bingo games and card games and bazaars. Winning the war became a national obsession, spurred on by the thought that the more we did, the quicker we'd get our boys back home.

We bought war stamps and Victory Bonds and we gave what we could to the Red Cross and all the other similar organizations we believed in. We prayed in church at special services and we invited to our homes the boys in uniform who were far away from their homes.

We worked for wages that were much too low, but we chalked this up too to the war effort. Women packed boxes of precious and hard-to-get food and sent it away to soldiers and civilians overseas that they often didn't know. We painted our legs in lieu of nylon stockings and girls working in war industries even gave up their lunch hours on the job to continue their volunteer work.

Yes indeed, war was a full-time occupation for all.

Effie Donnell
Islington, Ontario

THE FIRST thing that pops into my head is the rationing. We never seemed to have enough stamps for the things we wanted most. Of course you could always trade with your neighbours. My shortage was always tea, even though my son, Laurence or husband, Hal hardly drank any at all. They preferred to have milk with their meals but I drank tea by the gallon, which meant that I was always on the lookout for someone who wasn't quite so addicted. I think, all in all, we did pretty well and it wasn't so bad at all. Certainly nobody went hungry.

The other thing was volunteer work. There was plenty of that. I

May Birchall modelling a lime-green, spun-rayon dress suggested for purchase as part of the c.w.a.c. discharge clothing allowance of $100, Glebe Collegiate, Ottawa, October 23, 1945. (Photo by Lieutenant Allan / DND, Public Archives Canada)

belonged to several organizations — my church, the IODE and a number of service clubs, and in all of them we were trying to come up with new ideas all the time on how to make money for "the cause." We were regularly sending out bales of clothing and bedding and how we ever managed to come up with so much only heaven knows for sure. There were teas, church suppers and rummage sales going on constantly — anything at all to raise a few bucks.

In those days, the baby cereal, Pablum, came in round boxes and one of our groups decided that it would be a good idea to collect these boxes from any of the young mothers we knew and turn them into money. We covered the boxes with different patterned prints and tartans and put on handles made from used clothesline cord. We got 25 cents each for the plain ones and 35 for the tartan. Just about anyone who was a knitter bought them to carry their materials when they went visiting or to a bridge game. They were a very popular item and easy to sell. I made dozens of them.

Then there were the aprons! You could get five yards of factory cotton for a dollar, so if you cut that out evenly you had enough material for seven pretty aprons using little bits of different coloured cotton for the pockets and ties. At 35 cents each, we more than doubled the money we spent for material.

At our private bridge club games, instead of giving high and low prizes we donated the money to the Red Cross.

The Red Cross supplied us with lengths of woollen material to be made into skirts and those of our members who had sewing machines would take them home and finish them off. Different groups knitted literally hundreds of pairs of socks that were sent off through the Red Cross to our servicemen. My three brothers in the air force reported that they were kept well-supplied this way.

It seems that everyone, regardless of age, was doing something for the war effort. All of the schools had different programs. In my son's Grade Six class at Victory Public School, each of the students could choose his own way of raising money. Laurence decided to collect old newspapers and he was out every day with his little C.C.M. wagon calling on all the neighbours. When he figured he had a big enough pile, he called the Pullman Salvage Company in

Toronto who came out and picked it up. It turned out he had several tons and he was a very proud boy when they mailed him his cheque, which, at $18.00 a ton, amounted to quite a bit to add to the rest that his room had collected. His class won the prize for collecting the most money, all of which was turned over to the Red Cross.

Old bottles were carefully washed and their labels removed, and they were sold to hardware stores at two dozen for 25 cents. They needed them as containers for oil and turpentine. In those days the ragman would go up and down the streets, and you bartered with him for any old clothing you might have on hand. More money for the war effort.

One of the things we did, which was a constant reminder to us of how lucky we were to be living in Canada and not in Britain, was to send food boxes to relatives overseas. There was a limit of 22 pounds placed on these boxes by the government, but we were able to send tins of canned meat and anything else we could squeeze in up to that limit — things they couldn't get usually, including the sweet biscuits that the English are so famous for. We'd get letters back saying things like "English biscuits sent to us from Canada? And we can't even buy them over here for love nor money!" Oh, they were so grateful. Long after the war was over, we would still get letters from those people telling how much those boxes meant to them.

I guess though, it does take something like a war to bring out the best in all of us. As hard as we worked over on this side to help out, we still had no conception of what those people in the war zones were going through. Not one of us ever had to spend even one night in a bomb shelter, did we?

Harry Cook
St. Catharines, Ontario

I WAS WORKING in a small mining town, Duparquet, Quebec, about 35 miles northwest of Noranda in the early part of the war. At the beginning of summer, 1940, a military training program was started and one man who had some military experience was given the task

Toronto Transit Commission Reserve Army Float, April 10,
1943. (Courtesy the National Archives of Canada)

to recruit all those who might be interested in getting involved. Since we all worked for the Beattie Gold Mine and the majority of us were on shift work, it was necessary to form three sections of about 20 to 30 men each.

I think we only had one little book of instructions between us at the start, to tell us how we should go about forming a militia unit, so a lot of it was more or less by guess and by golly. The first thing we did was to appoint a group of acting sergeants and corporals, some of whom had a little background of parade marching, but little else. Then, after it was felt that we acting N.C.O.'s were sufficiently trained, we, in turn, trained the other men to march and turn, and to take route marches down to the lake, which was about a mile away and then back again. Since there were no uniforms, all of the acting

N.C.O.'s wore berets along with different coloured arm bands to distinguish the different ranks.

It was all pretty informal stuff but we took our job seriously and in time we became very proficient at everything, including our marching. They were doing the same sort of thing in most of the other towns too, and as things progressed we were given wooden rifles to train with. It wasn't long before most of us were very good at the business of rifle drilling, even though those precious wooden rifles weren't ours to keep. They had to be shared with all the other towns in the area, meaning they would be taken from us after a drill and transported to the next town where their militia force would be waiting to practise rifle drill too. Surprisingly, though, we all managed to get pretty good at it.

After a while though, we got a little bored with the make-believe guns and the marching drill, so the word was passed around while we were on afternoon shift at the mine, that the next morning we were all going to show up at the school yard and put on a real show. Sure enough, all the boys were there on time with real rifles and shotguns, and Johnny Vasko, who worked at the ore crusher plant, brought his accordion along to supply the music.

Well now, I'll tell you we put on a show that would make any military outfit proud. With marching music and real guns we had the time of our lives pulling all our little tricks. We marched and we turned and we put on a rifle drill, the likes of which was never seen before or since in that small town. We sure enjoyed ourselves that day and so did everybody else. It really was a day to remember. I guess it was one to forget too, because somebody up top didn't think it was quite the right thing to do. They said we didn't follow proper military procedures. How about that? We were told not to do it again. *C'est la vie!*

Later, during the winter, we were issued with greatcoats and forage caps from World War One, which was fine except that we decided to keep wearing our own fur caps because they were much better for that cold climate of northern Quebec. We must have looked quite a sight — a militia unit marching group with the only military clothing being greatcoats that were one war late!

We did attain some distinction though. One Sunday, all the militia units from all the towns gathered in Rouyn–Noranda and had a real parade through the two cities. They tell me it was the very first parade ever held in northern Quebec, so I guess we made it into the history books.

As time went on, all of those who could opted to join the regular services. Our acting militia sergeant, George Forster, went into the airforce and I went into the navy. Did all of this militia training help us at all? Well, perhaps it did. One thing for sure, we certainly did know how to march and rifle drill. I can't remember though, that they gave us any extra pay for that.

The vast majority of Canada's present population has no memory of the Second World War. They know it happened, but all of their knowledge of the 1939–45 conflict is second-hand. They've read about it or heard relatives talk about it but they have no personal experience of what it was like to be living in a country that was waging a full-out war against another country.

I asked my own son, who was born after the Second World War ended, what that worldwide conflict means to him.

Russell McNeil
Nanaimo, British Columbia

MANY OF MY generation count the days of our lives from the close of the Second World War. We personally know nothing of that frightful period in human history. We have read countless stories about the war and seen hundreds of films about its sad history.

Unfortunately, for most of our youth, most of what we saw or heard or read was softened by time or mellowed by romantic recreation. We saw that war as a great struggle between good and evil; a struggle which saw a powerful but cowardly enemy go down to defeat at the hands of weaker but braver Allied forces. There are exceptions. In the movie *Sophie's Choice*, a concentration camp victim is forced to choose between her little boy and her little girl; one must die, one will live. If she doesn't choose, she will lose both. As a father of three, I cannot think of a more vicious torture on the mind or on the soul. But I am told that such acts were routine in that war.

We know from realities such as these that there was little which was soft, or mellow, or romantic about those days. It was a mean time that brought out the best and the worst of the generation before ours. It was a mean time that ruined its sons and daughters on both sides, oppressed entire peoples and corrupted truth.

As parents today, we cannot understand where the mothers and fathers of those years found the courage to carry on, after losing their children to the war. As adults today, we try to imagine how we might feel if we were forced to wear a yellow star, and to abandon our livelihoods, homes, and rights to basic human feelings. We can only try to imagine how we might feel if those we love today were taken away, beaten, tortured, raped, and murdered.

Where is the romance in that? There is none. These are the blackest of memories. The millions lost on both sides of that awful war are lost for eternity. Their children will never be. I see no romance in this.

The men and women in the generation before mine did what they had to do. They crushed an evil idea. In the Germany of the 1930s it was called National Socialism. Like all evil, this lie was masked in other lies and promises of a better life. It is ironic that the idea sprang up in a great land, amongst a caring and compassionate people, no different from the people in the towns and cities in Canada. Yet the idea took root in spite of this, and attracted the worst of any country's criminals.

The terrible sadness is that evil never dies. At best, it is only controlled. When the controls fail the evil can take root again — anywhere. It could happen here.

We can only hope and pray that the impossible sacrifices of my parents' generation has taught our generation to recognize deceit and evil, and that they have provided us with the tools to keep those ideas under control.

Bob Bolster
Nepean, Ontario

I WASN'T OLD enough for the war — that is to be playing an active part in it — but I sure do remember what it was like on the home front.

I grew up in my grandfather's house and the whole world for us was his Atwater–Kent radio. It was the stuff of imagination and entertainment for us but, especially for Grandpa, that little radio meant that all important news of the war.

The war seemed to be in everything we did. In school, the government had a system going where they would pay any of us kids five dollars if we would learn the Morse Code. Needless to say, I took advantage of that and was very happy the day my cheque for $5.00 arrived. Five dollars in those days was big bucks.

Down at the butcher shop, there was a constant stream of people coming in to donate the fat they had saved from their cooking. The butcher was in charge of collecting it and turning it over to the government for use in explosives or something like that.

It used to be a big deal for a kid during those war years to get a ride in a car because, first of all, there weren't many private cars, and secondly, there wasn't much gasoline around to keep them going. What gas there was was used very carefully on essential trips or for business. I remember this gold-letter day when Louis David, who was manager of a local clothing store in our town, invited me to go with him to Morrisburg, which was about 18 miles away from Chesterville where I lived. He wanted to get some rum or beer or something like that, and that liquor store in Morrisburg was the closest place you could buy booze. He didn't want to go on a long trip like that all by himself. I couldn't believe my good fortune. This would be my first trip out of town in a car, and to think I'd be going in such an automobile — a 1938 Buick. What prestige!

Well it was prestige all right — until we actually got out on the roads. I don't know how many people remember this, but in those days of the war, nobody ever got through a trip of more than a few miles without a flat tire. They were using some kind of imitation rubber in tires and inner tubes, and they might as well have been using chewing gum. Perhaps that *is* what they were making them from. Who knows? In any event, before we got back home again that day, we had nine flats, and each one meant jacking the car up, getting out the tire irons to get it off the rim and then fixing up the inner tube with these rubber patches and glue. Then it was letting the car down again off the jack and hoping against hope that there would be no more that day. I remember making a mental note to have an excuse ready if Lou David ever asked me to go with him again. Those pleasure drives were just too much hard work.

By the way, does anybody else besides me remember what they used to call the Victory speed limit? It was 25 miles per hour, and it applied only in the U.S. I think we were still flying around the highways at 30. Driving a car became ever more difficult as the war went on, because at one point you couldn't buy a tire or a tube for love or money, even those imitation rubber ones. People are ingenious though. Women learned how to braid long pieces of hemp rope and pack them down tightly into the tires instead of inner tubes. That worked pretty well too. Not quite as smooth a ride but at least no more flats.

Listening to my favourite shows on the radio was a lot more fun. At 6:30 every evening, Grandpa would let me tune in "L for Lanky." Great show. Chock full of action. I can still remember the way it started with the announcer ordering us, "Don't touch that dial — it's L for Lanky." For me, it was time to soar off into the clouds with the crew of a Lancaster bomber and be part of the action in Grandpa's war. I never did figure out why the CBC chose the Lancaster as the hero airplane for that program when everybody knows it was the DC Dakota made by Douglas Aircraft that was the real workhorse. The Mosquitoes, made, I think, by deHavilland, were no slouches either, even if they *were* only made of plywood.

There was lots of war news on the radio, with the topper being Lorne Greene's late night newscast. "The Voice of Doom," everybody called him. There were lots of reports coming over too, from

CBC reporters who were right over there where the war was going on. It seems to me, though, that an awful lot of those "Canadian" reporters had English accents.

During the early part of the war, there were still a lot of hobos and bums left over from the Depression "riding the rods" of the CPR and they would drop off in towns along the way to try their luck with the local people. It was said that if they had luck at any of the houses they would put a big X there in chalk, so that their friends who came after them would know where they could get a handout. There was plenty of reason for bums while the Depression was on, but when the war came and the army was looking for men, and the war factories were offering lots of work, people had little patience or time for roving bands of beggars. When they came to our door Grandma would sometimes tell them that she had nothing or that her husband was the chief of police. Neither of these stories was true, but it was enough to get rid of them.

Another thing that the railroads brought through our town were the long 25-car troop trains with German prisoners going off to the camps out west or up north. We kids used to gather on the station platform and put our thumbs to our nose and wave our hands back and forth while the train was stopped for water. Maybe we were too young to join the army, but at least we could let those Germans know what we thought of them. There were plenty of armed guards with rifles on those trains who warned us kids not to agitate the prisoners, but we did it anyway because we knew all about Nazis and how they treated their prisoners.

"Rosie the Riveter," kind of a tribute to all those women who were working in the war industries, was a very popular song, and just about everybody was collecting some kind of scrap for the war effort. I especially remember the drives they put on for old pots and pans, and anything else made out of tin or aluminium. Grandpa owned a variety store and he tossed in anything and everything that was made in Japan — pots, pans, the whole works, including all of my poorly made Japanese toys.

My Aunt Betty had a 1938 Ford that carried a green AA sticker on the windshield, which meant she was allowed a bit more gas because she was a school teacher and needed her car to get to work. Her biggest problem all through the war was trying to find silk stockings with the seam down the back. She had nice legs and she knew it, so a "disaster" for her was getting a run in a precious stocking.

When "Musical March Past" came on the radio at 8:25 in the morning, that was my signal to start walking to school if I wanted to get there on time. I'd rush home again at noon though, because I wanted to hear the radio soap operas as much as I wanted to eat.

Kilroy Was Here was a bit of wartime graffiti that was scrawled on every bare piece of wall everywhere — at our school, on fences and even in churches, not just in our town but everywhere else in the Allied world. I never did find out who this guy Kilroy was, but he must have been a great traveller.

Everything was scarce and some things were impossible to get, things like gum boots that were made of rubber. They were a part of every kid's outfit in pre-war days, but I must admit I didn't miss them one bit, because our Ottawa Valley winters were so cold it felt like you were wearing two blocks of ice on your feet. Besides that, they were smelly, even worse than the canvas sneakers we wore the rest of the year. Parents resisted throwing them away though. When they got holes in the bottom they'd patch them up with the same stuff they used to fix inner tubes.

There were ration stamps for sugar, tea and meat and people in our community used to trade them around like baseball cards. I can't remember anybody not being able to get enough of any of these things because they didn't have stamps. Liquor was also rationed, but those who wanted it always seemed to get what they needed. Of course, in the valley there were lots of illegal stills.

That's the way the war went in our valley town, and I suspect it was much the same all across the country. When 1945 arrived, I turned 13, and although Grandpa was still listening to the war news with his usual ferocity and total concentration, his health was starting to fail. In the U.S., their great wartime leader, Roosevelt, long showing the effects of the strain of war, died on April 12. Grandpa followed him to the grave just nine days later. Too bad they couldn't have stayed around just a little longer for the final victory. They would have enjoyed that — Grandpa especially.

On V-E Day our whole town went crazy with joy. What a celebration! My uncle Roland Carr — most people called him "Roll Car" — got drunk, and the word got back home afterwards that he was lying with his head in the gutter and missed all the fun. It sure was fun though, as well it should have been. It was a long hard war and people needed a bit of relaxation. Even Uncle Roll.

Jean Lucier
Deep River, Ontario

THE THING I remember best about the Second World War was that I was finally going to have a father. The day the telegram arrived, I flew out the door of our living quarters on the top of my grandfather's house on Campbell Avenue in Windsor, Ontario, and down the stairs to the street. I was screaming at the top of my voice for the whole world to hear, "My daddy's coming home! My daddy's coming home!" It was probably the happiest day of my life.

And yet today, I still wonder just why I was so happy. You see, I was not yet six years old and I had no memory whatsoever of my father. He went away shortly after the war began; he was wounded in that ill-fated raid on Dieppe and he spent the rest of the war in German prison camps. I only knew what he looked like from the pictures my mother showed me. He didn't really know me either, because I was just a baby when he left, and if he didn't know me, he knew my baby brother Bobby even less. Bobby was born after his departure for overseas, so he never even saw his baby boy. The war did strange things to families.

Dad was C.S.M. of the Essex Scottish Regiment that was decimated at Dieppe in August, 1942. He was one of the lucky few who survived, but I don't remember any of that. What I do remember though is the day that my daddy came home and the crowds at the Windsor train station. I remember what seemed like millions of

*Private G.R. MacDonald, Toronto Scottish Regiment, giving
first aid to an injured boy, Brionne, France, August 25, 1944.
(Photo by Ken Bell / DND / Public Archives of Canada)*

people, and the crush of human bodies, all of them anxious relatives and friends of the returnees. And I remember spotting my dad with mom getting off the train together. She had gone to Toronto the week before to meet him, and then went with him on a tour of the north making speeches for the War Bond Drive that went on, even though the war was then over. That was the first time I had ever seen my father and mother together.

They were way over there with all those people between us and I was over here propped up on my uncle's shoulders pounding him on top of the head and crying, "Put me down! Let me go! I want to see my daddy!"

I did see my daddy that day, and he hugged me and kissed me and called me his little girl. I didn't know how to act with him, because he was really a stranger and I was very shy. It took a while, but it wasn't too long before he became my dad in every sense of the word. Then I had a hard time trying to imagine what it was like when he was away.

I guess it was 45 years ago but I can still cry about it. That's all I can remember about the war.

Dan Konig
Toronto, Ontario

I WAS EIGHT years old on September 10, 1939, the day that Canada entered the war against Germany and as far as I was concerned, my birthday was far more important than any old war.

I had been looking forward for weeks to the party my parents had promised me and nothing was going to spoil that. Anyway, kids in those days were far less sophisticated than today's youngsters, mainly I think because there is so much more information available to them now coming in from all directions.

In our house at that time we had only one radio, a big one that was my father's pride and joy, and it was never turned on unless he was there, mainly I suppose, because it operated on batteries which ran out of power very easily. That meant that if the radio was going to be turned on at all, you would sit down and listen. You were expected to do that. None of this walking all over the place and listening on the fly. Radio listening was a serious business. That also meant I didn't do any listening at all, unless I happened to be in the room when father had the set turned on.

That also explains why I didn't know anything at all about the war that had been threatening in the late thirties. The only thing I ever read in our daily newspaper was the comics, and our teachers at school never got into anything but the three Rs. None of us kids knew anything about what was happening in Europe, and we couldn't have cared less.

On September 10, I had been out playing around after school trying to kill time until 5:00, which was the time Mother told me to be home to get washed up for my party. On the dot of five, I ran through the kitchen door expecting to see all kinds of good food laid out for the festivities. I stopped and looked around and couldn't believe my eyes. There was nothing. Even the fire in the kitchen stove was out. Perhaps, I thought, they're pulling a surprise on me.

Still full of expectations, I ran into the living room but it was even darker and emptier than the kitchen. I was all set to start crying when I looked over to the corner where mother and father were both intently listening to the radio. They were staring at it in the same way that people look at their television sets today. Father's face was even glummer than it usually was and there were tears streaming down mother's face.

"What's wrong?" I asked, in a panicky voice, "Is my party off?" By this time I was crying too.

"Danny," my father replied, "The war is on. Canada has just declared war on Germany."

"What does that mean?" I cried, "What's that got to do with my party?"

I'm telling you honestly I didn't understand any of it. I didn't know what a war was. I knew nothing about the international tensions that had been building up all through 1939, and the only thing I knew about Hitler was that he was a funny-looking man with a moustache. I had seen cartoons of him in the newspaper.

Father, who had emigrated from Europe in the 1920s, sat me down alongside him and tried to explain as best he could the horrors of war as he remembered them, to an eight-year-old who knew nothing about current events.

I listened as he talked, but not much was getting through. The only thing I understood was that it was getting awfully close to 6 P.M., the time my party was supposed to start.

When he finished, my mother slipped out to the kitchen and started to rattle some dishes and make food preparation sounds. I washed my hands and face and combed my hair and waited for the three friends I had invited to arrive. Father stayed where he was with his ear right up to the speaker of the radio.

My friends came, all at the same time, and we had sandwiches, cookies and milk and mother gave each of them a piece of cake with a candle in it to take home with them. We played no games and nobody even sang "Happy Birthday." I guess the mood wasn't quite right for it with mother's face all wet with tears, and father filling the room with the sound of the war news. It was the worst birthday party I ever had, before or since.

Everything changed around our house after that. Daddy, who never had money for anything, except what we absolutely needed, came home one day with a big wooden crate and opened it up right there in the living room. It contained the biggest radio I had ever seen, and he told me it had the latest of everything on it, including a very powerful short wave. It was an electric-powered model that didn't need batteries he said, and it could bring in every country in the world. He set it up in the same corner where the old one had been and he dragged that one down to the basement.

That was it. From that moment until the last day of the war, that radio was his only companion. He didn't play games with me anymore and he and mother didn't go anywhere. While he was home, he didn't do anything but search around the dial of his radio for war news. It didn't matter what language. He could understand all of them, it seemed.

My father worked as a projectionist at the local movie theatre, which meant that he was also getting a full war diet there on the

Movietone News that they showed along with the movie. Then there were the propaganda films and the National Film Board documentaries like the "Canada Carries On" series. He was being soaked in war news during his every waking hour and he never seemed to get enough.

When he got home every night around 10:00, on would go the radio for the CBC National News and then, when that was finished he'd switch over to shortwave. I don't know what time he'd finally go to bed, but mother told me one time that she didn't know either. She said she was always asleep by the time he was ready to give up and climb the stairs. The only thing we did know, just from looking at him when he came down in the morning, was whether the news was good or bad. It was all reflected in his face and in his eyes. When it was really bad the whites of his eyes were all bloodshot.

When the announcement came over his radio that the war had ended and the Allies were victorious, Father let out a whoop and a holler that, I swear, was loud enough to wake the dead. That evening, we all went into town and celebrated along with everybody else. The next night when he came home from work, he didn't even turn the radio on. After that, he seldom stayed up long enough to hear the national news. He started listening to music programs and drama, and he bought me a brand new baseball glove, a bat and a ball, and he would bang out a few tough ones for me to catch. Not only that, he never talked about the war again.

He turned out to be a pretty good guy once he got that war out of his system.

Betty Storosko
St. Catharines, Ontario

I REMEMBER the war years mainly because of my dad who served in the army from 1939 to 1945. He joined up because he was born in England but had emigrated to Canada in 1925 and he wanted to help his new country.

As I was only six years old in 1939, I don't remember him actually joining the forces, but I do remember the day my mom, along with my sister Louise and I, travelled from Port Dalhousie, where we lived, to St. Catharines by streetcar. Then we switched to a bus which took us to Niagara-on-the-Lake where Dad was taking his basic training. We thought we had travelled quite a distance but it wasn't really very far. Of course when you combine a streetcar and a bus with a child's curiosity and sense of adventure, I suppose even a few miles can be quite a distance. Also, not many of us had cars in 1939, so distances appeared to be quite different to us then.

The three of us stayed at a rooming house for two weeks and we watched as the soldiers did their drills on the Fort George grounds which seemed to be filled to overflowing with tents. I can remember the day Dad came home and announced that he had earned his first stripe — having made the highest score on the rifle range. That was a proud day for him and for all of us.

Later Dad was shifted up to Campbellton, New Brunswick, which was a bit closer to our home, but still a long distance away. Nevertheless, the three of us went by train to see him before he left for overseas. The train was crowded with service men and their families who were trying to grab at each little bit of togetherness while they could.

We spent about a month in New Brunswick until Dad left for England. The next day we left for home, the three of us crying all the way.

The next thing I remember is Mom working on the local fruit farms during the summer, and riding a bike to get there. In the winter she wore overalls and a bandanna and worked in a munitions plant. Louise and I would go to movies together on Saturdays and sometimes we would get in free if we brought an aluminium pot or a jar of grease for the war effort. Sometimes we would go out in the fields together, and collect milkweed pods which were also used for the war. We heard they used them in the making of parachutes.

I remember, too, books of ration tickets, some were pink, yellow, or brown, and were used for sugar, tea, and meat.

We wrote lots of letters to Dad in England and also to his army buddy Jack. They kept Dad in England because they said he was a bit

Louise and Betty Storosko (front, left to right) *with friends of
the family, R.T. Pennock and his wife, Margaret. (Courtesy Betty
Storosko)*

Betty Storosko (left) *and sister Louise with their father, on leave,
1941. (Courtesy Betty Storosko)*

too old to accompany the troops to the European battle zones, and that's where he stayed till the war was over. I still treasure a couple of those letters he wrote me.

Another thing I remember is how hard my mother worked while he was away. She put every cent she made on the mortgage because she wanted to have it paid off by the time he got back.

At school we knitted little squares to be made into afghans, and Mom, when she wasn't working, belonged to a group which they called the Duration Club. They packed parcels at the local armouries to send overseas.

The three of us, Mom, Louise, and I, would have parties with the children and wives of other soldiers. I remember too that Mom always cried when they played war songs, especially "There'll Always Be an England."

On V-E Day, when the war was finally over, Mom was working as a waitress at a small inn at Lakeside Park. I remember how she, nor anyone else, wanted to work because all anybody wanted to do was celebrate, and that's what we did.

The next thing I remember is Dad coming back home, and we unpacked his kit and he gave us all little souvenirs he had brought back with him. It was all very wonderful to finally have a father. We talked a lot that evening, especially Dad and Mom. Louise and I just sat on the floor looking at him while we played with his gas mask.

Peter G. Breithaupt
Willowdale, Ontario

I REMEMBER the date well — it was August 4, 1941 and I was walking to the store for something as important as a Buck Rogers comic book, when I met my oldest brother Bill, who was on his way back to our home. He told me that he had just enlisted in the Royal Canadian Air Force. He was 21 years old. I have always regretted that I did not join him on that walk home. Little did I realize then, the succession of events that would follow in the next few years would severely wrench us from the comforts of a peaceful Canadian home.

Peter Breithaupt in front with dog, Skipper. Standing, left to right: *brothers Doug, Bill and Hughes, Mom and Dad.* *(Courtesy Peter Breithaupt)*

Bill took his Elementary Flying Training in Goderich, Ontario, and from then on it was the coming and going of a brother on leave that began to change our life pattern.

My second oldest brother, Doug, joined the RCAF. After earning his wings he was posted to Dauphin, Manitoba, as a pilot instructor, Doug also returned home on leave. It was upsetting for my parents having two of their sons training for battle.

Then Doug transferred to the navy. He wanted to see more action than was available as an instructor in Manitoba. He joined the Fleet Air Arm as a fighter pilot and went to Scotland for further sea training.

Brother Hughes tried unsuccessfully to get into the RCAF too but at that time the air force had sufficient pilots so he joined the infantry. Fortunately, at the time that Hughes joined up, there was a distinct impression with most people that the war was being won by the Allies, an impression that proved to be correct. Hughes never did get overseas.

However, we were not to be satisfied with just three sons in the service. There was to be an "addition" to our family. During the Second World War, there was a Norwegian air force training base in Gravenhurst, Ontario, and as the fates would have it, a Norwegian pilot came down from this base to share our house. He was a splendid fellow who dated a friend of our family and, incidentally, married her when the war was done and took her off to Oslo.

He was tall and rather reserved and when he told us a story with no names about an incident that happened on their base, we rather suspected who the culprit might be. It seems there was a party in the Norwegian Officers Mess and more than a few libations must have graced the dinner table. Later in the evening, one of these officers became highly annoyed with his Commanding Officer and took the C.O.'s picture off the wall of the Mess and pushed it down into the toilet in the washroom. As I say, our friend didn't supply names with his story, but we had our suspicions.

Yes. Those were years of upheaval and anxiety that tended to drive up the temperatures of even the seemingly placid. In our home we never stopped wondering how the boys were doing. Would all of them come back alive?

Then there were the other things — the shortage of gasoline, the rationing of food, the Victory Bonds and the Victory gardens, war films and posters that warned about letting out the secrets of war because one never knew who might be listening. There was the good work being done by the Imperial Order of Daughters of the Empire, and the Red Cross workers making blankets and knitting socks. Mother's fingers never stopped. And the music that will remain etched in our brains until the day we die — Marlene Dietrich's haunting "Underneath the Lamplight," Gracie Fields' "Wish Me Luck As You Wave Me Goodbye" and, of course, the inimitable voice of Vera Lynn giving heart to all of us.

The worst of all, was the day that dreaded telegram arrived

stating simply that Flying Officer W.R. Breithaupt was "Missing in Action" on a night intruder mission over Germany. Then the months of waiting and hoping that somehow Bill would survive. Sure, it was false hope but it was, at least, something to cling to. Life has to go on. Which is worse — "Missing in Action" or "Killed in Action"? Perhaps the former. Mourning is put partially on the back burner and to some degree is able to share a place with hope, however small that hope may be. It was a long time afterwards that we heard the whole story.

The night of 12–13 September, Bill and his navigator, Jim Kennedy, in the Mosquito vanished without trace into the night of fog and war, and it was not until two years later that the villagers of Ransbach, Germany, were to recount the story of how two English fliers came to rest in their churchyard.

Somewhere between 2300 hours and midnight a Messerschmidt 110 had attacked the Mosquito, set it on fire, then overshot. In the last few seconds of his life, Bill had aimed at his assailant and shot down the '110. The Mosquito then crashed, killing its occupants. The German crew bailed out and told the story of the gallant fight. Flying Officer W.R. Breithaupt had become an ace on the night of his death.

One day in September, 1943, Bill, along with his navigator Jim Kennedy, were flying their Mosquito on an air-search mission over the North Sea. Just off Newcastle, England, they located a dinghy with five almost frozen survivors inside. They were able to summon a rescue craft to the scene so that situation ended happily. But when Bill's time came there was no happy ending.

Forty-four years later, my wife Maureen and I rounded out yet another chapter of memories reflecting on those years of the Second World War. In response to my query, John A. Gardam of the Commonwealth War Graves Commission in Ottawa replied:

Thank you for your enquiry. J17 271 Flying Officer (Pilot) William Ransom Breithaupt died 13 September 1944 at age 24. He is buried in Rheinberg War Cemetery, Ruhr, Germany, Plot 18, Row B. Collective Grave 21–22. I enclose copies of the burial register pages

*pertaining to your brother, directions, a site plan of the cemetery
and a map.*

In the Canadian Aviation Historical Society, Fall 1967 issue, Hugh
Halliday wrote an article, "Five Down and Death." I quote this
article in part:

*On 7 July 1944, the London Gazette announced that the two men
(Breithaupt and his English Navigator, Flying Officer J.A.
Kennedy) had been awarded Distinguished Flying Crosses.*

Maureen and I flew across the "pond" and drove from Amsterdam to visit Bill's grave. Rheinberg is approximately 30 miles over
the border from Holland. As we parked, we could see the Stone of
Remembrance, the Register Box and the huge Cross of Sacrifice at
the rear of the well-groomed cemetery. It was surrounded by lush
green hedges with tall trees arching over the gravestones as if to
protect this sanctuary.

Since so many years had passed since Bill's death, Maureen and I
assumed that we should now be accustomed to the tragedy of war
and that our visit to this unquestionably special place would be
conducted in a reasonably objective, mature and dry-eyed manner.
We were wrong!

We paused at the Register Box. In this cement enclave, protected
from the weather, was a very simple register book — not unlike a
copy book from school. Glancing through it we read many comments written by relatives and friends of the dead veterans. I wrote
after Bill's name, "He got them on the way down."

There were 3,326 bodies in that cemetery, all of them from the
Commonwealth — Canadians, Australians, New Zealanders, South
Africans, Indians. There was one from the U.S. and one BBC war
correspondent. The one thought that Maureen and I shared at that
moment was simply, what a profound pity.

Close to the Cross of Sacrifice, we found Plot 18, Row B, Collective grave 21–22. Bill and Jim. On Bill's gravestone was the inscription, *For 'Bright Eyes' Brighter Skies.* Bill had the nickname of Bright

Eyes. The inscription was written by our father, W.W. Breithaupt, a veteran of World War One.

Tears blurred the vision, and my chest started to heave uncontrollably with a grief that had been buried for more than four decades. This 58-year-old man cried like a baby for a brother he had never had a chance to know properly.

Every year since peace was declared in 1945, I have watched veterans from both world wars maintain a stolid appearance while silently weeping at the cenotaph on the "eleventh hour of the eleventh day of the eleventh month." These old and aging men were all youngsters when the folly of man swept them off to fight in distant lands from which many never returned. Such waste. And yet, it is vital to emphasize the heroic actions of men such as Bill and Jim, and the thousands of others who possessed that sterling capacity to defeat the enemy and most assuredly, help provide those on the home front with 'brighter skies.'

G. Kingsley Ward
Markham, Ontario

FEW PEOPLE realize the effort that the Commonwealth War Graves Commission has gone to since it was formed during World War One to honour the war dead of the Commonwealth countries. At the end of the war it went to a lot of trouble first of all, to leave the bodies where they fell and secondly, in Churchill's words, to leave them where something would be remembered in three or four hundred years from now. Certainly and surely they did that. They rebuilt the cemeteries and they built the memorials, and most of them including Canada's own Vimy Ridge were only dedicated two or three years before the Second World War started. But the people who have taken the time and the trouble to get in touch with the Commission in Ottawa have found that they can get complete information on relatives who died in the wars.

The Commission will tell you where your uncle or grandfather or whoever you're interested in is buried, or is remembered on a

Canadian Military Cemetery and Memorial to the Missing,
Groesbeek, Holland. (Courtesy G. Kingsley Ward)

memorial if his body was never found. It is relatively easy then for
these relatives to make that trip overseas to visit the cemetery or the
memorial. The Commission doesn't assist you financially but they
will give you all the information you need.

If anyone wants information on the resting place of a family
member who was a veteran killed overseas, they should get together
the full name of the person, the rank, serial number, if they can find
it, the regiment he served with and the approximate date he was

killed. Then they should write to the Commonwealth War Graves Commission, Parliament Buildings, Ottawa.

They will send you back a letter telling you exactly where this person is buried and the location of the cemetery. They will give you the location of the grave within the cemetery.

When you get there you will find a book at each of the cemeteries that gives all the particulars about those who are buried there, including the names of the parents and the home town.

One of the most moving experiences anyone can have is to visit a war cemetery and walk up and down those rows of crosses and read the names and the ages of those who died in the full bloom of youth. It's shattering when you walk into one of the large cemeteries, for instance in Etaples where there's 12,000 graves and also in Ypres, Belgium, where there's another 12,000. You think of the lives lost, most of them under 25 years of age. You think of the suffering of mankind as a result of war. There's a real poignancy in such a visit. The strange thing about it, is that such a visit is not really a sad thing to make. I've talked to so many people who have made these visits and they always tell me that they are very pleased they've done it, and have made solemn vows to themselves that they are going to go back.

I've been involved for about ten years now with an organization called the Vimy Ridge Group that pays special attention to the war graves and monuments. We have written a book about the commission and its work entitled, *Courage Remembered*, and I think the title says it all. We are remembering these courageous young men and women, whether they're in the Dieppe cemetery or the Calais or the cemeteries in Holland where a lot of our Canadian soldiers died.

You can drive by some areas in France and you'll find that in a stretch of two miles you'll pass 12 war cemeteries. There are about 2,500 cemeteries under the jurisdiction of the Commission but there are about 25,000 that they also partially look after. People should know that if their family has a veteran buried, they are entitled to have a headstone from the Commission if that veteran died within a period of 21 months after the war ended. That allows for those who were injured during the war and died some time afterwards. Graves such as that will be looked after in perpetuity by the Commission in the same way as if the veteran had died on the battlefields of Europe. The local members of the Canadian Legion across the country help to keep the Commission up to date on the graves of veterans and the condition they are in. They'll even take over the graves of veterans when there isn't any family left or when the family is not able to look after the grave.

PART 4
COMMUNICATIONS

For an understanding of what was going on overseas on the battlefields of Europe, those of us at home depended on a relatively small group of people who were right up there on the front lines — unarmed, but every bit as vulnerable as the troops they accompanied. These were the war correspondents and photographers whose job it was to record in print, sound and pictures, the fury of battle so that we could be fully aware of what war was like and how it affected the men and women who were fighting those battles for us. Their stories kept us up to date on the progress of the war.

We eagerly awaited each newspaper and radio report. In those pre-TV days, the newsreels in the movie houses satisfied and horrified at the same time. These correspondents were in the thick of the battles and many lost their lives along with the men whose exploits they were covering.

Ken Bell was a war photographer, a member of the Canadian army, and it was his job to be with the troops to record on film anything and everything that was going on.

Ken Bell

MOST OF THE soldiers who fought in that war were glad to say goodbye forever to the battlefields when it was all over. Some who have made trips back did so because they wanted to see again some of the places they had been, or people they may have known under wartime conditions. What they really wanted to do, I think, was to wipe from their minds the nightmare they lived and to see it all again in a different and more peaceful light.

*Personnel of the Highland Light Infantry of Canada milking a
goat.* **Left to right:** *Private F.L. Galvert, Lance-Corporal
Gooding, France, June 20, 1944. (Photo by Ken Bell / Public
Archives of Canada)*

In my own case, going back afterwards became almost an obsession. I've done it so many times just to see the faces and places
I photographed so many years ago and then to take those pictures
again in the changed conditions of peacetime. I wanted to see the
changes that the non-violent years had wrought.

The first time back was in 1949, four years after the war ended. At
that time I took a series of black and white pictures which I jux-

taposed with pictures of these same people and places taken while the war was on. The changes in just four years were quite dramatic.

Twenty years later, I did it all again only this time, I took the pictures in colour. It was something I wanted to do for the 25th anniversary of D-Day — to photograph the places that were wrecked by war and then to see the same places and the same people as they appeared after a quarter century of peace. The faces and the surroundings were so dramatically different and the results are as strong an anti-war statement as you would ever wish to see. I don't think people can ever be reminded too much of how horrible and destructive to humanity war can be. I made another trip over in the early eighties and took more pictures for the 40th anniversary of D-Day in 1984.

It was a fortuitous thing that I did keep going back to these places so many times over the years, because I got to know a lot of those people from Normandy, Holland and Italy who were in my wartime pictures. Even finding people I hadn't seen in forty years wasn't all that difficult because people don't move all over the place like we do here in North America. Often they end their natural lives in the same house they were born.

A good example of that sort of thing is in this baby I photographed shortly after D-Day. She was only a few seconds old when I took her picture in a house which our army unit had taken over. The mother went into labour while I was there and I really didn't know what in heck to do except to send off an urgent message for an army medical team which was nearby. They arrived just in time for the doctor to successfully deliver the baby. When he brought him out of the room I took pictures of this little bundle. I felt like a father to this little girl.

Five years later, when I went back, I took her picture out in the yard of that same house playing with her rabbits and her bicycle. Twenty-five years after, when I went back she was already married and had a one-year-old son of her own. Then, the last time I was over, her little boy was a 20-year-old man who was already planning his own marriage. To me that represented the continuity of life. The baby girl whose picture I took that day in 1944 was a mother and

Captain E.L. McGivern and Captain J.H. Medhurst examine the top of a pill box, Dieppe, France, September 3, 1944. (Photo by Ken Bell / DND / Public Archives of Canada)

would probably soon be a grandmother. It struck me then, that here was a family living a happy and normal life that could easily not have happened at all if that young mother had died in war, and so many other young people her age did.

You go back to these places today, to the beach at Dieppe, for example, where so many died, and it's very hard to imagine what it looked like at that time with the beach just a mess of coiled barbed wire, military equipment, guns, landing craft and dead bodies. Today, the waves are breaking gently on the shore, the sun bathers are stretched out all over the white sand and you wonder — do any of them even know what happened here just over 40 years ago? Probably not. Then you pray to God that nothing like that will ever be allowed to happen again.

It was a horrible time for anyone who was there, regardless of the role they played. There was a great toll on both sides and also among the civilian population who were guilty of nothing except the fact that they happened to live there.

I was a war photographer, of course, but that didn't lessen the danger. There were six of our number killed and a great many others wounded, but we were very proud of the part we played, especially the fact that the very first photographers of the Normandy invasion used around the world were those of Canadian photographers. Dick Malone, who headed up the Canadian Army Public Relations group, had everything so well-organized that our D-Day pictures were sent out from the beaches along with the wounded men, and were then wired around the world within hours.

I was just as scared for my life as any soldier on that beach. A shell coming from the enemy side doesn't have any sense of discrimination whatsoever. It doesn't care if you're a Red Cross person or a padre or a photographer. The only difference, I suppose, is that the man with the rifle is the enemy's first target and he is forced to stay in his position. Our advantage over him was that we could move around in performance of our tasks and, as you know, a moving target is harder to hit. Aside from that, everyone there was fodder for the guns.

I've often thought that the work I did on those European battlefields was probably the most important thing I did or ever will ever do in my life. It was real. Everything else in my life following the war has to be considered superficial, because all of that is done for different reasons, for money or pride or whatever. What you do in a war is done because it's your duty to help in a common cause; money or pride doesn't enter into it.

It was a great morale booster for troops to see a photographer up there, being part of the team doing the same kinds of tasks that everyone else was doing. All photographers were trained soldiers and their main aim, like that of everyone else, was one of survival. You can't take photographers when you're dead so you had to learn quickly how to look after yourself. Any man who landed on those Normandy beaches in June, 1944 had to do that. There wasn't much about what we were doing there that you could learn from a training manual.

The truth is that all of us who came in off those landing barges were as green as grass. We were well-trained but as innocent as babies of what we were about to do.

It took a while for all of us to even recognize the sounds of war — a sudden air burst and the whine of a shell or a bomb. It soon became obvious to all that if we were able to survive that awful first month in Normandy, we had a very good chance of going the rest of the way. After the first onslaught at the beaches, the casualties usually were the green troops who were just coming in. They couldn't learn fast enough to protect themselves from injury or death.

It wasn't a pleasant time and it wasn't romantic. War is never pleasant or romantic.

Victor Albota
Ottawa, Ontario

I THINK it's more the small incidents about war that we remember rather than the big ones.

During the Second World War, I was a photographer stationed at RCAF Eastmoor Number Six Group Bomber Command, about 12 miles from York, England. On one of my days off, I was just wandering around taking pictures of anything that interested me. In the heart of the city are the famous ruins of an old abbey; it is just a beautiful place to relax in a park-like setting. There were lots of

Victor Albota with Margaret (right), *the little girl whose photograph he took in York, England, to send to her father stationed in the Middle East. The other girl is her cousin, Valerie. (Courtesy Victor Albota)*

people there that day, just taking it easy like I was and having a break from the war, including one pretty little red-headed girl about three years old.

I pointed my camera and waited for the right moment and took her picture with the ruins of the abbey in the background. With that memory safely on film, I kept up my wanderings when a woman about my mother's age approached and asked me if I had just taken a picture of her granddaughter. When I replied that I had indeed taken a picture of a charming little redhead, she told me that her son, the child's father, was stationed in the Middle East with the British army engaged in the battle against Rommel's forces. She went on to say that film was very hard to get in wartime Britain, and that the few snapshots they were able to send him of his daughter

The crash of a Lancaster at Eastmoor after returning from a raid in Germany in 1944. (Courtesy Victor Albota)

were not too good and they hadn't been able to send him any more. She wondered if it would be possible to get a copy of the one I had taken so she could send it on to him. I told her I would be delighted.

The picture turned out beautifully and I made a large copy of it — 20 by 24 inches — and sent it to the address she had given me. With that done I thought no more about it until several months passed by. One of our men at the base asked some of us one day if we would like to attend a birthday party in York for an English girl he was going around with at the time. Since none of us had ever been inside an English home we all readily accepted, more out of curiosity than anything else.

It was a good little party and we met some very nice English girls there. We were given some very welcome cakes and cookies, the likes of which we hadn't seen since we left Canada. It was a real touch of home.

*Rebecca, the camp mascot of 432 Squadron, 6 Group Bomber
Command, Eastmoor. (Courtesy Victor Albota)*

You can imagine my surprise when one of the older ladies came
over and said that she was the woman whose granddaughter I had
photographed in the park. She said she was so pleased to see me
again and she thanked me over and over for the picture which she
said was a big hit with the father who was with General Montgomery's staff in the desert. She said that even the General himself had
expressed admiration for the picture.

Mrs. Wedgewood was the lady's name, and she told me that her
other son, Peter, was in India and since his room was not being used,
I was welcome to use it any time I needed a place to stay when I was
in town. I usually stayed at a hostel on my visits to York but there
came a time, much later, when I couldn't get into the hostel as all the
beds were taken. So I 'phoned the lady and told her that if the offer
was still open I was ready to accept it. She told me to come right over
and was I glad I did. I never had it so good. I had a beautiful room,

Photographer Victor Albota. His photograph was taken at
6 Group Bomber Command, Eastmoor, in 1944. (Courtesy Victor
Albota)

breakfast in bed and the run of the whole house. Not only that, she
insisted that anytime I came to town, I was to come and treat her
home as if it were my own. From that time right up to the end of the
war, I stayed at my "home away from home" whenever I had a night
off. It sure helped this soldier in coping with those frequent bouts of
homesickness.

On my return to Canada I kept up a correspondence with my
"English Mom" until she died in 1975, and I still exchange letters
with her daughter. I still wonder at the fate which caused me to take
a picture in a park in 1943 resulting in a friendship that has lasted
almost half a century.

One of the other things that I shall never forget also happened in
1943. In the fall of that year I was sent on a refresher course to bring

This bomber, part of the 6 Group Bomber Command, Eastmoor, carried out 80 raids over Germany prior to 1944. (Courtesy Victor Albota)

me up to date on the latest in aerial cameras. It was an RAF course held at their research station in Farnborough.

When I got there, I was constantly being bothered by this loud whistling noise that began at odd times; it irritated me that I couldn't figure out what it was. Whenever I asked any of the English airmen at the base about it, they wouldn't answer me at all and they'd give me this strange look which seemed to say, "You're hearing things."

One day I spotted a fighter plane which was flying very low and which whizzed by at a terrific speed. Besides that, the thing I noticed immediately was that it didn't seem to have any propeller! I kept watching, horrified, because I assumed that this was one of our planes which was heading for a crash because it had lost its "prop."

When I didn't hear the expected sounds of an explosion, I just assumed that the pilot had been able to bring it down safely at the airfield which was just out of my sight.

When I spoke about this to a group of these English airmen not one of them even acknowledged having seen the plane. Was I crazy? Was I seeing *and* hearing things?

Later on, one of these airmen caught up to me and pulled me aside. In a conspiratorial voice he whispered, "What you saw was a jet plane being tested. It's a very secret project, and you must do what we do. You can't discuss it. You mustn't even mention the whistling sound, the lack of a propeller or the high speed at which it travels." I thanked him for letting me in on the secret.

After suffering with my secret for a while, I could no longer stand it, so I mentioned very casually to some of the Canadian airmen in our photo wing that I had seen this fighter plane with no propeller flying low at a very high speed over the base. I was greeted with great hoots of laughter and asked what kind of a goof I was. They accused me of coming off a drinking binge and asked if there was a pink elephant at the controls of the plane. After that I kept the knowledge completely to myself.

Nobody believed me anyway until some time later when reports started to come in that the Germans now had a fighter plane with no propeller that was shooting down and playing havoc with the American Daylight bombers that were carrying out raids on Germany. It was only then that my comrades believed my story and that I had been the first of our group to see the first British jet plane.

Bob Bowman
Toronto, Ontario

WHEN THE Second World War began, broadcasting was still in its infancy. Although radio's potential was starting to be realized, nobody had any clear idea of what this new child on the communications block was capable of becoming. There were, however, many of the bright new generation attracted to the medium who were

willing to try anything, and that's what they did. What's more —
they made it work.

Nobody anywhere had broadcast a war before, so those of us who
took up the task in 1939 were operating on virgin ground. We just
had to make up the rules as we went along. No matter what the job
we were called on to do, we early correspondents and technicians
had to invent the way to do it.

The CBC was only three-years-old when war was declared. It was
the organization on the spot, expected to do the job because, after
all, nobody else had the necessary money, personnel or equipment.
The time had come for the broadcasters who were accustomed to
warm and comfortable studios, to get out in the field and show what
we were made of.

The first one to feel the stress of this new-found role for the
fledgling corporation was me. I was just a young reporter from
Ottawa whose job, up to that time, was Director of Special Events.
Sounds big but it wasn't really. My only function was to do what was
called "actuality" programs. I was the man who would do such
things as live reports from lonely lighthouses and coal mines. During one broadcast about fishing in Buckingham, Quebec, I actually
caught a trout and fried it during the program. At the time this was
considered something of a coup, a first in this new game of broadcasting. The war changed all that though. There would be many
more coups of much greater significance in the months and years
ahead.

In early December, 1939, about three months after the war
started, my boss, Ernie Bushnell, asked me to go down to Halifax as
quickly and secretly as possible. All he said was that this was "war
stuff," and that when I got there I was to seek out a General
Constantine, sidle up to him as unobtrusively as possible and whisper the word "Constantinople" in his ear, which was some sort of a
password.

Naturally, I was pretty excited about all this so I rushed home,
threw a couple of things in a bag and took the overnight train down
to Halifax. I had no idea what was going on, but when I arrived, it
didn't take me long to figure it all out. There were five ocean liners

lined up along the wharves and there was a big battleship out in the stream; our Canadian First Division was about to sail. I had an official pass to be there so I had no trouble locating General Constantine who was easily the most important-looking person around.

So, I sidled over and whispered "Constantinople" as I was told to do, and sure enough, it worked. The General said he was expecting me and he explained what he wanted me to do. "Your job," he said, "will be to record a program about the First Division sailing, with the troops marching on board the ships and that sort of thing, and then I want you to hold that recording until we land at our destination before you put it on the air. There must be the utmost secrecy about all of this up until the time you do that."

Well, naturally I agreed to all of this, that is, until I heard through the grapevine that Canadian Press was sending their man along *with* the troops. I thought, "By golly, if CP can send a man, so can the CBC."

I went out and immediately put a call through to Gladstone Murray, who was president of the CBC at that time. He was as indignant as I was about all of this, so he went to work on his sources in Ottawa. Within a day I got a call re-assigning me to sail with the troops on one of the ships, the *Aquitania*.

The CBC then rushed my engineer, Art Holmes, down to Halifax to go with me and by the time we got to England, we had with us not only a recorded broadcast of the ships setting sail, but also a lot of recordings we made with General McNaughton and some of the troops on board.

So there I was in Britain with only two shirts left in my suitcase for a period of time that looked like it might be the rest of the war. I had word from Ottawa to stay on in London until further notice and to start sending broadcasts to Canada from there. After I replenished my clothing supply, one of my first transmissions back home was from British Columbia House in London, which was opening up a canteen for Canadian soldiers where they could get hot dogs, apple pie, pork and beans — the kinds of food they were missing in Britain. I had booked the transatlantic circuit for half an hour for this broadcast, fully expecting the ceremonies to go at least that long. Instead, all the formalities were over in ten minutes and I was left with twenty minutes of air time to fill, for which I hadn't made any plans at all. I was desperate.

Then I got the idea of asking each man, as they were filing past the food tables, to identify themselves and to send a short message back home. The twenty minutes just flew by and the reaction to that broadcast back home was fantastic. The CBC got all sorts of letters and phone calls from relatives of these men in Canada and one lady sent me a cable which read, "I heard my son's voice tonight. God bless you."

That was the beginning of broadcasts which featured our troops coming on the air from the war zones and sending messages back to their folks. It was, without a doubt, the most popular thing we ever did.

While I stayed on in London, my recording engineer, Art Holmes, went back to Canada for a while where he designed and had built a mobile broadcast unit which contained all the equipment we needed to do broadcasts from just about anywhere, and we got some of the greatest material with that unit that ever came out of any war. Art was a dedicated genius who spent just about every night out with his van recording the sounds of war. Some nights he'd just stop his van in Hyde Park recording the sounds of the bombs falling and the big anti-aircraft guns going off. I remember saying to him once, "Look Art, don't spend every evening recording bombs. Stay home some nights and take it easy." He promised he would. The very first night he did stay home his apartment was hit by a bomb and although he escaped, he had to spend the rest of the night digging himself out. He also lost his hearing in one ear. So much for my good advice.

One of the things that was really tough, something that reporters don't have to contend with today, was the lack of really portable equipment. Tape recorders hadn't yet been invented so that our "portable" things in reality weighed hundreds of pounds. It took two men to move any one of the pieces, and there were several pieces that made up a unit. We were recording on acetate discs at that time and we would have a devil of a time trying to keep the unit from bouncing around in the bombing and gunfire. This would knock the cutting needle out of its grooves and we would have to start all over again. An alternative to this was a machine which recorded on wire but we found this unreliable. The wire would break and tangle up. So, we stuck with the acetate discs and the heavy equipment as the lesser of two evils.

When we finally started getting out to the actual battle fronts we found ourselves working in a cloak-and-dagger world. We were always briefed beforehand by a commander who would outline what was going to happen and what was expected of us. First of all, we'd get a phone call at our London Headquarters that would always be couched in kind of a code. If the caller said, "The balloon is up," this meant I was to report to Canadian Military Headquarters right away, dressed to go.

Well, this day I got the call that "the balloon is up" and I was sent down to Portsmouth and taken to an underground cave and there was Lord Louis Mountbatten, the Head of Combined Operations, and he had before him a map or, in fact, a sand-table of the whole of Dieppe, the country surrounding it, the beaches and everything else. He went over that with me and told me what we were going to do and what the objectives were. If Mountbatten said, "Walk that plank and jump into the sea," you would walk the plank and jump with no questions asked. He had that commanding presence.

So, we boarded the ships, the six war correspondents who had been chosen to go, but they called the raid off because of rough weather. That was in July. In August, I got the message, "the balloon is up," and this time we were taken to Bath and I said to Cliff Wallace, our PR Officer, "What's up?" Well, he just looked and sort of nodded with his head to follow him. He took us out in the garden where there was one of those latticed summer houses where he could be sure that there was no one to overhear and he said, "The Dieppe operation is on again, boys."

The fact that we were going there after a four-week lapse really shocked me because of the security aspects. The troops were the same ones who knew where we were supposed to go the first time, and it was only natural that they would have talked about it among themselves in the pubs and other places. It was entirely possible that the destination was no longer a secret.

Nonetheless, they put me on a tank landing craft and at dusk we sailed out of New Haven. I'd had an awful day — no food, no rest, nothing.

I went up on deck and settled down on a coil of rope. I was totally exhausted, cold and hungry but I went to sleep almost immediately with my greatcoat wrapped around me.

When I woke up there were red flames in the distance over the port bow and the sound of faraway gunfire. I found out that East Flank Command which was going in ahead of us had run into a German convoy going down the coast, and the shooting started. That gave the enemy at Dieppe the alert that something was happening out there. The result was that when we started to storm the beaches there was no element of surprise whatever. In my opinion, General Roberts should have turned the whole thing around and called off the attack. However, as we know, he didn't, and with the element of surprise lost, our troops were just decimated.

The Royal Regiment had 96 percent casualties. As the men got out of their landing craft on the beach they were just mowed down. My fellow correspondent, Ross Munro, was with them and I remember when he came over to my ship in a little rowboat he was just as white as a ghost from what he had seen.

The commander of the ship I was on made three efforts to land the tanks we were carrying and each time we almost got blown out of the water. The shells were landing all around us and it was a miracle we weren't blown to hell. In we'd go, in and out, and back again but we couldn't get near that beach. I spent the whole time of the action at Dieppe just circling around in that ship as it tried to get near the shore, so what I saw most of all was the air fight that was going on over my head.

That was unbelievable. There were planes falling out of the sky, just fluttering down, like leaves coming off the trees in autumn. The gunfire was absolutely dreadful. The noise was something you could never imagine.

I have a picture that was taken by Fred Griffin of the Toronto *Star* who was on another tank landing craft about 300 yards to the right of ours. It shows our craft being attacked by Stuka dive bombers coming right down on us. He said, "There goes Bowman." He told me that later when he gave me the picture. The bombs from those Stukas exploded all around us and we were submerged in water but we didn't sink.

Finally, the order came through from Command Headquarters for us to turn our ship around and get out of there and that the action was terminated. I don't know that I have ever been so grateful for anything in my life as I was at the moment we sailed away from there. As we got farther out in the Channel it suddenly became quiet — the disastrous action at Dieppe was at an end.

The following day I was back in London putting my story together from notes that I was able to make while this nightmare was going on and later on that night I was able to broadcast my story back to Canada.

Later on they got all the correspondents together and told us their version of what had happened. I didn't know until a quarter of a century later that every word of what they told us was an utter lie. They told us, for example, that we'd shot down 176 German planes and that we'd only lost 30 or some ridiculous figure like that. We were told nothing but utter bunk in their attempts to mislead us about an action that was sheer folly from the start.

Art Holmes
Toronto, Ontario

BOB BOWMAN AND I literally dodged those bombs during the whole time of the London blitz, and we literally had to invent the means of reporting this first broadcast war.

I was in high school when this marvellous invention was just getting started in this country in the early 1920s and I knew, even then, that radio was going to be my life's work. I loved the technical part of it and had no desire at all to be in front of a microphone.

As soon as I got my high school diploma I found work at Marconi's small station in Toronto. I had other radio jobs too, in rapid succession, all of them in radio. I was an operator on Great Lakes ships and transatlantic liners, and was one of the first employees of the new Canadian Radio Broadcasting Commission when it was formed in 1932. When the CBC replaced the Commission in 1936, I became one of its first employees. Although I didn't realize it then, I was laying the groundwork for my most important job of all in the Second World War.

The biggest challenge that faced the CBC before the war had been the Royal Tour of 1939. It too was something that had never been done before and we had to figure out how to do it. That wasn't easy, especially when we arrived in little towns with no facilities whatsoever for handling a radio broadcast. There was nobody in most of these places who had even seen the inside of a radio station and not very many people had radio sets in their homes.

What that meant was that we had to invent what amounted to portable radio stations. We had two of these which were operated by two separate teams who had to move across the country by train. While one team was setting up and overcoming problems in one place, the other team would be setting up and getting ready in the next town, and we were always working against the deadline of being ready when the train arrived with the King and Queen on board.

The fact that there was no such thing as tape and that we had to use these big, awkward and very heavy disc recorders was a monumental problem, not the least of which was that they had to be kept perfectly level at all times. On land you could do this by means of jacks, but on the ocean it was quite a different problem because of the roll of the ship.

That's what Bob Bowman and I found when we were suddenly put on a ship and told to interview the troops on the way over. We had no time to figure things out in advance and when we did record we were afraid to even test the recording because the same rolling ship might ruin what we did have. If that heavy needle came out of the groove in our soft disc it could cut the whole thing to ribbons.

When we got to London, we found that the BBC didn't have the facilities to play back what we had recorded because we had been operating at 60 cycles and they were using 50. Everything seemed to be working against us but, once again, by trying this and trying that, we did invent a way of solving the problem. But Bob and I realized we were going to have to build some special equipment if we were going to report a war from the battlefields.

We spent some time looking at the situation in the battle areas of Britain and we visited the Maginot line in France to see what they had and what we were going to need. Then I sat down and drew up some specifications for this mobile equipment van and I went back to Canada to have it built. I returned to London with my van by May or June, 1940 and right away began recording all the activities of the Canadian troops.

When Goering's Luftwaffe began the massive bombing of London, things became very difficult. Those huge explosions made it virtually impossible to record anything unless I found a way to cushion against the shock. I worked on that for days and was finally able to rig up something that worked for all but the very biggest shocks. I knew it would be historically important to get the sounds of the bombing of London and the whole Battle of Britain recorded, because I realized that nobody else was doing it, not even the BBC. I'd be out there most nights racing around in that van trying to get closer and closer to the places where the bombing was heaviest. I wasn't trying to be heroic; it was just something I felt I should be doing.

Some nights the bombs fell so close that my recordings would be ruined, but after a while I learned to gauge how loud an explosion was going to be by the amount of noise the bomb made as it was falling. Then I would just lower the volume on the recorder and turn it up again after the first shock.

I didn't worry about being hit by a bomb because I figured that could happen during the Blitz no matter where you happened to be. In fact, since you didn't know where one of these things was going to fall, there was no sense in running away because you could be running into it when you thought you were escaping.

After the BBC learned what I had been doing that *they* hadn't, they started borrowing my recordings of the bombs so they could use the sound to accompany their broadcasts. We did that all through the Battle of Britain. We even went down to Dover to record the sounds of the dogfights going on in the skies there.

By experimenting all the time, we developed our own unique equipment that turned out to be better than anything anybody else had. Because of this, we were called upon to do recordings for just about everybody — Americans, Britons, Poles — you name it. Canada really did lead the way in that area. The BBC made some good equipment but the problem was they tried to make it too good, with the result that it was too heavy to be portable enough for war.

Besides working with Bob Bowman, I also worked with some of the other Canadian correspondents on the battlefields of Europe — in Normandy and Italy and all over. At the time of Normandy, Marcel Ouimet, Matthew Halton and I were the first three people in Canadian uniforms to enter Germany.

It's funny, you know, but those recordings I made during the war have been used in countless movies and TV shows all over the world. It's really strange even now to be relaxing at home watching a movie on TV and to suddenly hear one of my own bomb sounds being used as a sound effect. I know they're mine because I can recognize every one of them. I always think of them as my babies.

The Second World War was, in many ways, the last of the old-fashioned wars, those that were waged largely out of sight and sound of the people back home. It was the last pre- TV war. Without television and satellite transmission, the only way most of us could get a picture of what was going on over there was through newspaper and newsreel coverage, a lot of it already out of date by the time we saw it.

Listening to recordings of the war correspondents, half a century later, I am amazed at how good they were. Many of them were former newspapermen who had never spoken a word into a microphone before accompanying the soldiers into battle. They marched into battle alongside the soldiers, or maybe a few steps behind, carrying their typewriters and other journalistic paraphernalia, writing their scripts in bomb craters and ditches and empty barns alongside the front lines.

Then, they would have to find a way to get these recordings out of the battle zones to some point that could relay them to someplace for broadcast. They swam across rivers, they hitchhiked rides in army vehicles and airplanes and sometimes they got killed alongside the men of the military. They were men of the military themselves although not officially. They ate with the soldiers and sailors and airmen, got wet when they got wet, were frightened when they were frightened, and were just as lonesome and anxious for the war to be over and done with.

Their work was remarkable. In fact, they painted as good, or better, pictures with words than television cameras ever could. Because they had only their voices as working tools, they had to try harder.

What follows is a word-for-word transcript of a report by the CBC's Matthew Halton written during the D-Day operations on June 6, 1944. To get it back to England for transmission to Canada, he had to scrounge an airplane ride from the Normandy beaches to the BBC studios in London where he voiced his report on June 8, two days after the first assault.

Matthew Halton
Toronto, Ontario

THIS IS MATTHEW HALTON of the CBC speaking from England. I came back this morning from France. France . . . where our assault formations are ashore and now fighting like wildcats to hold the bridgeheads . . . to hold them against German generals and German armies who know that in the next few days they either throw us into the sea or lose the war.

I've come back for a few hours to tell you what I can of what I saw in the few immortal hours in which we crashed through the famous German West Wall. And so began the liberation of France . . . of Europe and of the world.

I went in with the Canadian assault formation. I've come back to tell you how those superb British and Canadian assault troops went almost contemptuously through minefields and curtains of machine gun fire to clear the beaches and storm the casemates, and rush the pill boxes and kill the Germans with the bayonet . . . those that didn't surrender, and many did surrender, and then push on to their objectives miles beyond.

I've come back to tell you what it felt like when the dream came true, the dream of going back to France, what it felt like — to swim and wade to shore and go up the shell-swept beach unto the wild, weeping, lovely welcome of our liberated friends. But where and how should one begin? . . . and what should one say after taking part in one of the greatest dramatic events of all time?

At this moment a feeling of unreality comes over me. Only three days ago we went aboard our assault landing craft in English harbours for the start of the mighty enterprise. What lay before us we didn't know. We knew that some of us would not come back. That hour seems a lifetime away because since then we've lived a lifetime. Since that hour we have crashed into France.

For my own part I can only say how strange it is to be back in England and saying . . . I've been to France with the assault and I've come back. I've been up the beaches that one had dreaded so long and seen this great event in history, and I'm back in England talking about it.

First, I must say that I can't satisfy the hunger that you must have for concrete news. We just can't afford to tell the Germans anything of value. I can't describe our order of battle — who was on the left of the British forces . . . who in the centre? . . . and . . . who on the right? You know we are in Normandy between the mouth of the Seine and the Cherbourg Peninsula but I cannot name the towns and villages. I can't describe what our fire plan was as we came in from the sea . . . nor the secret weapons that helped to get us ashore . . . nor the way we fool the Germans about time and tide . . . nor the tanks and guns we got ashore . . . nor the number of prisoners we've taken . . . nor many other things. I can only describe some of what I saw in those two splendid and terrible days.

First there was the strain of the last hours in London . . . waiting for the telephone to ring and summon us away. And then there were the few days spent in the loveliness of the country. The country had a special beauty and a sharp poignancy now that one was leaving it on such a dangerous adventure.

One thing I shall never never forget is being wakened just before sunrise on that last day by the dawn chorus of the singing birds . . . dozens of them, especially the nightingales. Then there was the exciting hour when we were briefed . . . the hour when we would learn at last what the world was holding its breath to know . . . where we were going and when . . . and it was to France.

Most of us had guessed France, of course, but some had thought Denmark . . . and some Holland. I'd guessed that we would smash in between Calais and Dunkirk and make a bold effort to cut France off from Germany.

And so, at last, we went aboard our ships. Then there was a 24-hour postponement . . . and the awful strain. We waited tensely all one day lest there be news of a second postponement. The weather didn't look too good. But then the word came to go and the greatest armada ever seen steamed out toward France . . . and the dark. We waved goodbye to England long before sunset and we gasped and we gaped at the wonderful sight as the hundreds and thousands of invasion craft, flotilla after flotilla, deployed into lines astern . . . warships and big troop carriers and headquarters ships and assault landing craft . . . and tank landing ships . . . and assault landing craft of every description covering the waters in every direction.

People on shore were waving. They must have known that this was it . . . that this was the eve of D-Day.

In the lounge of our ship that night we pored over our maps . . . but then we played bridge or gathered around the piano and sang. We were going where our fathers and brothers had gone 25 years ago . . . and we sang the same songs they sang. There was one we sang more than others . . . "There's a long long trail a-winding" . . . and I began to wonder if it wasn't a dream after all . . . playing bridge and singing as we approached the beaches of Hitler's Europe.

The assault was to be in broad daylight. We were to go in on a rising tide so that there would be just enough water to carry the assault craft over the underwater hedgehogs and mines but not so much that the marine engineers couldn't get at the obstacles to blow them up. But the waters were rough. Even heroic commando sappers couldn't always do their job . . . and some craft had to go ashore where no lanes had been cleared.

It was absolutely astonishing to stand on deck in the early morning before H-Hour, the moment when the battle was to start. It was bewildering. There was this enormous armada at anchor right off the coast of France in broad daylight and nothing was happening. Not a thing. Not a gun. Not a bomb. It was fantastic . . . at top dawn with the sky overcast, and not a thing to be seen or heard. A vast flotilla on the coast of France. We stared at the villages and the tall church spires of Normandy, and there was not a sound.

But at last it started. The enormous bombing and shelling of the coast defences. We came in from the sea that morning with a terrific volume of fire power. The hundreds of aircraft were dropping thousands of tons of bombs. The cruisers and destroyers were going close in to pound the shore batteries and casemates. And we had other weapons. In a few minutes we could hardly see the beaches for smoke.

And then . . . at last . . . H-Hour . . . and at H-Hour there was a sudden and almost frightening silence. The fire program ceased. It was the moment for the assault troops to go ashore following the sappers who were clearing gaps through the mines. Armoured bulldozers went in with them to make exits from the beaches . . . and other vehicles to blow up the mines and throw bridges over the concrete walls.

At H-Hour, the small infantry landing craft were in on the rough rising tide and thousands of troops were jumping ashore. At first, the volume of enemy fire was not too terrible. The barrage and the bombing, as we expected, had stunned the Germans, if it hadn't killed them, and this gave most of the assault troops the crucially precious few minutes to jump and wade and get ashore and go into action.

By the time the Germans came to, these incomparable storm troops were rushing the strong points. We got over some stretches of beach almost without opposition. On others there were fearsome bloody fights.

Our casualties were actually lighter than we expected in breaking into France . . . and we hadn't expected too many, but there were losses. The Germans were behind their concrete with heavy machine guns and field guns registered on the beaches. At best we had to lose men. And when I got ashore a few of the finest soldiers that ever attacked were lying dead in the sand or floating in the water.

I was with the Canadians . . . and I say the Canadians had everything. Wonderful skill as well as wonderful dash. Before the assault began I felt that the optimism of the officers was too high. I would say to them, "Yes, but suppose you don't get to this lateral road or that high ground . . . or some other objective at a set time? What then?" And always the reply came, "But there's no question about it. We will get there. We'll get farther." And they did.

There were delays that day on some beaches . . . but when D-Day ended we had all our objectives and more. There was one great regiment none of whose men had ever seen battle before who fought like tigers all day . . . and at night had taken some high ground beyond their objective many miles inland.

I suppose that the most surprising and wonderful thing that happened on Tuesday was what did not happen. At best we expected ferocious sea and air battle round and above us. We expected that some of the German shore batteries would be intact . . . big guns with a range of many miles . . . and here was a target of thousands of ships. We expected that at any cost the Germans would throw hundreds of bombers in against us. We expected the sky to be a cracking inferno of air battles with planes crashing into the sea everywhere. We expected that some at least of the German submarines and E-Boats would get in among us. But there was nothing . . . and believe me, nothing was wonderful that morning.

In the first hours I didn't see a German plane. There didn't even seem to be many of ours. We began to say, "It looks as if the German air force has been destroyed after all. Surely they'd use it now if they'd ever use it. Where were the fearful rocket devices they threatened us with? . . . and the radio-controlled bombs and gliders? . . . and the secret devices by which they could practically stop the whole invasion by pressing a button in Berlin? Was it all a myth?"

It looked like it. And some were even saying the West Wall itself was a myth. But if it was, believe me it was democracy in arms that made it a myth. The Wall was there all right. Not as bad as we expected . . . but it was there. It was British and American skill and firepower and, above all, the heroism of the assault troops that scaled the wall. And as for the shore batteries, they must have been put out of action by the bombers during these past few weeks . . . and by the commandos and paratroops.

I've been through many battles but I was never as excited as when my time came to go ashore . . . for this was France and the beginning of the end. The rough swirling tide carried our assault craft over the obstacles and we jumped into more water than we expected . . . six feet of it . . . so I had to swim a yard or two with my pack and two typewriters . . . before I could wade to shore. Then the struggle across the soft sand. Five minutes that will always be vivid in my mind.

A few shells were falling on the beaches . . . a few mines still exploding. The whole beach covered with small craft. Men at work organizing the beaches already. Bulldozers widening the exits and laying the wire carpet. Ammunition and tanks and supplies and vehicles and guns . . . coming ashore as far as the eye could see . . . on that strange historic morning.

In the sands, the dead who have made it possible. The first German prisoners sitting in slit trenches . . . some sullen, some smiling. The wounded Canadians and everywhere the soldiers and vehicles rolling forward into battle and down the lovely little lanes of Normandy. And the first German aircraft diving in at last to drop a few bombs and open up on us with their cannon guns.

At first glance you may have said, "What an unbelievable pandemonium." But there was no pandemonium. There was order and organization and skill as well as heroism. Everything planned to the most minute detail . . . and working smoothly there on the beaches of France . . . and they had to work smoothly. This was only the beginning. The great battles were to come.

I went over the beach and down a lane with Major Roy Oliver, a British officer . . . and my friend Captain Placide Labelle. We spoke to the first civilian we saw. He was an Italian. Then I saw men, women and children taking shelter behind the hedge. I went over to them. They embraced me and I made a little speech in French. We went on down the lane and I saw a French woman putting roses on the face of a dead Canadian. A woman brought me eggs and strawberries and cream. In a half-daze I began to write. We had broken in. We were in France.

This is Matthew Halton of the CBC speaking from England.

Matthew Halton
Paris Report

THIS IS MATTHEW HALTON of the CBC speaking from Paris. I've just returned from Berlin. In Berlin at ten minutes past 12 midnight this morning, Central European time, Air Chief Marshal Sir Arthur Tedder, Deputy Supreme Commander of the Allied Expeditionary force, rose to his feet beside Marshal Zhukov, Stalin's second-in-command, and turned to Field Marshal Keitel, the German Legate.

"Have you received the document of unconditional surrender?" he asked. "Are you prepared to sign it and execute its provisions?"

Keitel, the Junker of Junkers, fixed his monocle in his left eye. He held up the document impatiently to show he'd received it and he said, "Yes, it's in order. I'm prepared to sign."

At fifteen minutes past twelve, Keitel took the glove off his right hand and signed the document which ratified the unconditional surrender of the German Power already given at Reims 23 hours before, and this time it was in the ruins of Berlin.

The ceremony which ended the war at Reims, France, had taken place in a technical school. By a strange coincidence, the ceremony which confirmed the surrender in Berlin was also held in a technical school. This time in a suburb of eastern Berlin. The technical school in Reims was chosen because it was the headquarters of the Allied Supreme Command. The technical school in Berlin was chosen because it was the only big building the Russians could find that was not destroyed.

Air Chief Marshal Tedder of Britain and Marshal Zhukov of the Soviet Union and a French general signed on behalf of the Grand Alliance. Keitel signed for the beaten foe. Tears ran down the cheeks of his tall, handsome aide. But if Keitel realized that this was a historic moment, he gave no sign. He turned to his weeping aide and said, in our hearing, "You can make a fortune after the war writing a book about this."

Keitel is still Prussian. He's not finished. He's just taking a rest. Under the military ribbons and medals on his chest, Keitel wore the Order of Blood, a golden party emblem that Hitler conferred on all Field Generals as opposed to staff officers. By wearing that medal, in the opinion of the British General, Keitel was saying, "I come here as a Nazi as well as a Prussian." The Germans left the room. An elaborate banquet was immediately spread in the conference room, a banquet that ended only when we left to go to our aircraft at six o'clock this morning.

The famous Russian prosecutor, Viscinsky, said in a brilliant and bitter speech, "When those men left this room, Germany was torn from the pages of history, but we shall never forget and we shall never forgive."

Marshal Zhukov's strong, stern face relaxed into a smile but it seemed that the Russians were no longer separating the sheep from the goats.

Perhaps it's because some of we observers of these solemn events have hardly slept a wink in three days and three nights that we feel bemused and in a dream, but really, is all this true? We were in Berlin. We heard "God Save the King" played at the Templehof Aerodrome. We've seen the fourth-largest city in the world in utter ruin — ruin too appalling and frightening to gloat over — with the fires still burning and the smoke pall hanging over the dead city, and the few erect German civilians sitting like scarecrows in their heaps of rubble to watch the British and American and Russian tanks go by.

We had been at . . . Stalingrad, and now in Berlin we heard on the radio the voice of Winston Churchill saying the German war was over. The voice seemed not so eloquent now as in the dark hours when it rallied Britain to its finest hour, but it was enough.

There were no more than 25 of us in the Dakota aircraft which carried the Allied delegation to Berlin. We left Reims early on

Tuesday morning. We landed at Stendahl Aerodrome on the west bank of the Elbe to wait for the German delegation coming from Flansborg on the Danish–German frontier and for the Russian fighter aircraft which were to escort us to Berlin.

The Germans arrived first. Keitel was received by Major General Kenneth Strong, a British staff officer at SHAPE, who has been the arranging genius of all these long, drawn-out and delicate negotiations.

Then, there was a roaring in the sky and the Russian fighter escort arrived, and we took off for Berlin. For 20 minutes we watched the Red Star fighters dipping, soaring and circling, and we strained our eyes for Berlin. Many thousands of British and American aircraft had come this way during the last five years, running into a tempest of steel that has cost us many of our finest lives. And now we came, in luxuriously appointed passenger planes in perfect safety, to watch the last scene in the long ghastly drama of the war.

The RAF and the RCAF have dropped a total of 45,000 tons of bombs on Berlin and the American air forces have dropped about 20,000. Now we saw the result, and what we saw is the most staggering sight in the world. As we flew low over the wooded lakelands west of Berlin, I recognized the great Olympic Stadium but I recognized nothing else. Even from the air we could see that Berlin was gone.

Air Chief Marshal Tedder was received on Templehof Aerodrome by General Narineenen, Zhukov's Chief of Staff. The flags of Britain, Russia and the United States, held by three Russian officers, floated in front of the Guard of Honour. There was a silence for a few seconds. The band struck up and there on Templehof Aerodrome, we heard the strains of "God Save The King." It was followed by "The Star Spangled Banner," and then, the Russian national anthem.

The Guard of Honour, consisting of three companies of Russian guards, marched past Tedder and his delegation in magnificent, if melodramatic, style. Field Marshal Keitel, Admiral Von Friedebourg and their aides watched the scene. It was unforgettable for us, and doom for them and the things they stood for.

A procession of 40 cars now left Templehof for Marshal Zhukov's headquarters. We'd hoped that the crowning triumph of the war would take place in Hitler's Chancellery, but when I mentioned this, the Russian General Berzerin, commander of the Berlin garrison, laughed.

"Wait 'til you see," he said. "The Chancellery, like all the rest of Berlin, is *kaput*. Nothing but rubble and dirt. But wait 'til you see."

We drove north toward the heart of Berlin and what we saw is, I repeat, too appalling for gloating. We saw the fourth city of the world in such complete and overwhelming ruin that I really doubt that it can ever be rebuilt. Multiply by 500 times the obliterated sections of London's east end or the area around St. Paul's, as they were the morning after they were destroyed, still burning and smoking with nothing but jagged edges of brick and stone against the lurid sky, and you have Berlin.

We drove to the Place Bel Alliance and then turned east along the main street running east through Berlin. It made us shudder. We saw there what could happen to civilization, and will happen, if there's another war.

The Russians have paid many warm tributes to the Allied air forces which destroyed Berlin. The best expression of this appreciation was given by General Malinen as he drove with Air Chief Marshal Tedder. "Look," he said, "Someone was here before us."

The eight-mile route to Zhukov's headquarters in the suburbs was lined by Red Army guards and by Russian women soldiers. One of these handsome, radiant women stood at each corner with signal flags. We passed buildings still burning and a number of German Tiger tanks and several Russian tanks wrecked in the ferocious 11-day battle in the streets of Berlin.

To see Berlin, you know at once that the last stand of the Nazis in their capital was a suicidal and mystic frenzy. There was nothing here to fight for but chaos and the body of Goebbels.

I shall long remember the German civilians, old men, children and women, whom we passed on the way. A few did lift their heads in interest when they saw the British and American flags with the

Russians', but most of them were indifferent scarecrows. There weren't many. We saw no more than four or five thousand. The Russians told us there were roughly two million people left in the city of the original five-and-a-half million.

"Where are they?" we asked.

"They've built caves for themselves in the rubble," said the Russians, "and they're afraid to come out."

We reached the end of our journey and Marshal Zhukov came out of his headquarters to greet Marshal Tedder, Deputy Supreme Commander of the AEF. On one hand, Tedder, that strong and brilliant but charming, unpretentious figure in the blue uniform of the RAF. It was fitting that an officer in that uniform should be in Berlin at this hour. On the other hand, Marshal Zhukov, one of the greatest soldiers of the world. To look at, here was no flashing Napoleonic figure. Zhukov is thick-set with a large head and strong heavy features. Except for his uniform he looked more a politician than a soldier, yet this man has proved himself one of the most bold and imaginative captains of history. Now, in a school house in Berlin, the largest city ever to be taken by storm, he received the western Allies and sat down with them to take the unconditional surrender of Germany.

The preliminaries lasted ten hours. There was no important problem to solve, but there were many details of formality and certain delicate questions of precedence. The Allied delegation with its secretaries and war correspondents shared the same large room. Drafts were typed and retyped in the most informal setting imaginable. Russian girls brought beer and cheese. Russian officers in many varieties of uniforms came and went. The lights went out and a Russian soldier came in to repair them. We heard Mr Churchill on the radio. But surely it couldn't be true. We sat in Berlin to hear the great Prime Minister announce the end.

Today, I heard from a man who certainly should know an estimate of what it cost the Russians to reach the end and come to this triumph in Berlin. Between 12 and 15 million dead, at least, of whom about half were soldiers and half civilians. There were times, said this Russian general, when we had to lose half a million men at a time to save the army itself, to keep the army in being.

Marshal Zhukov was the Master of Ceremonies at the banquet which marked the victory, the end. The banqueting and the toasting went on all night. In one of his many speeches the Marshal said, "Our ally, Great Britain, has suffered much and fought gallantly. During that fight she has produced some famous war leaders. I lift my glass now to the great Air Marshal Tedder, aide to the great General Eisenhower. Look 'round Berlin and you will agree with me that the Germans will remember for a long time his technical and operational skill. Let's drink to him and to continued success to the British nation, and to the continuing friendship between Great Britain and the Soviet Union. That friendship is necessary for the future of mankind."

Marshal Zhukov said that with warmth and the most evident sincerity.

All 'round us, in a hundred square miles of utter and appalling ruin was the warning that friendship between East and West was no luxury but the bare necessity for the continuing life of civilization.

This is Matthew Halton of the CBC speaking from Paris.

This is Matthew Halton speaking from Paris. I am telling you today about the liberation of Paris and I don't know how to do it. Though there was still fighting in the streets, Paris went absolutely mad. Paris and ourselves were in a delirium of happiness yesterday, and all last night, and today.

Yesterday was the most glorious and splendid thing I have ever seen. The first French and American patrols got into the outskirts of Paris the night before last. Yesterday morning the soldiers were coming in, in force. I came in with them . . . with French troops, into Paris.

I believe the first Canadian to enter Paris was Captain Colin McDougall of the Army Film and Photo Unit and I think I was the next. We came in from the south along the Avenue de l'Italie. For hours we had strained our eyes for the first sight of Paris and then suddenly there it was . . . the most beautiful city in the world . . . and the people surging into the streets in millions.

I don't know how we got along those streets. We were among the first vehicles and the people just went mad. We drove for miles, saluting with both hands and shouting, "Vive La France!" 'til we lost our voices. Every time we stopped for a second, hundreds of girls pressed around the jeep to kiss us and to inundate us with flowers, but as we drove along the Boulevard St. Germaine towards the river and the bridge leading to the Place de la Concorde, the crowds thinned out because there was fighting just ahead in the Chamber of Deputies. There was machine-gun fire, rifle fire by German snipers and an occasional shot from a tank. For half an hour we watched the fighting . . . a battle in the streets of Paris. It was indescribably dramatic . . . fighting . . but yet the people frantic with the joy of liberation.

We saw Germans stop fighting and come with white flags to surrender to the French soldiers lying behind their barricades. At times bullets splattered the walls around us. No one seemed to care. Then I asked a policeman how I could get 'round the fighting and across the river to the opera and the centre of the city. I asked if there was still fighting 'round the opera. The *gendarme* at once telephoned his friends . . . who responded by sending a car to lead us 'round.

From that moment on, I knew what it was like to feel like a king. Three people . . . came and got me . . . two young men and a beautiful girl . . . an actress . . . one of the loveliest women I've ever seen. They broke into tears when they saw I was Canadian and they kissed me 20 times. Then, they took me in their car and we drove through the wildly cheering crowds with our arms around each other. We crossed the river to the Île de la Cité . . . the cradle of Paris history . . . and there we were now . . . hand-in-hand with history. Then we drove past Notre Dame . . . and up the Avenue of the Opera. Here the crowds were just beginning to come into the streets . . . mad with happiness. My friends were shouting, "Il est Canadien" . . . He's a Canadian! . . . and I knew what it was to feel like a king.

We were all kings for a day. In fact, when I asked the proprietor of the hotel whether it would be possible to get writing paper, he said, "You can have anything in the world you wish. You are a king."

Men, women and children kissed us and thanked us for coming. Walls were knocked down to produce stores of champagne hidden from the Germans. In a few hours we made friendships that we'll treasure all our lives.

The only sad thing . . . it seemed to me . . . was that British and Canadian troops who have done so much and suffered so much, were not taking part with their American and French comrades in the entry into Paris. They should have taken part in this glory. For years we've dreamed of this day and tried to imagine what it would be like, and the reality is even more wonderful than I ever expected.

Paris is not only the most beautiful city in the world, Paris is so much more than that. Paris is a symbol. Paris is victory, freedom, democracy. In some ways, Paris is all that we fought for during these long terrible years. The fall of Paris was one of the darkest days of history. Her liberation is one of the brightest.

The last time I was in Paris was on August the 25th, 1939. On that day the world was out of control and rushing toward the abyss . . . and France knew already that she was doomed. Five years later, to the very day, I returned to Paris with the liberating army. It's a moving thing for which I have no adequate words.

For weeks as we strained towards Paris, there was the fear that the city might be destroyed. If the Germans held Paris as they've held places like Caen there would be nothing for it but destruction . . . but happily, things have gone otherwise. The City of Light is not destroyed. She hardly seems to have changed. The dream has come true. You can still stand in the Tuileries Gardens in front of the Louvre and look across the Place de la Concorde and up the Champs Elysèes to the Arc de Triomphe . . . the most splendid view on earth. Yes . . . and driving up the Champs Elysèes yesterday, we knew what it was to be a king.

I drove up there with my friends. Sometimes we were all in tears. One youth with me is a descendant of Jacques Cartier. He has fought the Germans inside Paris and elsewhere for four years. His father and his brother have been killed. I talked all night to these people and their friends. Sometime I'll tell their story.

When we got into Paris yesterday, the Germans, under General von Choltitz, the military governor of Paris, were still holding out in five places . . . the Military College, the Chamber of Deputies, the Senate . . . and the Place de la Concorde and the German headquarters at the Opera. But just after noon yesterday, the German governor asked General LaClaire, commanding the French forces, for an armistice. At half past three the armistice was signed. At that hour, Paris was free after eight days of fighting in the streets. The armistice was signed by General LaClaire and by Colonel Roule. An hour later, General de Gaulle was in Paris making a triumphal tour. He went first to the Hôtel de Ville, the historic Town Hall of Paris, which had been seized four days ago. The General made a sober speech. He said, "Germany trembles, but she is not yet destroyed. Combat is still the order of the day. We must enter Germany as conquerors."

One of the most moving things I've ever seen was the entry of the French troops into Paris . . . French troops who had continued the fight for four years and now had come home. The reception sent chills tingling down our spines. They're in American battle dress, in American tanks and half-tracks, but the colours of France were painted on each vehicle, and each one bore the name of a French town or a French hero or a French sentiment.

At times, however, this unforgettable parade turned into battle. Once, at the Sorbonne, Germans concealed in a building fired into the crowd. The Germans were attacked and killed but there were other such incidents. The men warned the crowds that there were still Germans in this street or that.

But Paris was mad with joy and followed the French tanks down the street and into action. It was absolutely fantastic. Occasionally amid the delirium, people formed groups and stood at attention and sang "The Marseilles." Never did the words seem more apt than now: "Against us sets the bloody flag of tyranny. The day of glory has arrived." Then there'd be more shooting, and then again the cheering and the hand-clapping would sweep down the streets as more troops appeared. And by now the streets were beds of flowers. Can you blame me if I call this fantastic?

Paris is free. Paris is happy again. This is Matthew Halton of the CBC speaking from France.

Bombardier C.A. Flanders writing a letter from the deck of his houseboat on the Scheldt River, which was home for some of the gun crew. Antwerp, Belgium, October 2, 1944. (Photo by G. Kenneth Bell / DND / Public Archives of Canada)

Lorne Greene
Toronto, Ontario

THAT "VOICE OF DOOM" nickname was started by one of the
newspapers in Winnipeg during the Battle of Britain. London was
literally being destroyed by bombs, so when I would be continually
reading these bad reports on the national news every night, I just
naturally started giving it everything I had. As far as I was concerned, bad news was *bad* news and I wanted the listeners to understand that. That "Voice of Doom" tag just came naturally, I guess.

However, I remember one night later on in the war, I looked over
the newscast beforehand and saw that for a change, most of what I
had to report was good news about the Battle of Libya, which was
then raging. On my own, I decided to preface that night's newscast
with the words, "Ladies and gentlemen, for a change, most of the
news tonight is good." The result was that I was called in later by the
chief news editor, and chastised for editorializing, something that
we were expressly forbidden to do.

I felt pretty badly about this at the time, but a few days later,
hundreds of letters came rolling in from listeners saying that they
were tired of bad news and that it had been so good to hear my
comments that night.

Bob Christie
Toronto, Ontario

I WAS ONE of those who joined up very early in the war. My
background was some radio announcing, some acting in amateur
groups at university, and on Saturday nights, some amateur acting
at CFRB in Toronto. Those were the days when anyone would go on
the radio for no pay at all just to get the experience. Lots of
experience but no pay; that's what I got.

After I joined up, because of these meagre qualifications, I was
chosen along with five or six others to form a radio unit under

another radio man, Bob Keston, who was to be our Commanding Officer. The truth of it is that none of us, including Bob, had much of an idea of what we were doing, or supposed to be doing, but we were willing to give it a try. We were told that our job was to provide entertaining programs for the troops. When we asked what sort of things we were just shrugged off with a, "You know — records and things like that." That was about the sum total of our mandate and we took that for what it was worth. We did disc jockey programs, although they weren't called that in those days, we read letters and news from home, told jokes and all of that sort of thing. We were just flying by the seat of our pants and inventing things as we went along.

The boys in the camps here in Canada seemed to like what we were doing. At least they didn't complain. We didn't complain either because we were having the time of our lives, operating our own equipment and, in short, gaining our radio education as we went along. We acted, announced, did all the office work ourselves and cooked our own meals. One day I would be frying up the eggs for our group and the next day I would be the lead actor in a melodrama.

This all changed when we went with the troops over to Britain. The BBC supplied us with technicians and all of a sudden we were an "official broadcasting unit" working behind the Canadian lines, where our main purpose changed somewhat. Here, we were told that our job was to counteract the German propaganda that Lord Ha-Ha and Axis Sally and others like that kept feeding across to us. It was also our purpose to bring a touch of home to these youngsters, most of whom had never been more than a few miles from home before.

Every day at noon we relayed the CBC Farm Broadcast to them by shortwave directly from the CBC. Some of those farm kids used to weep openly when that came on the air. You wouldn't believe how homesick some of them were. We also had a great collection of records and a lot of remote dance broadcasts that had been done in different hotels across Canada. It was a great thrill for the boys to hear someone like Mart Kenny and his Western Gentlemen doing their show from "the beautiful Banff Springs Hotel in Banff Springs, Alberta," for example.

These broadcasts would be sent over to us on big 16-inch discs called transcriptions. It wasn't just the famous big bands like Mart Kenny that we would get either. We'd have the orchestras from the smaller centres around Canada too — orchestras that a lot of these youngsters had danced to. In short, we tried to bring them as much of home as we could.

Wherever the army moved, we were right behind them. We gave Canadian news and we broadcast whatever we could find about Canada to take their minds off the job they were being called on to do. When the war was over, I would be delighted when I'd meet some ex-soldier who would tell me that I had greatly helped save his sanity. It was very rewarding to hear something like that.

When I came back to Canada in 1945, I didn't have any clear-cut idea of what I was going to do, but I did know I wanted to stay in radio and in acting because, after all, that was the only thing I knew how to do.

Andrew Allan's "Stage" series, which started while the war was on, was already well established by this time, so I made a date to have lunch with Andrew to talk about some possibilities for me. We were to meet at the CBC cafeteria in Toronto and I remember when I showed up there I was still wearing my uniform, as I was still not fully discharged from the army.

I was so anxious to meet with Andrew that I showed up about an hour early for our date, and while I was wondering what to do with this time, two old friends from our pre-war acting community, Grace Matthews and Jane Mallett came along, each of whom took me by an arm and said, "Come with us."

It turned out that auditions were being held for the part of George in a series to be called "George's Wife," which was a new series to replace the one that had been running throughout the war called "Soldier's Wife."

I got the part of George that very same day. I couldn't believe my good fortune. Here I was not yet out of the army and I was already a radio actor in Canada. Perhaps this peace was going to be even better than I thought it would be.

Gordon Keeble
Toronto, Ontario

I WAS ONE of those serving on the home front. I was chief announcer at the CBC in Toronto and we were called upon during those years to do a lot of wartime propaganda material, dramas and programs which reflected life for all of us in a country at war. It was pretty serious stuff, and all of us looked at what we were doing as being important to the war effort. We didn't take our tasks lightly but sometimes, some very funny things happened.

In those years everything was live. The recording of programs was unheard of, so that whatever you did in the studios went out on the air to the listening audience, warts and all. That meant, of course, that you had to be very careful of what you said or did. There was no way of taking anything back. As they say, the best laid plans of mice and men — and even broadcasters — often go astray.

During one of our big dramatic shows, our time to go astray came about. We were putting on a play about a submarine patrol and Alan King was playing the part of a submarine commander. At the point in the play where he was to bring the sub up to the surface — a very tense and dramatic moment — the sound effects man gave us, as called for, great bubblings and other appropriate noises as the sub broke through the surface of the water.

It was supposed to be the absolute climax, but he must have turned a wrong dial or something, as there was this great clanging of a streetcar's bell and the sound of a motor car starting up and driving away. You have to admit that's a pretty good trick to have happen when we're supposed to be out there surrounded by nothing but water in the middle of the Atlantic!

For a moment there was nothing but complete silence. Then one of the actors couldn't hold it in any longer. I think it was Alan King. He started to laugh. It was like one of those situations in church where something suddenly strikes you as very funny and you have to let it out. That one little laugh spread to the whole cast and the whole place erupted. Everyone in the cast was laughing uncontrollably and all of this was going out over the air. Even the technician at the controls was so overcome by this ridiculous situation of a streetcar and a motor car out in the middle of the Atlantic alongside a sub coming to the surface, that he forgot to pull the plug on the broadcast. The producer, Andrew Allan, normally a man who was totally in control of all situations, had tears running down his face. I guess it must have gone on for a couple of minutes before someone thought to kill the feed to the listening audience. What happened next struck us as almost as funny as the streetcar bell: the announcer, after order had been restored, went on in the stuffiest of stuffy CBC styles and said, "Due to technical difficulties we are unable to continue this program." Then he started to laugh and the whole thing started all over again. We never did finish that drama.

Wayne and Shuster
Toronto, Ontario

WHEN WE were in the armed forces, the army decided they were going to do a radio show, and they started picking a cast from the many entertainment people who had already joined up. We had gained some little success during and after university, so they asked if we'd like to participate. Well, we sure did and they didn't have to ask us twice.

They were planning a radio program called "The Canadian Army Show" and in addition to all the service people they were going to have some big-name guest stars. The first was Jack Benny, who was about as big a name as you could find at that time, and we were asked to write the script for him. Now this was big stuff for us because before that, we were only writing material for ourselves. Anyway, we barrelled right into it and you can imagine how thrilled we were when Jack said he liked the script very much.

"The Canadian Army Show" came out of Montreal and it was a great success with the listening audience, so we just went on from there and built a regular half-hour program called "This Is the Army," which also found a great acceptance with the public.

Things were rolling along nicely with the program and then one day, the whole group of us were called together and told that since

Ptes. Vera Cartwright and Enid Powell lend contrast to the Nazi costumes of Sgt. Frank Shuster, Sgt. Johnny Wayne, all from Toronto and Captain Ralph Wickberg, Winnipeg, at Canadian Army Show, Bonville, France, 30 July 1944. (Photo by Ken Bell / DND / Public Archives of Canada)

we could put together such a successful radio program, we should try our hands at a stage show. "Why not give it a try?" we said, so we went enthusiastically into that.

Jack Arthur, who had made a name for himself producing stage shows for the Canadian National Exhibition, was hired as the civilian producer. Vic George, a broadcaster from Montreal was to be co-producer for the army and Rai Purdy of CFRB in Toronto was to be second-in-command. In addition there were also a lot of other people who had been with the CBC before the war.

Geoffrey Waddington became our musical director and Bob Farnon, who had been with "The Happy Gang," became the musical conductor. We did the book and lyrics for the show and we also played the leads.

It was a good show and, once again, wonderfully received by everyone who saw it. It too was called "This Is the Army" and we toured that stage production all across Canada. It was just a great team effort and we were all so proud of it.

The next step by the army brass was to take the show overseas, as had been done with the other Canadian show "Meet the Navy" which had also been a smash success. They decided though, that instead of taking it to London, England, as they had with the navy show, it would be better to take our program and play directly to the troops in the field.

So, when we went over in 1943, we split up into five compact units, each with its own trucks, lighting system, and generator. It was a good idea and we were so very flexible and self-contained, we could go into any town and set up in any old field or any place we wanted. We were right in the tradition of the Dumb bells of the World War One.

What we liked most of all about this was that we were meeting, sitting with, and talking to, soldiers from everywhere in Canada. We were getting an unparalleled chance to see what they liked and didn't like and we were learning what made people laugh in all parts of our country. It gave us a glimpse of Canada we would not have gained in any other way.

Bernard Benoit
Montreal, Quebec

I ALWAYS associate the beginning of the Second World War with meeting the girl I married. It was in September, 1939 that we met, and although we didn't marry until 1945 because I was overseas with the army, we carried on our love affair through the mail for those very long six years.

I was with a branch of the Canadian Army Intelligence Corps called Propaganda and Psychological Warfare. We did a lot of different jobs, including the interrogation of war prisoners. It was our job to get information from these prisoners which could be useful to our side. It was also part of our job, through propaganda and other means, to convince those we were fighting against that they had lost the war and that the only sensible thing they could do now was to give themselves up. We were trying to do this by every means possible; dropping leaflets from airplanes, sending those of our own men who could speak German across the lines to infiltrate their units and so on. At the beginning, in Normandy, we were even using loudspeakers to gather up prisoners, urging them to come over to our side. We just brought a big bank of these speakers close to the line and invited them over, promising to treat them well and trying to assure them that no harm would come to them and that they could soon be home with their families. Do you know, we got quite a few prisoners that way. Those who did come across told us a lot about what was happening in their lines, what the state of morale was and what the rumours about upcoming battles were. It's amazing how much they knew, and how valuable that information was to our planning officers.

Our unit constantly changed its role and its duties as the war progressed, doing things that had to be done depending on the needs of the moment. We even helped in the publishing of newspapers. That part was very interesting and we had people on the newspaper staffs who spoke German, Ukrainian, Russian, French and English. I was the one for French, and we also had Dutch as well.

(Courtesy the National Archives of Canada)

We needed Dutch-speaking men very badly once the action moved down into the Netherlands, and we were very lucky to get a fellow who came from the Dutch Underground. He did translation, wrote articles for the newspaper, broadcast propaganda to his own underground and sent fake messages over to the German troops. What he did for us during the Netherlands campaign can only be described as invaluable. He got along so well with the Canadians that after the war he decided to become a Canadian himself. He came over here and found a job as a broadcaster with the CBC International Service using the same skills he had developed with us.

I was in the army for the whole period of the war really. At the beginning I was a cadet officer at university in 1939. When I decided to enlist in the regular army, the only thing that changed was that I became more active and I finished my training course in tanks. I became one of the first French-Canadian officers in tanks. There were three of us in all, and I went overseas as a member of the tank corps. Then, while waiting in England for something to happen, I discovered some French-speaking fellows were needed for the Intelligence division and I was transferred over to that.

Many of the men in my section were being parachuted into France to work in the Underground network there, but I wasn't chosen to do that, which was a fortunate thing for me in the long run, because I probably would have ended up under six feet of earth as a lot of those men did.

As soon as the war was over, my fiancée came over to England as a member of the United Nations Relief Agency (UNRA). We were able to get married in London, but, as it turned out, we weren't together there for very long. We both wanted desperately to get back to Canada but with the numbers of troops who wanted that as much as we did, we had to wait our turn.

It was January, 1946 before my wife got home on a commercial ship and I got back one week later on a regular troop shipment. We were finally ready to start on the road of life together. It was a good marriage and one that lasted for 42 years before she died in November, 1987.

(Bernard Benoit's wife Jehane was the well-known culinary authority known as Madame Benoit.)

Jack Donahue
Calgary, Alberta

ALTHOUGH I was certainly of an age to do so — 23 when the war broke out — I didn't run off and immediately join the colours. Circumstances and my background were not conducive to such action. Let me explain what I mean by that.

My mother and father were both born in Kingston, Ontario, within the civilian portion of the community where soldiers from the nearby military establishment had not exactly endeared themselves to the townspeople. I don't know exactly what it was, but apparently there was always a great deal of conflict between those two worlds.

I was born in 1916 while World War One was raging, after my parents had moved west to Winnipeg. When I was about 15, and no doubt feeling very much a man, I walked into the Minto Armouries there and joined the militia with the Lord Strathcona Horse Cavalry. This would be about 1931 shortly after the Depression got into full swing. Lots of young fellows were doing that sort of thing at that time and it was considered very much the thing to do — to become a part-time soldier. I took my uniform home and hid it from my parents, but not very well, because my father soon discovered it and ordered me to march right down there and resign. Naturally I did just that, because those were the thirties, not the sixties, and youngsters did what their parents told them to do. So that ended that portion of my military career.

After high school and during my four years at university I worked as a "stringer," a freelance reporter, for British United Press and I liked it so much I joined them on staff after my graduation. It was shortly after that when war broke out and, as a budding young journalist, I saw the war as a source of story material. I was about 23 by this time and more anxious to learn my craft than I was to enlist.

Being a child of the Great Depression, I feared unemployment more than the army or the war.

It was during this time too, that I met and fell in love with my future wife Colleen. She agreed to marry me but only after a delay of about a year. This was fine with me except for the fact that it would be getting pretty close to the time when I would be called up for military service. I had no desire to be dragged into the army by my heels and so Colleen and I made an agreement that I would enlist shortly after the wedding — which I did about 50 days later.

There was a certain branch of the service that interested me greatly — Army Public Relations and this arm of the service during the war was a very early part of the beginning of public relations in Canada. That's where I served my time as a soldier.

What we did was provide the facilities and the planning to assist newspaper and radio correspondents, and photographers with their jobs and to get the news back to Canada. We had to plan how those reporters would be fed, housed, clothed, moved about, and how to get those stories, pictures and recordings out of the war zone. By the way, there was no such thing as tape recording at that time. The recording was all done on reels of wire. It was our job to get those things out of the war zones and over to the U.K. And then from there to the newspapers and radio stations in Canada for broadcast.

This was a very big job. The key person who did the planning was Dick Malone who, after the war, became publisher of the Toronto *Globe and Mail* before he retired. He was my Commanding Officer. He was a master at planning and he developed a system that was really the finest public relations organization that the Allies had.

The communications that we had were outstanding. Canadian war correspondents were able, as a result, to get the first stories out to the world on the invasion of Sicily, the invasion of Italy, the capture of Rome, the invasion of Normandy, the liberation of Paris and the liberation of Brussels. That's a pretty impressive record.

When I first arrived in England from Canada, shortly before the Normandy invasion in 1944, I was here only a few days when I was assigned to the headquarters of the Supreme Allied Commander, General Eisenhower, which was exciting stuff for a young guy from the Prairies. My task was a pretty small part but we were planning how the newspaper copy, films and wire recordings would get from far shore in Normandy back to the ports in England, and then from the ports back to the University of London which had been taken over by the Ministry of Information. From there it was turned over to the newspapers and radio stations in Canada which then broadcast it to the world.

I also helped to plan those centres in the various ports that would first receive the copy. For example, correspondents who went in on D-Day carried canvas bags with the word PRESS stencilled on them in big red letters. Then back in these ports we had soldiers stationed who wore armbands with lettering that duplicated what was on the bag. Then, also on the bag, there was a tag which gave instructions on how to close it and what to do with it. It was the job of the individual correspondents to just throw their bags onto the landing barges that would be going back to the ships to collect more men. The ones in charge of the barge would then throw these bags up to the sailors on the ships. The sailors in turn, would read the tag and then when they got to port they would just throw these bags to the soldiers on shore who were wearing these armbands. Back at the centre we had Dispatch Riders whose job it was to tour around these places and bring the bags back. We would then log the material in and figure out the fastest way to get it back to London. It all seems very complicated and fraught with risk as you talk about it, but actually it was very simple and it worked.

Dick Malone told us of a recent innovation that helped our efforts tremendously. He said it was possible to marry an army standard wireless set, which I think was called a number 36 set, with a high-speed teletype that could send by wireless. With a normal army set a correspondent would be lucky to get out twenty words a minute but with this rig, it would be a hundred words a minute. Malone saw to it that this was done when everybody else said it couldn't be done. Our correspondents took these rigs with them to the beaches of Normandy and were the only ones to do so. The British on our left flank were left in the lurch as their communications for PR failed, as did those of the Americans on our right. The result was that both groups had to come to our Canadian unit to transmit their copy. We were happy, of course, to clear their copy, but only after we cleared our own.

One good thing about all of this is that the censors didn't get in our way. The actual censorship was very rational and sensible. Our unit had a transportation section which provided the jeeps and the drivers to move the correspondents. Each jeep had a Conducting Officer like myself, and two war correspondents sat in the back. We tried to make sure that these correspondents were non-competing, for obvious reasons.

Then we had a censorship section and a transmission section. The censors would censor the copy and the only thing that would be held back would be information that was considered advantageous to the enemy. That's the only thing. For example, when the RAF accidentally bombed the Canadian troops in Normandy, soon after the invasion started, there were heavy casualties and the correspondents were allowed to write that story.

There were other instances too, like the quarrel between Eisenhower and Montgomery. Eisenhower himself cleared that story, and the correspondents were allowed to write about it. So, as you can see, there was no holding back. If there was propaganda at all, and I don't know that there was, it certainly didn't come from the field. The correspondents were always briefed in advance of battles. They were told what the intention was. Then they went and saw it for themselves. If it didn't work out, they were at liberty to say so.

All in all, our systems worked beautifully and, as I've said before, they were great examples of Canada showing the world how to do it.

Jack Nissen
Willowdale, Ontario

THE ROLE played by radar in winning the war is almost inestimable and I suppose since I had been involved with radar almost from its conception, there weren't many people around at that time who knew more about it than me.

I had been intensely interested in electronics for as long as I can remember and when I was just a boy of nine or ten, I used to make pocket money by fixing my neighbours' radios. I remember one woman paying me with half an apple. So that will give you an idea of what the times were like. I didn't care about the fees though; I was just fascinated with radios and any new one I could get my hands on to fix was all the payment I wanted.

When the war came along I was up to my ears in this new technology and worked on radar long before it was even called radar. It was very secret work and those who were in that field worked under conditions that could almost be described as "cloak-and-dagger."

I remember once when I was sent on a very clandestine mission during the disastrous raid on Dieppe. The other men who were sent with me had orders to kill me if I should fall into enemy hands, so that the knowledge I carried around in my head would die with me.

I had been working with British radar since 1937 and I'm not being immodest when I say that, at that time, I knew everything there was to know about it. However, it wasn't so much the radar secrets that our people were worried about at Dieppe, it was something else I was working on in secret. This new thing was called Centimeter Height Finding (CHF), a vital part of a new secret weapon called the Magnetron which played a big part in winning the war.

This was a fantastic British invention and our side was scared that the Germans would get even an inkling that we had made this breakthrough. The Nazi mind would never be able to accept that anybody but one of their own could come up with something as radical as a radar using microwaves, which is basically what this new invention was. Little did they know that we had already done it with this thing called Magnetron. At the very time I had become involved with Dieppe, I was already using it on my night-fighter radar station to improve the height finding.

We were terrified that the Germans would discover we had this invention if they captured me during the Dieppe operation. We weren't too worried about normal radar because we knew that they were as advanced as we were in that direction. We knew everything there was to know about their radar and they knew as much about ours.

The Magnetron was incredibly top secret, because one day we hoped to make radars with it that would defeat the Nazi U-boats which were playing havoc with Allied shipping in the early years of the war. The radar we were using in the U-boat war was not very effective and we knew that once we got Magnetron radar going we would beat the underwater menace. In fact, we eventually accomplished that dream in just three short weeks in 1943. It was our H2S radar that finally beat the U-boats and rendered them virtually impotent. They couldn't hide from us anymore.

At that time I had memorized in detail all the circuit diagrams of our radars. There weren't really a lot of them. We had the CH, the main big radar that did all the work during the Battle of Britain, and we had the CHL which was a backup for the big one which could see a bit lower, and we had the little box called the Transfonder, which every airplane carries today, and we had the CDU which was a radar that allowed you to see U-boats from the shore and maybe shoot at them. That wasn't too effective.

What I was sent to determine at Dieppe was whether or not, in my opinion, the particular type of radar they were using had been turned from a non-precise, ordinary radar like our CHL into a precision radar. The only way for me to find this out, something I discussed with Don Priest and other colleagues in England before I left for Dieppe, was to get close to the enemy's radar station which I could see from the beach.

I was instructed to do this up-close inspection while there was a big air fight going on, so that I would be able to observe how they were using their radar — whether they were sweeping continually over 360 degrees plotting aircraft, as they had done the year before, or whether they had turned it into a radar that could follow individual aircraft.

At the time there was a big difference of opinion at our headquarters in Britain as to whether or not that had been achieved. Professor Linderman, who was Churchill's scientific adviser and friend, insisted that nobody would make a precision radar on such a low frequency. He was wrong; the Germans were such incredible engineers that they had done it. It was a precision radar they had, and I had determined that bit of knowledge on the beach at Dieppe that day.

Now that I had this information it was terribly important that I should convey this knowledge back to my superiors in England as quickly as possible. I was at this time about 150 miles from my headquarters in Britain and it was, of course, my hope to get back there. The immediate problem for me at that moment was that there seemed to be very little hope that I or anyone else would even survive. We needed a plan.

I came to the conclusion that the only way I could let the people in England know that this was indeed a precision radar, was to put into effect a plan that Don Priest and I had hatched before I left for the Dieppe raid.

Don Priest said, "You have to get near enough to that German radar station so that you can see where the main telephone wires are, and you have to chop them with an axe or a hatchet. This will force them to revert to their MCW plotting as they always do when their telephone lines go down." So I did that.

I chopped the wires leading into their radar hut and found myself, miraculously, still alive. Of course at this point I didn't know if I'd achieved anything or not. Then, by crawling and running and jumping behind this and that, I was able to make my way back to Murray Austin, one of my colleagues, who was waiting for me with what was left of my group.

Of the 120 men in A company there remained only about 12, and my group was down to about seven. However, our part of the mission was a success because we were able to establish that the enemy did indeed have precision radar. Back in Britain, we immediately started taking counter-measures. Our superiority in the field of radar was one of the reasons we were able to win the war. For one thing we wouldn't have been able to survive the Battle of Britain without it. That's how important it was.

Jim Anderson
Ancaster, Ontario

IN 1940, I was turned down by the Argyle and Sutherland Highlanders, a militia unit in Hamilton, because of a slight hernia. I will never
forget how devastated and disappointed I was, because there was
nothing I wanted more in life at that point than to serve my country.
With all of my friends already in uniform I felt as though somehow I
was failing them. The problem was that I couldn't see any way of
rectifying the situation. I thought if you were turned down once,
that was it. So for more than a year I just moped around and went to
my job every day with a heavy heart.

Then, in late 1941, I learned that the RCAF were training people
for some secret radio detection work. That sounded pretty interesting so I signed up again, hoping that if I were once more rejected, I
might at least be trained in some sort of civilian capacity.

While waiting to be called by them, I was drafted for a six-week
stint in the army but this time they never discovered the hernia.
During that short army duty, the call I was waiting for from the
RCAF Radio Detection Unit came through and to my great delight, I
was immediately transferred to the air force.

I spent the next year learning about radio detection waves at a
school in Clinton, Ontario, and on Langara Island in the Queen
Charlottes off the coast of British Columbia.

I was no blood-and-guts kind of person, but I did want to be
involved in the war in some way, even if it meant just going through
it with a screwdriver and a volt metre fixing things, which is what
I first thought this Radio Detection Unit (RDU) would be all about. I
soon found out though, that I was involved in something that was
very important and very secret.

I was surprised to discover that this radio detection was the early
and experimental form of radar before it was even called radar. The
first name it was given was RDF, range and direction finding, and it
was very hush-hush all the way through. We had no textbooks or
anything like that because we were studying it as it was being

Dismantling a concentration camp. (Courtesy Jim Anderson)

invented. What we were learning came straight from the experimental labs, through the instructors and then into our heads. Our instructors would be teaching us things today that they themselves had only learned yesterday.

All of this was taking place at the Clinton Air Force school and it was so secret that every page in our notebooks was numbered so that they couldn't be removed and taken from the classroom by the students. It was a court martial offence to write something on an envelope or a scrap of paper and take it out of that room, even in the case of a circuit that you were trying to memorize. You had to carry it all in your head.

There was barbed wire all around the compound where we studied so that everything that went on in there could not be observed or overheard by anyone who was not involved. Even on leaves, we were strictly warned not to discuss any aspect of our work even with fellow students. If you were on a train for example, and a military policeman heard you talking about it you'd be in big trouble. You couldn't even discuss it at meals. Radar was to be kept within the confines of that compound only.

All of the equipment we were working with had some sort of explosive destructive device on it so that you could blow it up if there was any chance of it falling into the hands of the enemy. That was one of the nerve-wracking things all the time. You'd be thinking, "What if I'm wrong when I do this or that — if I do this will it blow up in my face?"

It was a strange feeling to know that you were working on something so secret and so valuable that it was more precious than your own life, but you do get attuned to it.

In France, we had a small group of the RAF Regiment with us. They had an armoured car with them and they were there to give us some protection at night, mainly from enemy forces who might be creeping and crawling around. Night watches could be very nerve-wracking because we were always in dark and lonely areas. Our unit of 15 men was considered very small and we operated almost independently of everybody else. We had five trucks and a jeep, and we were given our orders through the wireless. They would give us a "pre-location" where we would search for a stake driven into the ground. I never did find out whose job it was to put that stake there although we figured it must be someone in the Resistance. Anyway, we would go to this spot and after a bit of searching we would find this fresh stake on a high point of land. Then we would crank up a little telescopic aerial which was powered by the equivalent of a motorcycle engine. The reason for all of these things was to provide navigational aids for our planes as they came in on missions. All of the planes would be provided with special maps showing the locations of these points. It proved to be a very accurate system.

Operating alone like that in enemy territory was a bit hairy and scary, especially if you were in Germany, and especially towards dawn when you'd see all the landscape littered with leaflets dropped by our planes during the night, calling on the Germans to sur-

Hitler hung in effigy. (Courtesy Jim Anderson)

render. I used to think, "Boy, I hope our guys know we're here before they start dropping bombs."

As the war started to wind down and the Allied victory was in sight, there wasn't so much need for our radar unit to be on the job so that meant I had more time to roam around and see what was going on. I went to some of the liberated concentration camps, which is something I shall never forget. I was at Buchenwald when the Allied tanks were knocking down the barbed wire fences and liberating the inmates. The horror of what I saw at that time is just about impossible to describe. I had my small box camera with me and I took pictures of some of it.

There were great piles of bodies in several locations and, as you can imagine, an overwhelming stench. To this day I feel very bad about the revulsion I felt towards some who came forward and put their arms out to hug and embrace us. Most of them were filthy, wasted, scabby and toothless, and I have to confess that I just wanted to turn away from the sight. At that time, of course, we didn't know that most of these people were political prisoners whose only "crime" was being a Jew or opposing Hitler and helping the Allies. We thought they were just a bunch of lawbreakers who were probably serving sentences for crimes they had committed. Later, we found out that many of them were civilians who had helped us in many ways all through the war by hiding escaped Allies soldiers and things like that.

I was violently sick several times as we went through there. The living were more dead than alive, just bones covered with skin, eyes peering out from deep caverns in their skulls and covered with running sores. The stench was overpowering. Dead flesh was the smell of Buchenwald. They had six furnaces there going day and night burning dead bodies. At one of the camps, they would cut fancy tattoos from the skin of the bodies and have them made into lampshades. The whole place contained all of the horrors of hell.

I was sorry, and I still am, that our unit had just blundered upon this place as we were making our way around the country, while the war was coming to a close. There was no reason really, for us to be there. We had no jobs to do. It's just that we came upon it and we went in to see what was going on.

In a way, I'm glad we did see it though, because I took four horrible pictures that end any doubts for anyone who says it never happened. There were thousands of these emaciated, walking skeletons around when I got there. Buchenwald was a huge camp. Many of them were so anxious to get away from there, that they were walking and crawling towards the gates and the holes in the barbed wire. We were trying to convince them to wait for the Red Cross and the other help that would be coming but it did no good. They just wanted to get away. It was my feeling that some of them knew they were going to die anyway, and they wanted to die outside the gates. I'm sure a lot of them wouldn't have made it more than a quarter of a mile down the road.

What I find rather frightening now is the realization that the majority of people alive in the world today weren't even alive when

Victims at Buchenwald. (Courtesy Jim Anderson)

all of that went on. It's hard to convince many young people that there was evil to such an extent in the world such a relatively short time ago. When you think about those camps you have to conclude that the prison guards themselves had to be devoid of ordinary human emotions to be so ruthless in their treatment of other humans. I think, frankly, that if I had been one of the prisoners there I would have taken the easy way out and just died. You have to admire those who survived.

I very often think about those four years of my life, what I did and what I saw, and the question always occurs to me, "Was it all worthwhile?" The answer, for me, is always the same, "Yes, it was." I remember talking with a woman from Holland who said, "Thank God you came." She was speaking of the whole of the Allied forces. God only knows what the world would be like today if Hitler had won the war. In the case of that woman from Holland, her gratitude to the Canadian forces who liberated her country was understandable. The Dutch people lost more of their countrymen than the total number of Canadian servicemen who were killed in the Second World War. It was a horrifying thing for them.

Am I glad I was in it? Yes, I am. If the part I played made even a modicum of difference, it was worthwhile. I'm glad I survived. I still have two arms and two legs. I had a few close calls but I was lucky. When the war ended, I was still in my twenties and I've always considered every day since then a bonus day.

PART 5

VETERANS

Eileen Addicott
Glace Bay, Nova Scotia

I HEARD a lot about war growing up, as I did, between the two great wars. My father was a genuine war hero. He never told me that, but I did hear it from the other kids whose fathers had told them. I knew he had lots of medals, because I had seen them in their cases in the top drawer of the dresser in his bedroom at home. He never said much about them or the war, except perhaps when he'd be drinking, and he did do a lot of that. As far as my mother was concerned, that's all he brought back from the war, a love for alcohol that she didn't know he had when she married him about five years after he returned. I guess he must have been on his good behaviour while courting her, because there was lots of drinking later. The truth is that I remember more about his drinking while I was growing up than anything else about him.

He managed to get into the war and get shipped overseas before his seventeenth birthday. He was athletic, extremely strong, and apparently a real brain. The army was his kind of thing, and he advanced rapidly in the ranks. Before his eighteenth birthday he was a Regimental Sergeant Major, the youngest ever in the Canadian army. Those who were there with him say he was afraid of nothing, always out in front of the other troops. When the war ended, the only scar he carried home with him was a minuscule fragment missing from the end of his thumb, and a small piece of shrapnel in one of his knees.

217

He also brought home the Military Medal, which was second only
to the Victoria Cross as a decoration for bravery. The Armistice of
November 11, 1918 brought peace, but it also brought the end of the
glory days for my father.

Back home, there were no big honours or big jobs for the returnees, no matter what they had done in the war. My father was a coal
miner's son before he joined the army, and his only post-war reward
was a job in the coal mine. I'm sure that must have been a terrible
letdown for him, and I'm also sure — after many years of reflection
on his situation — that this, rather than the war itself, could be the
cause of the drinking.

It was a commonly accepted fact of life in those days that "once a
miner always a miner," and if you didn't like it, that was just too bad.
There was nothing else available in those one-industry towns of
eastern Canada.

So, Daddy the war hero became Daddy the coal miner and took
his place beside his father and his brothers in the bowels of the earth.
He never uttered a complaint as far as I know, but when he got
drunk, as he often would, his talk was all war talk. He became like a
lot of the other miners who lived only, it seemed, for the release of
Saturday night booze.

The final nail of destruction in my father's life came as the result
of an accident in the mine when his right arm was torn off under a
fall of stone. After that, his drinking escalated to the point where
Saturday nights could be any night of the week. He bitterly resented
the fact that he had survived the war virtually unscathed and that
now he was a "cripple" as a result of his "goddammed job" in the
pits. He would not tolerate anyone's sympathy, and he would practically bite the head off anybody who tried to help him with a simple
task like tying his shoes.

In leisure activities he worked at becoming the best at what he
did. He was the best ice skater in town and, even with one arm, the
strongest and best swimmer. He would dive into the Atlantic waters
off Cape Breton and swim out of sight, not returning, sometimes,
for hours. He even became a hero once again when he saved the life
of a drowning girl who had ventured too far from shore. He dove

into the water and reached her just as she was going down for the third time. Somehow, using his teeth as a grapple, he managed to pull her to shore. His picture appeared in all the local papers the next day and later on he received a National Life Saving award.

When the Second World War came in 1939, Daddy received a letter from the Defence Department in Ottawa, inviting him to re-enlist as a Commissioned Officer whose duties would be to organize and instruct in the army that was being readied for overseas. I had never seen him so happy in my life. He was going back into the organization where he had achieved success and his coal mining days would be behind him.

Even Mother, who had long ago ceased to be a loving wife for him because of the excessive drinking, was happy for him. She helped him with the letter of reply he had to send back, and she helped him to compose the proper words to use in explaining that although he now had only one arm, he would still be a most able soldier, as he was in the first war.

I went to the Post Office with him to mail the letter and he joked and talked with everyone he met on the street. All he had to do now was wait.

As it turned out, he didn't have long to wait. In less than two weeks the reply came back. They thanked him for his interest and explained that when they had written to him in the first place, they weren't aware that he had lost an arm. They were sorry, they said, but under the circumstances he could no longer be accepted into the army. They ended the letter by thanking him for his "courageous and kind offer."

Daddy got drunk that night and a lot of other nights too, as he searched for war news on his radio.

He was still around when the war ended in 1945, the same year that I presented him with his first grandchild. How proud he was but, sadly, not for very long. Daddy died before my baby, his beloved grandchild, reached his first birthday. He was only 49 years old at the time.

I wish I had known him and understood him better.

Ella Trow
Toronto, Ontario

THE COMING of the Second World War seemed to bring about a change in everything so far as our way of life was concerned. The Depression years, although terrible for an awful lot of us, also brought out the best in people. There seemed to be more concern for one's fellow man. Those who had a little more seemed to be willing to share with those who had been hit the hardest by the collapse of the economy.

The war, although it signalled the end of the Depression, just turned our lives upside down. My brothers and my husband went into the services and most of my friends were in the same boat. In fact, a lot of my friends and neighbours were killed in the war.

Toronto, where we lived, became tremendously crowded because of the servicemen who came here with their families. Then too, there were the war industries that located here bringing in a huge number of workers and *their* families. I don't believe that the Toronto I grew up in existed at all once the war started. In my mind, the changes were not for the good.

My Toronto before the war was a much better place to live. It was a prettier place and not nearly so polluted. I think people were much more considerate of each other and I know that there was a lot more politeness. Suddenly, there was crowding and pushing and you had to line up for everything. So many things changed overnight that it was difficult for people of my generation to absorb it all.

I think too, that it was the war that changed people's perception of marriage, something that my generation found very difficult to come to terms with. In my day, marriage was thought to be forever and divorce was unusual. Most people would only talk of some couple getting divorced as if it were the greatest of scandals.

Marriage was something entered into very seriously and engagements would last at least a year or two, the waiting period being used to plan the big day. The war brought about the quick romance and the even quicker marriage, before a couple even had a chance to get to know each other. This led to quick divorces or just plain abandonment in many cases.

The war took over our whole lives. Most of us were so idealistic. The boys and men did not enlist for excitement or love of conflict. Most of them felt that a horrific force was loose in the world and that it must be stopped. The women worked in war industries, canteens and clinics, and they sewed and knitted and packed. They took men's jobs for the first time, mostly the hard and dull ones. It was a time too, when no service man or woman was ever neglected, regardless of rank. Hospitality was almost universal. We may have been naïve but no one could fault our effort.

Who now remembers or even cares about the truly gallant service men who are left, or about the families of those who did not come back? I would not want my sons ever again to serve on foreign soil. I have to conclude that this war was no more noble than any of the others that have gone before. We can only assume that this too was a war about greed, as was the peace.

Our ill-equipped and under-trained forces were stupidly and recklessly sacrificed in Hong Kong with unbelievable ineptitude. Even "Mother" Britain who needed our personnel and support so badly had treated our forces carelessly and even cruelly. We know now that the tragedy of Dieppe never should have happened. It was just a disastrous and bloody dress rehearsal for a triumphant D-Day, planned mostly by people who would not be involved themselves in any of the action.

My younger brother was one of those in charge of one of the landing craft that landed on the beaches of Dieppe, and he was later decorated because he got all his men out safely. He was one of the few lucky ones who had good fortune on his side that day. He wasn't totally lucky though, because he had to limp his way through the life that was left to him. But then again, he did come away with a life yet to live, which was more than a great many of those young innocents who landed there on that August morning in 1942 ever got. How were they to know that they were just being thrown in "to test the waters?"

There were good things to remember though, about those years. There was the selflessness and the kindness of so many people in an amount that is hard to realize today. To counter the sadness we also had exciting and happy times. There were surprise parties at a moment's notice, going away parties where the guests of honour may never have been seen again. The good part was that at least we had the satisfaction of knowing that they left with good memories and heroic plans.

Then there were the wonderful times when we could welcome them home for long or short leaves, or occasionally, for ever. There were the travels across Canada to new places where our men were stationed, and there were the joyous welcomes awaiting us when we got there. There were the strangers we met who became dear, lifelong friends.

It was a romantic time in spite of everything — the sudden love affairs where time was felt to be running out, the engagements, the weddings, and the honeymoons. Young wives who had never been more than a few miles from home before, were now crossing the country with their babies to spend whatever time there was with their husbands, in whatever circumstances they happened to be in.

Who could ever forget crowding around the radio for the latest war news, the wonderful feeling when all was going well, the despondency when it wasn't.

When the war was over, and the men came home to pick up their lives again, things weren't nearly as good as they thought they would be. They found, first of all, that the war wasn't nearly as decisive as they had hoped or that any of us had hoped. It was our dream that this would be the last war the world would ever see. Instead of that we are today never without terrible wars all over the world.

Victor Laurin
Buckingham, Quebec

ONE OF my earliest memories is of the day four of my uncles came home from overseas. I was just a toddler when they left, so I hardly remember anything of them being gone or about them actually leaving. I probably slept soundly through the tears which flowed freely, I'm told, on their departure. Each came back though, and it is that memory I recall. What a day that was!

The church bells rang out, a red fire engine sounded its siren, and a joyful parade wended its way through the gravel streets of Buckingham. A stuffed pig hung in effigy from the back of a truck — a pig, they told me, that symbolized the defeated enemy.

By this time, I was not even five years old and could scarcely be expected to comprehend the horrors of war — of human blood soaking the soil of some foreign land. How could a young lad know that our family was lucky — that there were thousands of Canadian soldiers, fathers and uncles and brothers, who would never return home?

I didn't know then, either, that Canadian women also served their country during those war years, at home and abroad. Nobody told me that. I thought that only the men went to war and the women stayed behind to do things here — like my Aunt Barbara for example. I remember that she worked in a small building not far from our house that had been converted into a munitions factory. It was there that she went every day, and we children often chatted with the guard at the gate. It seemed like a pretty safe place to me — a good place for a woman to work.

In later years, my wife's stepmother told me how she cared for the wounded in Great Britain during the war as a physiotherapist. She came over to live in Toronto after the war, and told me much about those times when not only men got killed in war, but whole families in their own homes in the cities. She told me many things about war, things I will not likely forget.

I have learned a lot more since then from my comrades at the Royal Canadian Legion that I was allowed to join as a fraternal member several years ago. I have come to respect and appreciate what the Canadian Legion and its members are all about. It can all be summed up in two words — *love* and *respect*; love and respect for each other.

The Legion, you might say, is an organization of survivors. Many of its members returned from the wars and achieved success in life in varying degrees. For some, it was great success in business and in other professions, and as husbands and wives, fathers and mothers.

There were also those who survived the battles and returned home bearing invisible scars, the kinds of scars that in their mind, can only be erased by alcohol. These old soldiers were victims too, just as much as their buddies who never returned.

Let's take the case of a man we'll call Willy Johnson, about whom Mike O'Reilly wrote an unforgettable poem called "Be Quiet When Willy Walks By":

Did you see the old boys
with their uniforms on?
They were marching down
Main Street today.
Some helped the others as
they went along,
But their minds seemed so
far away.
And when they laid the
wreath at the top of the hill,
I saw some of them cry,
as they thought of the
friends they knew long ago,
in ages long since gone by.

And old Willy Johnson, he
walked all alone,
As the rain came
tumbling down.
And someone laughed
when Willie drew near,
For he was the drunk
of the town.
Then one of the men came
over and said,

Y'know Willy's one hell
of a guy,
If it wasn't for him
I wouldn't be here,
So be quiet when Willy walks by.

He sold all his medals a
long time ago
for the hope that a bottle
can hold,
But it's hard to crawl out of
the cracks in your soul
when the last of your pride
has been sold.

But deep down inside,
there's a heart of pure gold
And a spirit that money
can't buy.
So, remember my friends,
and bow to the truth.
Be quiet when Willy walks by.
Please be quiet when Willy
walks by.

Michael O'Reilly, 1986

There is a helping hand reaching out to the Willy Johnsons through
the various affiliates of the Legion all across the country. War does
bring about a lifelong fellowship among those who stood together
against the enemy.

Al J. Elder
Calgary, Alberta

MAYBE IF one waits long enough all stories have a happy ending, but sometimes it's that waiting period that kills or destroys the people involved.

I am only a minor player in this story that started in Middleton-St. George, England in 1943. I was an aero-engine mechanic by trade, the NCO of an aircraft called *H. Harry* piloted by H.A. (Smokey) Reid. I had the responsibility of servicing this airplane and keeping it in top shape for its missions, a job I always took very seriously.

On this particular night, the weather was beautiful as the *H. Harry* left on one of its regular night runs over enemy territory. As far as I was concerned, it was just another mission and one from which Smokey and his crew would return as usual in the morning. As was my habit, I waved to the plane as she rose from the airstrip into the night sky and I made my way back to my barracks and bed.

The next morning, I was shocked and saddened to hear the announcement over the P.A. system at our base that *H. Harry* had failed to return from its mission. In these cases we always assumed that the worst had happened, and that we'd lost some more of our friends.

Shortly after this, I volunteered for service in Japan and the fate of the *H. Harry* and her crew gradually faded from my mind.

In June, 1945, one month after the end of the war, I was back home in Canada and I had a 30-day leave to play with. What better Canadian thing to do than to spend it at the Calgary Stampede, so I put my thumb to use and hitchhiked from my home in Saskatchewan to Calgary, all set for the good times to come.

The first thing I did was to head for the beverage room at the York Hotel for a nice cool beer. As I settled down at a table, I happened to glance over at the next table and when I saw who was sitting there, also having a beer, I almost died from shock. It was none other than my friend Smokey Reid of the *H. Harry*, the same

Smokey who was "missing and presumed dead" the last time I heard of him. But here he was, as alive as I was, and all dressed up in "hospital blues," the garb of the patients at the Colonel Belcher Hospital down the street. When I had recovered enough to go over to his table and speak to him, he told me that he and his friends had just sneaked out of the hospital for a "quick one," but he had enough time to tell me the story.

On the night of their last run, Smokey and his crew were shot down over Sweden, and had to bail out of their plane. They all made it except one crew member who got caught up in the doors of the bomb bay and went down with the plane. When Smokey came to, after hitting the ground, he wrapped himself up in his parachute and went to sleep, glad to have survived and to have escaped from the hell of their mission over Berlin.

When he awoke the next morning, he found that he had a badly twisted neck and was unable to move his chin from its resting place on his right shoulder. He was eventually found, and placed in protective custody in Sweden before his repatriation to England and then home to Canada. He told me he was glad to be in the hospital here in Calgary, because perhaps they would be able to find out the cause of the constant pain he was in. We shook hands and said goodbye as he headed back to the hospital and I to the thrills of the Stampede.

I never heard any more about Smokey until several years later when I read a story in the paper about a former RCAF pilot, Harry Albert Reid who was arrested for trying to hold up a branch of the Bank of Montreal in Calgary. It was my friend Smokey! What had ever happened to turn this hero of the war into an outlaw?

For eight long years, Smokey had been living a nightmare. He was in constant, fierce pain from his neck injuries. He couldn't work and he kept getting turned away from doctors' offices and hospitals because they could find no reasons for his "so-called" pain. They kept referring him to psychiatrists who told him, "It's all in your head." He couldn't get anybody in the medical community to listen to him anymore, and he couldn't even get a pension from his time in the air force. Harry and his wife were forced to live in poverty as he couldn't hold down even the most menial job. He tried everything, but the pain became even more unbearable.

Then came the bank robbery business which came out of his desperation, and out of that came a doctor who finally found his trouble. X-rays showed he had a broken back all of that time, a time when he had often wished, I am sure, that he had died that night in 1943.

That was 1951, the last time I heard anything about Smokey. I can only hope that it was the end of his long nightmare. I've tried to track him down many times since then, but I haven't been successful. That's such a long time ago. He probably wouldn't even remember me now.

Barry Broadfoot
Nanaimo, British Columbia

WHEN I joined up in the first place in 1942, I was still underage at 17, and I had been itching to get in since the war started, but they weren't too enthusiastic about taking a skinny 14-year-old kid. I held my breath, so to speak, until my seventeenth birthday had just passed, and then something happened that propelled me right into the middle of it. I got word that a friend of mine, who was just two years older than me, was killed in action on the Western Front. This was a good friend, someone I had almost hero-worshipped, and the news of his death hit me like a ton of bricks. When he joined up and went overseas he was attached to an English unit, and he'd write letters telling me everything that was going on and what was happening to him. He was more than a best friend; he was more like a brother really.

When he got killed in action I was totally devastated. I didn't know what to do, but I knew I had to do something. I was full of grief. I didn't want to be with my family or with anybody else. I wanted only to be alone. That night I went over to a park near our

*Paratroopers enjoy a game of gin rummy in front of a huge
"farewell" sign at the First Canadian Repatriation Depot
recreation hall, Thursley, England, May 22, 1945. (Photo by
Arthur L. Cole / DND / Public Archives of Canada)*

home and just wandered around for hours full of rage against Hitler
and all of those German bastards who killed my friend.

The next morning I told my mother that I was going down to the
recruiting office to join up.

"But Barry," she said, "you still have a year-and-a-half to go
before you're old enough."

"No Mom," I said, "I want to go now and nobody's going to stop
me."

I guess she knew what I was feeling, because she never said
another word to try and stop me. By late afternoon that day I was in
the army, and I was there for the last two-and-a-half years of the war
as an infantry man, which really wasn't my first choice. I grew up on

the Prairies, and didn't have much love for the dust of the Depression years or the mud that came after the infrequent rains.

I tried the air force first, because I thought it would be cleaner and neater, but they didn't express any great desire to have me, which might have been a good thing as it turned out, because I found out after the war that the highest fatality rate in the services was in Bomber Command which was, after all, what the RCAF was all about. So it was the infantry for me.

I didn't get to shoot Hitler during the next two-and-a-half years, although I was ready, willing and able, and I didn't locate the Germans who killed my friend. I just managed to do my infantryman's job and survive the war in one piece. I don't think the war had any great psychological effect on me, except for the ambition it gave me to do something with my life afterwards. My army buddies and I had done a lot of talking about this while we were "over there" and there was a lot of talk about how badly the soldiers were treated after World War One ended, and how so many of them had ended up bitter and disillusioned by the uncaring attitude of a government that no longer had any interest in their welfare. There was widespread unemployment when they got back, and the official attitude towards the World War One veterans seemed to be "Get lost. We don't need you now." Well, we were determined that this wasn't going to happen to us, but the truth is we didn't have to worry. When we came back, there seemed to be a complete reversal of that hard-hearted attitude.

When I came out and looked around at my options, I soon realized that I could immediately go to university on one of these Department of Veterans Affairs grants. Well, this was exciting, because I don't think that any Broadfoot in the west in my line of the family had ever gone to university — I would be the first. I could hardly wait to get down there and register.

I took an Arts course, because I had been involved in army newspapers and things like that when I was overseas. I didn't realize it then, but this eventually changed the whole course of my life.

I didn't really gain that much from the Arts degree itself in those four years, because I was always a great reader anyway. What it did, though, was to award me an official piece of paper which set me on the road to a career in the field of newspapers and writing. Maybe I learned a bit about psychology and sociology and those things, but it was the contacts I made and the people I met who were important.

We carried on those friendships all the way through life. The thing is, that there's a camaraderie there, a sort of buddy-buddy system like you find in an infantry platoon. You look after your buddies on your right and your left, and they do the same thing for you. A platoon is a cohesive unit, and that's the main fighting thrust of the infantry that wins the wars in the end.

You know, it's always been a popular sport with all of us in my generation to curse old MacKenzie King, the prime minister who brought Canada into the war, as a fumbler and a doddler but he was, in fact, a very shrewd operator. He brought out the very best DVA education program in the world. It didn't just apply to university. It applied to trade schools and all sorts of other things like that. A fellow in grade nine, for example, could go to a crash commercial school setup and get grades ten, eleven and twelve in six months instead of the usual three years. Those schools could do this because they just taught the basics, what you needed to know in order to pass those exams.

They were out to give us the time that we had lost during the war, and to set us back on the road. They were giving us back missed chances. Instead of someone starting out cold after the army, at some job like working at the bottom of the ladder in the CNR shops in Transcona, Manitoba, you could upgrade your education and become an engineer or a doctor, a newspaperman or an author, as I later became.

I will be eternally grateful for the DVA program, because for the first time really, when a war ended, a soldier's worth was appreciated. After World War One, the soldiers marched home to the bands playing after they got off the train and that was about all. After the music and the hoopla of the welcome home and the crowds dispersed, that was the end of it as far as anyone thinking of the soldiers' welfare. It was, "Goodbye buddy. Nice to have known you." Not so for us.

PART 6
INFANTRY

Jack Currie
Toronto, Ontario

I SPENT five-and-a-half years in Europe fighting that war, the biggest part of the time in Italy in some of the toughest battles of the
Second World War. I can tell you, it was no piece of cake either.

The "day" for us would start at midnight and end the next
midnight, so there was no such thing as a normal day. I can remember hearing things on the radio while we there, where the
announcer would say something like, "All's quiet on the Italian
front tonight. Just patrol action taking place." Well, if you were out
on one of those night patrols yourself, it was quite different from
what they were saying on the radio. It was your own little world
maybe, but those on "just patrol action" were always engaged in
some pretty tough fighting. Some of the time we were in tanks or
armoured cars, but if there was a need, we'd be on foot a lot of the
time too, engaged in some very tough one-on-one action with
enemy troops. "All quiet" didn't describe what we were up to.

We always had a pretty good idea of where the enemy was,
because we would hear the gunfire and see the flash of their guns.
Often on these patrols, we'd bump right into them in the darkness
and engage in face-to-face battle. At times like that, you would
naturally be scared, because you were in a fight where one of the
combatants was going to end up dead. Your job was to see that the
dead one wasn't you. This was a lot different than being engaged in
a full-scale battle with all of you against all of them. I found that once

235

Company sign painter Corporal Jack Reay busy at work on his famous sign. On the road to Falaise, France, August 13–14, 1944. (Photo by Lieutenant M.M. Dean / DND / Public Archives of Canada)

A soldier of the Second Canadian Infantry Division looks at a portrait of Hitler tacked to the wall of a house with a knife, Calcar, Germany, February 28, 1945. (Photo by George Kenneth Bell / DND / National Archives of Canada)

the battle started, things got going so fast you didn't even have time to think about danger or death or anything else. You're involved, and that's it. You just do what you have to do, and there's no time to be scared or to think about dying.

The fortunate thing is that we didn't have very many killed in our regiment, but we had an awful lot of casualties, an awful lot of wounded. For that reason we were getting new men all the time. In Italy once, we had a turnover of 3,000 troops after one battle, because we had had 3,000 casualties.

When I first went off to the war my Dad said to me, "Son, remember to keep your head down." Perhaps that's how I survived it all. A combination of keeping my head down and good luck.

When one thinks back, it's the camaraderie you remember best and you miss the most. Those men were your real true friends. Even

*Not quite like home but . . . what the heck. Members of the
Saskatchewan Light Infantry take advantage of a break in the
fighting to clean up in a mobile shower at Adrano, Italy in
August, 1943. (Courtesy the National Archives of Canada)*

now, half a century later, that's the spirit we find in our legion halls
and our other regimental associations. It's remained with us over
the years.

For some reason or other, the friendships you make in battle are
different from any other kind of friendships. The guy you served
with in battle is different than the guy you went to school with, the
guy you live with, or the guy you work with. There's something
between you and the man who fought alongside you that's different
than anything else. Perhaps it's just that you both faced death
together and during that time a special bond was welded.

There wasn't any of that glamour or glory about war that the
movies often try to depict. It was mostly downright miserable. It was

mud and cold and shortages — shortages of food, ammunition, clothing, and anything else you care to name. What made this so frustrating was that the only reason for all of this was because the stuff just wasn't getting through to us. We knew the supplies were out there somewhere, but we couldn't get our hands on them. This was especially true in Italy, because the Germans at that time still had lots of planes and U-boats, and they were sinking all of our ships that were coming through the Mediterranean. At one time, seventy-five percent of the stuff that they were sending to us went to the bottom of the ocean.

Lieutenant-Corporal R.H. Davies from Vancouver, washes Lieutenant George Cooper's back, with H.G. Dowdly from Newburgh, Ontario, and C.L. Halfpenny from Moncton, New Brunswick working the shower. Falaise, France, August 14, 1944. Lieutenant Cooper is from Ottawa. (Photo by Ken Bell / DND / Public Archives of Canada)

As I look back on it now, and watch young people around me grow up without war, I realize what it was I lost. I see them go off to university, start careers, get married, raise children, and all those other things, and I appreciate just what it is that we who went to war lost, and can never regain. We lost time — all those years when we should have been doing the same things. We lost five or six of the most valuable and formative years of our lives. Sure there was training when you came home. Our government did the best of any of the countries for its veterans, but it's not the same thing. Those years could not be replaced.

The most important thing though is that those of us who survived can always count our blessings just to be alive. We can also say that we had a part in a great adventure and a great cause. We who were in action in Italy did a lot of fighting. Sometimes we were in battle, day after day, for five or six weeks at one time. Just to come away from one of those battles unscathed was a gift.

Another way of looking at it is that of the five or six years that you were there, maybe only two years would have been in actual combat areas. The rest of that time you maybe lived it up pretty well. You had a good time among yourselves, and you saw a lot of different countries. It was somewhat like being a tourist except that there were a lot of people out there who were trying to kill you! Another thing you couldn't get rid of was that terrible ache you always had for home.

I remember those broadcasts by the German propagandist, Axis Sally, whose programs were aimed at the Canadian troops. We would listen to her programs because they were made up of good music and news from home. She knew how to tear us apart though. At the end of the program she would always play the sound of a freight whistle as it made its way across the Prairies. That was the thing that made us more lonesome and homesick than anything else she did or said on the broadcast. The lonely whistle of a freight train on the Prairies. For us, at that time, there was nothing that sounded more like home than that. You'd see the guys reach over and turn off their radios just as the train whistle started to blow, because they couldn't stand hearing it.

It's been a long time since that war, and a lot of veterans have the feeling that the sacrifices they made are being forgotten. Some feel that our Canadian flag is not respected as it should be. They are disturbed when they see some of our war memorials used for other things or being desecrated. They have the feeling that many of the young people don't even know or realize that the good life they have today wouldn't be here at all if it wasn't for those crazy Canucks who went off to fight in 1939.

I would never want to see our country go through something like that again, but we should be reminding our children more of what the world was like at that time. I can't understand why our schools don't have more Canadian history that tells what did happen, and about the part played by Canadians in doing something about it.

John H. Neff
Ottawa, Ontario

IT'S VERY hard, and most often impossible, to get old soldiers like me to talk about the horrors of war. It was, after all, a time when we had to become something other than what we would have been if war had not intervened. Without war, how many of us youngsters would have taken the life of another human being and looked upon it as a triumph? But that's the way it was in battle — kill or be killed.

Most of us who survived went back to our homes after the war, and tried to bury the horror of the things we had to do as soldiers. We had to start living normal lives. Our memories of the war would be, by choice, only the happier times. It was a time when we forged lifelong bonds of friendship and these are the things we like to remember.

Go along to any Legion hall sometime and listen to the stories that the old soldiers are telling. We don't fight our battles all over again. We don't even mention them. We talk about the good times; the leaves we took in foreign lands, the girls we knew, and the tricks we played on our soldier buddies. We'll resurrect the songs we used to sing together and we'll raise a glass to the memory of friends who didn't make it through. We don't glorify war; we have a mutual hatred of it and our most fervent wish is that it never happens again.

At the same time we are proud, as we should be, of the part we played in the destruction of an evil force in the world.

There's really no way to find out what it was like to be in the middle of a battle unless you can find a soldier who secretly defied regulations and kept a secret diary.

I was one who did that and so, just to give you a glimpse of that life, I'm going to open that diary to one day in my life in a battle situation. I was member of a tank crew, B Squadron, South Saskatchewan Regiment.

On August 20, 1944, we were in action at Caen. This was a couple of months after the D-Day invasion, and that was the day I decided to start making notes of what we were doing. It was a bad day for us. Of the 96 members of our squad who went into battle at Caen that day, 20 had been killed. Thirty-seven had been wounded and five had been taken prisoner. These are my notes for that day:

Sunday August 20, 1944
This is the day I thought would never end. At 2 A.M. things had quieted down a bit, and I left the tank for a few minutes to do a job we all should do at least once a day. I went to a ditch about 50 yards from the tank and as I sat there with my pants down, I heard a low whistle and a rustle nearby. Just then, someone fired a flare and there in the ditch I saw the biggest Jerry I have ever laid eyes on. To make a long story short, I beat him to the draw, as I had laid my pistol, all loaded for bear, on the ground in front of me. I went back to the tank without finishing my little job.

We could hear Jerry tanks moving around outside our enclosure. I remember going over to either the Major's or the Rear Link's tank and calling one of the officers' attention to these tanks, just in case they hadn't noticed them.

Just before first light, some Jerry planes flew over. At first light we could see the German tanks on the other side of the hedge — a couple of Panthers. Some of our tanks opened fire and one of the Panthers burst into flames. The other pulled away. A single sur-

*A short pause for the Lincoln and Welland Regiment at the side
of a road in Wertle, Germany, April 11, 1945. (Photo by
Alexander M. Stirton / DND / Public Archives of Canada)*

vivor got out of the burning Panther with all of his clothing burned off.

The German infantry tried to get past our position. We shot up several trucks and cut down their men on foot like cattle. Major Nash went in front of our tank to take a peek through a hole in the hedge and a couple of Jerries made a grab for him. I can still see him as he dropped to his knees and motioned to us with his thumbs to open with the machine guns. We sure cut a swath into that bunch. One came running forward with his nose hanging by a little piece of skin.

By this time we had quite a group of prisoners in our little corral, most of them wounded. Another wave of Jerries attacked and we drove them off once more. The wounded prisoners were loaded in

Sergeant C. Orton of the Highland Light Infantry of Canada with a jug of captured cider, France, June 20, 1944. (Photo by Ken Bell / Public Archives of Canada)

some Red Cross vehicles, which if I remember correctly, were German. With these in the centre of our convoy we drove off toward our Regimental Headquarters. Just as we started to move, Jack jumped off our tank and grabbed a P38 from a German officer who had just come in. It all looked so silly because Jack was unarmed himself.

As we moved back, dozens of Jerries came out with their hands up and we weren't in a position to do much about it. Some of them just followed our tanks back, rather than return to their own ss Officers. On the way back we nailed another Panther, and then, after reaching RHQ and turning over our prisoners to them, we just turned around and started down the same road we had just come up. We didn't get more than a mile when we ran into a whole convoy of Jerry half-tracks and trucks. What a slaughter that became. I have never seen such a mess of burned and blasted flesh. The blood was knee deep. About this time, our old tank decided to act up again and we lost another motor, but we still had enough power to carry on. How we cursed that tank as it sputtered along on three of its five engines. It was here, at about 1 P.M., we ran into a Tiger tank, and as brave as anything, we decided to take it on. At 3,000 yards I don't think we even annoyed him.

Around 4:00, we went back down through the orchards from which we had twice withdrawn and we formed up at a sort of crossroads just beyond the place we had slaughtered the light German column. We were told to stay there until we were relieved, and we were also told that at last light, all or part of A squadron would be down to help us. This never took place as A squadron got mixed up in a battle of its own.

Just at dusk we were warned that a column of 100 enemy armoured vehicles was approaching us from the southeast. We were able to knock out the lead tank and that served as a roadblock. The Germans then started to deploy and we were sort of surrounded while the German infantry kept sneaking up on us. We spotted one sniper in a tree and Nell fired off a 75 shell at him. The shell cut off the branch he was on, bringing him to the ground. He came forward to us with his hands up and looking very pale.

S.S. / M Billet and infantry troops of the Belgium Brigade on a street corner, Sallenelles, France, August 16, 1944. (Photo by Ken Bell / Public Archives of Canada / DND)

Finally it got dark, and with the darkness came the rain. We were helpless there in the dark without one soul on the ground to help us, but we stuck it out until about 1 A.M. when things came to a head. The Germans were all around us and we kept up a random fire and threw hand grenades into the hedges and ditches in an effort to drive them off.

I was standing on the back deck of our tank with a Sten gun and George Evans' tank was no more than 20 feet away from mine. I could hear movement about his tank and it sounded to me as if someone was pouring petrol over it. Suddenly, there was the flash of a grenade explosion and George's tank just went up in a sheet of flame. I could see a couple of Jerries duck under the Major's tank, but I held my fire because one of our Majors was standing near there, and I was afraid I'd hit him.

In a few minutes the Germans had two more of our tanks burning, and an order came that we should get out of there — it was every tank for itself. That, I think, was the wildest ride ever made by a group of tanks. It was blacker than the ace of spades with a constant rain falling, but yet the night was lit with burning tanks and buildings, along with the vivid streaks of tracer and gun flashes and the weird light of flares.

After what seemed like ages we finally halted. Only six of our 19 tanks were left.

The next time we stopped, we were on a main road and the battle still raged on around us in the darkness, but through it all you could still see the burning tanks, houses, and villages. Major Nash came over to our tank to ask if we could get through to RHQ on our radio.

Private W. Sutherland of the Westminster Regiment (left) *and Private V.A. Keddy of the Cape Breton Highlanders repacking rations in the supply depot for the men in the trenches, Cassino, Italy, April 18, 1944. (Photo by Strathy E.E. Smith / DND / Public Archives of Canada)*

As luck would have it I had been onto RHQ all along, and despite all the battle and confusion I was still right on the beam. Captain Gallamore, who was our rear link, was still back in the valley from which we had withdrawn. His was the only tank that hadn't pulled out, so that when I used the code sign to call the Colonel, it was old Guy Olmstead in Gallamore's tank who answered. As it turned out, that was the last time I ever heard old Guy's voice, because when Gallamore heard what happened, he tried to get to us but never made it.

Gallamore, Olmstead, and Crawford were taken prisoner. The other two crew members, Pashal and Colwell, were killed. God rest their souls.

At this point we still didn't know where we were, but we did know by the strength of their radio signal that we were somewhere near RHQ. So Major Nash asked the Colonel over the radio if he would fire a burst of Oerlicon straight in the air. When the Colonel did as he was asked, and we saw the burst in the night sky, we realized that we were less than a quarter mile from RHQ. . . . When our Major Nash told the Colonel on the radio that he would be willing to take our remaining five of 19 tanks back to the battle at the crossroads, I felt like punching him in the nose. I couldn't see the point of it, especially since we were just about out of ammunition and our gas gauge was showing EMPTY.

Well, we didn't go back. Instead, the Major and someone else ended up walking over to Headquarters and the rest of us just stayed put and moved over under our own power at first light. It was quite a scene. The field below RHQ was strewn with German dead which indicated that RHQ also had had a busy night.

The rest of the day was rather quiet as we just stayed in a patch of woods and watched thousands of prisoners file down the road past us. Our own infantry showed up in the meantime to help us and we felt much better, even more so when three more of our lost tanks showed up bringing our strength up to eight. Rumour had it that we had taken 7,000 prisoners and killed or wounded 2,000.

To end the day, we pulled our eight tanks out in an open field and formed a circle for the night as things were still a little sticky.

Author's note:

John Neff told me that his most vivid memory of the whole war was on May 5, 1945. It was in the morning of that day when the cease-fire was announced, and with that came the realization that he had survived the whole bloody mess. He was still alive. Of the 96 members of his squadron who had gone into battle together, 57 had been killed or wounded. Their average age had been 22.

For four-and-a-half years they had worked, eaten, slept and gone on leave together. "Most of them I liked, some I tolerated and a few I detested, but I think this would be true of any family," said John.

Robert F. MacIntosh
Kingston, Ontario

IT'S A FUNNY thing you know, but when you look back at the war, it's not the big things you remember. At least, I don't. I was in the army from day one right up to the finish, and during that time I had all the experiences that a soldier on active duty could possibly have. I had some close shaves with death and I lost some of my closest friends in battles during the D-Day invasion — which I went through without a scratch — and yet when I think about the war, it's always the little trivial things that come back. Things that bring a smile to my face. It's never blood and guts. Let me give you a couple of examples.

I joined up in England when I was 18. After basic training, I was sent to an Officer Cadet Training Unit (OCTU) near London. The Princess Royal was Colonel-in-Chief of the Royal Corps of Signals where I had been assigned, and one day there was great excitement in our barracks, because we were told that she was coming to inspect our unit. I, for one, had never come into contact with a member of the Royal family before so naturally, I was determined to make a good impression, and so I think, was everybody else. The whole place was shining in anticipation of her arrival, and that included every button on every immaculate and neatly pressed uniform. Our officers had devised two different schedules for her visit, one for

Wireless operator Private Mackeays relays news of the end of hostilities to driver Private Hugh McKerlain and a group of Seaforth Highlanders of the Canadian D Company, the Netherlands, May 5, 1945. (Photo by Michael M. Dean / DND / Public Archives of Canada)

indoors, in case it should rain, and another for fine weather. Not a detail was missed. The barracks buildings were cleaned up like I had never seen them before, and there wasn't even a scrap of paper blowing around in the whole compound. Everybody had been told how to act and how to address her if, perchance, she should stop to talk to any of us. Nothing could go wrong. Our officers had seen to that.

The Princess arrived and began her tour through the different parts of our establishment, dropping into offices and classrooms in a pre-arranged order. Then suddenly, there she was in our class-room, the face I had seen in newspaper pictures hundreds of times before. My face was turning red; I could feel that. I was dizzy. Maybe I was going to faint. She started down the aisle alongside the row of desks where I was sitting. "Please God," I prayed, "don't let her stop by me." My prayer went unheeded because suddenly, there she was, and she was asking me a question.

"What is that you're doing?" she asked.

"Practising rope splicing, your Highness," I gulped.

"Why?" asked the Princess.

Now this wasn't something I had expected her to ask, so I was completely stymied for an answer, and in my confusion I blurted out, "Your Highness, I haven't the foggiest idea." I could see the shocked look on the face of our Commanding Officer who was standing behind and to one side of the Princess, but it was her reaction that I'll never forget. She just stood and stared at me for a few moments saying nothing at all, and then moved on to ask a question of one of my classmates. I worried that she thought I might have been some kind of a smart aleck or showoff trying to impress my friends. In fact, I was secretly praying that she would just think I was stupid. The prayers were partly answered because that's exactly what the C.O. called me when I went to his office later for a full-scale dressing down.

When I think about the Normandy landings in which I was involved, the thing that always comes back is the terrible pain I suffered the day after D-Day. I suffered no injuries whatsoever during the invasion, but I suffered more than many. Anybody who's ever had a bad toothache will know what I'm talking about. My whole head felt as if it were on fire, and the throbbing was so bad that given a choice I would have preferred death if it were offered, but no such luck. The only army dental clinic I could find was an American one which was just setting up when I came across it. I was to be its very first patient as it turned out, and the young U.S. army dentist seemed glad to see someone in need of his services.

At the end of the session, he turned to me and said, "Since you're my first customer, you are eligible to receive our American Purple Heart medal which is awarded to wounded war casualties. You have lost some blood here."

I thought he was joking, but I knew he meant what he was saying when he took a small case from his desk containing ten Purple Hearts which were awarded to wounded American soldiers. He said that the ten medals in the box were, by special permission, for his first ten patients on the Normandy battleground.

I thanked him very much, but said that I couldn't accept it because I belonged to the British, not the American army. I thanked him profusely for helping me in my hour of need, and made my way back to my unit, minus the toothache but with a story to tell that nobody believes right to this day.

Irving Penny
London, Ontario

WAR IS WAR is war, to paraphrase Gertrude Stein, but the Second World War did have its lighter moments, without which, I suppose, we would have all gone crazy. Some of my own best memories happen to come from that war, as do some of my worst. It's the lighter moments I'd like to dwell on first.

The first platoon I went into battle with was made up largely of boys from the Kitchener, Ontario, area — boys with names like Steinmetz, Dahmer, Fruher, Friese and Schmidt and many others whose ancestors came to Canada from Germany. Many of these lads spoke fluent German, and at times, when we heard them in conversation we were apt to wonder if we had wandered into the wrong lines.

This ability to use the German language proved invaluable to one of our night patrols who encountered a much larger German patrol somewhere out between the lines. When challenged, it was a corporal from Kitchener who, in perfect German, loudly complained of being sent out to do all the dirty work while "you fellows in the big patrol merely walk around having a good time." This brought a derisive laugh from the larger patrol as they passed by in the dark, not realizing that the shadowy figures they could barely see, were, in fact, Canadian soldiers and not one of their own fatigue parties.

German officers and troops coming in to surrender and dump their arms, Utrecht, the Netherlands, May 8, 1945. (Photo by M.M. Dean / DND / Public Archives of Canada)

Another thing that used to give us great satisfaction and lift our spirits was the amazing accuracy of our Canadian artillery. I especially recall one bright morning on the Orsogna front when we were greeted by the sight of huge German flags flying from the tower in the wreckage of the town opposite our position, and others that were draped over some of our burned-out tanks lying between the lines. It was a perfect example of adding insult to injury.

Well, it wasn't long before a young captain of the artillery, armed with a board of instruments, arrived to survey the scene. Minutes later, a 25-pound shell smashed into the tower, levelling it and disintegrating the offending flag. In the next few minutes, each and every one of the other flags came to the same ignominious end.

The medical officers, too, lifted our spirits by the miracles they were able to perform in the most primitive of battlefield conditions. I remember one case in particular, when a friend of mine was hit by a sniper in the inner corner of the right eye, the bullet emerging from just below his right ear. Our medical men were able to go to work on him and they did such a good job that when I met him again, years after the war, he appeared to have suffered little permanent damage thanks to the battlefield surgeons. There were so many cases of that kind of thing, and so many other cases where they gave life and a future back to gravely injured men.

When one reads the literature produced since the war, one is sometimes left wondering where the authors got their information. For example, take the flood of books and articles about General, and later Field Marshal, B.L. Montgomery. One would think that this man won the war all by himself and that the soldiers adored him. I cannot speak for anybody but the P.B.I. (Poor Bloody Infantry), but among us, the man was detested. He had absolutely no respect at all for the lowly private or the N.C.O. and he treated them as so much cannon fodder, only good to be used for the glory of Montgomery. To us in the lower ranks, he was the most over-rated character of the Second World War.

Monty was all "spit and polish" whereas we of the Perth Regiment gloried in the name of the "Scruffy Perth" and we boasted of being a fighting regiment rather than a troop of parade-ground soldiers. That nickname was tacked on to us, by the way, after a totally unexpected inspection by a general, following field manoeuvres in England. Although our wonderful colonel defended his regiment, the name was picked up and proudly carried by those of us in the lower echelons.

If Monty was over-rated, by far the most beloved commander, as far as the ranks were concerned, was Field Marshal Sir Harold Alexander, later to be Lord Alexander, Governor-General of Canada. He was a man who took time to visit the front to talk and listen to the men in the ranks, as well as the officers. He also seemed to take the greatest care in keeping casualties to a minimum, in spite of the fact that some of the most difficult campaigns were successfully carried out when he was directing the action.

If most things about war are anti-human there were also some times of blissful quiet. I often think about a bright, sun-drenched hillside in Italy in a rest area a mile or so behind the lines. On that occasion, I was lying half-asleep on the grass listening to the booming of artillery and the staccato rattle of machine guns in the distance, thinking only how music-like all of this sounded. It was easy to imagine where Beethoven got the ideas for his great symphonies. He must have had moments like that.

The tragedy of war was not confined to the battlefield; it extended all the way back to the home front. One day, a handsome young man in our platoon who had married a lovely English girl while in Britain, received the news that his wife and their infant son,

German children displaying their surrender flag, Sogel, Germany, April 10, 1945. (Photo by A.M. Stirton / DND / Public Archives of Canada)

together with her parents, had been killed when a buzz bomb fell on their home. He was inconsolable.

Now I don't want to deprecate the assistance given to the Allies by the forces from the U.S., but it seems their filmmakers want the world to believe that the Americans won both world wars all by themselves. It is hard to forget that following the breakthrough of the Canadians at the Hitler Line and the drive of the British Eighth Army towards Rome, we were all stopped by a general order on the outskirts of the city in order that the U.S. troops could catch up and enter Rome first, thereby gaining the credit for its capture.

Let me say, too, that infantrymen on both sides of the war considered the American fighter aircraft of the Second World War to be the most dangerous weapon of all. Their strafing was deadly, and they could do it from a position that made them relatively immune from firepower on the ground. We used to say over there, that when German planes came over, we ducked. When British came over, the Germans ducked. When American planes came over, everybody ducked!

Brigadier General Denis Whitaker
Oakville, Ontario

IN THE FALL of 1944, the Allied forces in northwest Europe were closer than ever to victory. Before that goal could be achieved, however, the U.S. troops had to get through the Siegfried line, across the Ruhr River, and push through the Rhineland to the Rhine River, the last defence perimeter for the Germans. Everybody had the feeling that this was the battle to end the war, and Canadian troops were destined to play a major role in achieving that victory.

There were three main Allied armies involved in this operation; the Ninth American, the First Canadian, and the Second British. It was a time of extremely fierce fighting over a period of six weeks to clear the Germans from the west bank of the Rhine — six weeks of the war's heaviest fighting to liberate just 20 miles of territory.

I was a Lieutenant Colonel during that campaign, in charge of the Hamilton Light Infantry, and I can honestly say that it was the most gruelling battle of the war. The casualties were much heavier than they should have been, for two reasons. First, our infantry forces were seriously under-strength and, secondly, the higher-ups had been filling our shortages with men who were almost completely untrained for the job, men who had never done anything but cooking or office work and things like that. This resulted in even more casualties. Men were getting killed or injured simply because of their lack of experience in battle.

The weather conditions, too, were absolutely frightful. The planning for the campaign was done with the assumption that it would all take place over frozen, winter grounds. Instead, just before we started, there was a great thaw and rain and the whole terrain was turned into a quagmire. The mud was unbelievable. The ruts in the roads were up to three and four feet deep, and all of our armour was being continually bogged down. Because of this, it became more and more of an infantryman's battle most of the time. The heavy equipment became practically useless.

Add to that the fact that the Germans fought like hell — like demons. This was their last desperate stand for their homeland, and they were not giving an inch away. Then, of course, there was Hitler's order that there would be no surrender and every man was to fight to the death.

On our side we had a lot of dissension and disagreement in the top command. The major players like American Generals Bradley and Patten and Britain's Montgomery each wanted to be the "glory boy" who got the credit for ending the war. Therefore, there was no unanimity whatsoever on how the fighting should be done. That's not the ideal way to win a battle.

To give you an idea of how tough it was, all you have to do is think of it in terms of time. It took six weeks of intense fighting by those three Allied armies to gain those 20 miles, but once attained, it took only another six weeks to gain the next 200 miles, and bring an end to the war.

The Canadian troops played a very important role in the whole

Crowd welcoming units of the Ninth Canadian Infantry Brigade to Leeuwarden, Netherlands, April 16, 1945. (Photo by Lieutenant D.I. Grant / DND / Public Archives of Canada)

war — not just in the Rhineland — and in far greater proportion than its size would lead anybody to believe. I don't think that the majority of present-day Canadians realize that. Another aspect is that all Canadian soldiers were volunteers. Not a conscript in the lot — which was something unique among the participating Allied armies.

When the war was over, our troops came home and took up their roles in civilian life, and thought of the war and their part in it only as a job that needed to be done, and not something to dwell on forever. They more or less erased it from their minds. They never talked about it much, and therefore, there was the unfortunate impression left that the Canadians probably didn't do very much. Nothing could be farther from the truth.

Another problem was that even our great field commanders

during the war, men like General Crerar, were reluctant to blow their own horns afterwards, unlike the American and British generals who just laid down their guns and picked up their pencils to write about the parts they played in the victory. General Crerar is a good example of the Canadian timidity, or modesty, whatever you want to call it. He commanded a force of 470,000 troops, including British and American, in the Rhineland and he never even wrote his memoirs. Nobody else wrote about this truly great commander either.

How many people know that three out of four Victoria Crosses awarded in the campaign in northwest Europe were won by Canadians? How many know about the Can Loan plan that saw 650 Canadian officers being loaned to the British forces because they didn't have enough officers of their own to do the job?

The fact that our troops were all volunteers is a very important point that Canadians would do well to remember. Present-day Canadians somehow harbour the feeling that England beckoned and we went running. That's not true at all. We declared war on our own date, and we sent our own men over who fought against the Nazi regime for Canada, not for Britain or anybody else.

I don't think that Canadians today fully appreciate that, and I don't think they've been really interested until recently. There now seems to be a surge of interest among young people to find out about our history, and the Second World War is certainly a very big part of our history. What happened to those men on those battlefields marked them for life. It scarred them and changed them, and I think we are now just beginning to wonder, "How?" and, "What happened?". "Tell us about it," they say, "and maybe it won't happen again."

W.J. Rupert
London, Ontario

SELDOM HEARD or talked about is the role played by Canadian railroad men during the Second World War. During the war we weren't mentioned that often, even though our role was critical, and then after the war, it was almost as if we hadn't even been over there, for all the attention that was paid to us. Many of our veterans call themselves the forgotten people of the Second World War.

Who were we, and what did we do? Well, simply put, we were the men of the Royal Canadian Engineers, Railway Operating Division, and our job was to operate trains through Europe behind the fighting troops, taking in military supplies, food, ammunition, and all sorts of fighting equipment like tanks and guns. It was our job also to move troops and take the wounded back to hospitals from the front lines. Our job was just about anything that involved train transportation.

Lieutenant-Corporal W.T. Haggerty, Lieutenant-Corporal B.J. Doucette, Corporal A. Boudreau and CSM R.M. Cooper frying fresh eggs bought at the frontlines. At the rear of the group is Lieutenant-Corporal Tellum from Cape Breton. Normandy, France, June 8-9, 1944. (Photo by Ken Bell / DND / Public Archives of Canada)

The work we did was of immense importance, but because we were not in the front lines we produced no heroes in the traditional sense, and we garnered few headlines.

Because of our remote locations, away from the actual fighting, few of our men were killed, although many were wounded as a result of heavy bombings by the Germans. They realized the importance of knocking out the strategic Allied supply lines, so we were constantly under attack from the air.

When new boxcars were needed, and they were needed a lot, we were called upon to build them ourselves, sometimes at the rate of 40 or 50 a day. We made something in the order of 100,000 boxcars during the war. What's more, we had to do all of this while keeping a watchful eye out for the bombers and strafers. We were the lifelines, the blood of the fighting troops.

Throughout the war we were in the areas of heaviest fighting in Holland, Belgium, and France and near the end of the war, we operated right inside Germany itself.

It wasn't until 1943 that the Canadian government formed our group at the request of the British War Office, which had asked for experienced railway troops to assist in the operation of the British railways. They were suffering from tremendous shortages in manpower and equipment. That's when our first men went over.

Then, of course, with the anticipated continental invasion, we would be taking an active part in operations on the continent. It was all part of the master plan for D-Day and its aftermath.

The projected need for transportation of troops and supplies was obvious, and certainly vital to future operations. The Canadian government urged all eligible Canadians employed in railway trades to report for enlistment, and the response was immediate. Many of our men gave up important jobs with the railways in Canada to enlist with the RCE. They were more than anxious to do their part in winning the war.

From there on everything happened with lightning speed. Enlistees to the call, which first went out from the government in March, 1943, were taken immediately to the Stratford, Ontario barracks of the Canadian Armed Forces. There, they were given

*Canadian soldiers wounded and captured during the raid on
Dieppe, France, August 19, 1942. (Courtesy the Public Archives
of Canada)*

some fast training and by July of the same year — a bare four months
after the first call — they were on board the *Queen Elizabeth* troop
ship in Halifax, ready to sail.

By the end of the month, they were already in their barracks in
Colchester, England. In the meantime in England, another railway
workshop company had been formed. This was made up of Canadian railway men who were already in other branches of the armed
forces.

The groups from the workshop company and the telegraph
company were ready to go to work at once, while the operating
company required training in British rules, methods and operations. Before long, all of our groups were actively assisting in the
operation of the British Railways.

On July 1, 1944, less than a month after D-Day, the telegraph company had landed in France, and had communications ready for the operating companies when they landed on September 1.

After that, these same telegraph men kept moving ahead to Belgium, Holland, and Germany. In each case they had communications ready for the operating companies when they arrived.

Aside from the strafing, we also faced the most difficult job of adapting to the different European railway systems. Track switches were one good example. While Canadian switches operated mainly by electricity, the European ones still had the hand-operated type which required about 30 hand cranks to change the train from one track to another.

Also, boxcars in Europe were half the size of Canadian ones. This involved a great deal of getting used to, especially since members of the railway division were responsible not only for the movement of the trains, but for building the boxcars and maintaining them.

Although the men of the Railway Operating Division didn't experience much actual combat, we were always only steps removed from the ferocity of the action taking place all around us. Ours was considered a support role, but it was also a role that gave all of us a legacy of nightmares filled with ear-splitting noises of falling bombs and the strafing fire of airborne guns. All we could do was hide. We couldn't even shoot back. We weren't an armed contingent.

There were many dark days in the Second World War, but the blackest of all for Canadian troops was August 19, 1942, the day of the slaughter at Dieppe. Just the name "Dieppe" is enough to bring the memories flooding back in all their vivid horror.

The attempted landing on the beaches at the French port of Dieppe was the first attempt by the Allies to penetrate enemy-occupied Europe, and most of those involved were Canadians, fighting valiantly but suicidally, as it seemed the enemy just sat there waiting for them to come. Out of a total of 4,960 Canadian soldiers from the Second Division who set sail from England that day, 3,367 were killed, wounded or captured.

The enemy was everywhere as the unsuspecting soldiers tried to gain

German troops examining the bodies of Canadian soldiers and their wrecked equipment, Dieppe, France, August 19, 1942. (Courtesy the National Archives of Canada)

access to the beaches in their landing craft. The Germans were holed up and hidden in farm houses, and in every nook and cranny of the rocks. As the troops waded in from the water, they were met with a barrage of gunfire from every conceivable type of weapon — machine gun, mortar, and heavy cannon. Dive bombers screamed overhead, and the life expectancy of the Canadians could be measured in seconds.

Many died as soon as they left their landing craft, and the succeeding waves of troops that followed were similarly mowed down in the murderous fire of the machine guns. It was the worst kind of slaughter.

John Mellor, who now lives in Kitchener, Ontario was one of the fortunate survivors.

John Mellor
Kitchener, Ontario

DESPITE everything that happened, I still believe that our side learned a great deal because of the Dieppe raid, not only in tactics, but also in human behaviour. Having said this, I believe that the whole Dieppe operation was a terrible waste of human lives.

It was badly planned and badly executed, but I do think that some very positive things came out of it. Like Mountbatten, I am convinced that without the horrible lessons learned at Dieppe we could never have won the war.

Some weeks after D-Day, I had occasion to drive down that way again where the first Mulberry Harbour was built. It was amazing to see all these ships tied up at a breakwater that had been floated over from England. This was an artificial harbour — floating roadways made up of pontoon bridges. It was an astounding sight and one that couldn't be visualized while the battle was on. It just boggled the mind, and reminded you that despite what people were saying, there was a lot of planning put into that battle. The men weren't just dumped in there at a whim.

I have come to believe that without the lessons learned at Dieppe that we could not later have attacked a fortified port on D-Day and succeeded. Without Dieppe and the lessons learned there, D-Day would never have happened.

It's been said over and over again that the troops were just dumped into Dieppe by the operation's planners who knew full well that they would be slaughtered. I'm not saying that isn't the case, but it is very hard for me to believe such a thing. I can't believe that we were sent in as sacrificial lambs.

On the other hand, I did a lot of research on this after the war, for a book I wrote about the Dieppe operation, and I did find some evidence that seems to confirm the sacrifice theory. Stalin was demanding a second front. Churchill was actually in Moscow the day of the Dieppe raid. Stalin told Churchill that the British were cowards, and that if they didn't start some sort of a major operation soon the Russians would capitulate. It was a political necessity you might say, and if that is correct, it seems certain that we were just thrown in there. As one of those who was on the beach and saw men dying all around me, I would prefer to think that this wasn't the case.

The raid, in fact, had been cancelled at one point and all the guys had been sent on leave. There's no doubt that secrecy was broken at the time because these fellows just went to every pub along the southeast coast of England bragging that they had been the first to be chosen. It wasn't their fault. They had been told that the raid was off, cancelled forever. Then without warning, they were dragged back, put on the same ships and sent off to Dieppe. The original plan for the raid, which was almost public knowledge by this time, was put back into effect again. Can there be any doubt at all that the Germans knew we were coming and that they were ready for us?

It was all so stupid. The only thing the planners did differently was to change the name of the raid. They thought that would be enough to fool the Germans.

The Germans said there had been a red alert all along the coast. They had seen ship activity along the southeast coast of England, and they had bombed two of the ships but they said they did not know for certain that something was going to happen at Dieppe. They *did* know all along, they said, that there would be an attempt by the Allies to breach the lines at one of the ports but they said they didn't know where that would be, or when. They said they were prepared for it to happen anywhere along the coast, and to such an extent that they all slept alongside their guns at all times.

What is amazing is that none of this intelligence got back to Britain. All of this reinforcing with heavy guns, large movements of German troops along the coast and in the area of Dieppe; all of the things that one would think could not escape detection by our intelligence sources, and still our planners knew nothing of it. How could that be?

I think the major reason that the Dieppe raid failed, apart from poor planning, was our lack of heavy firepower. Mountbatten begged for a battleship or a heavy cruiser or whatever, and

*The fighting on the Italian front was thick and heavy at
Cartelnova on St. Patrick's Day, 1944. Here, Sergeant R.H.
Easby hands a message for delivery to a despatch rider at the
Fifth Canadian Armoured Division Headquarters. (Courtesy the
National Archives of Canada)*

"Bomber" Harris turned down his request for a heavy preliminary
bombing raid before they touched down on the beach although this
had been promised.

My Commando unit went ashore near a gun bastion. The
Number Three and Number Four Commandos were chosen to take
care of these coastal gun batteries located on either side of Dieppe.
These were huge 5.6-inch guns, in batteries of six, pointing out to
sea. They were capable of sinking any ship within a distance of
14 miles. This means that at first daylight, unless those gun bastions
were taken out, almost every ship in our invasion fleet would have
been sunk.

I was one of those Number Four Commandos, and we went in about a half hour before the main body of troops and climbed the cliffs in total darkness. We took out that gun battery which, as it turned out, was the only successful part of the raid. Number Three Commando went in on the other side of Dieppe, but most of those men were wiped out, although they did keep the gun battery quiet.

The Canadian troops were without a doubt, the best that the Allies had, very highly trained and more than anxious to get into battle. That was probably the reason they were chosen for this particular operation. However, they were doomed right from the outset. As soon as they dropped into the water from their landing craft they ran into this murderous barrage of gunfire. Many died before they took even one step forward. Those that followed had to step over their bodies and it was only a matter of seconds before they went down too. They didn't have a chance.

If they managed to get on the beach at all, they found it totally strung with entanglements of barbed wire 20 feet across and sown with mines. Even if they got across that, they came face to face with the actual sea wall itself, which was seven to eight feet high. That was covered with rolls of barbed wire too, on the top, and there were machine-gun posts all the way along.

The whole front itself, a mile long and crescent shaped, had boarding houses and hotels that were filled with hundreds of Germans with machine-guns and mortars zeroing in on the main beach. There were balloons over our landing barges that were supposed to protect us against low-level dive bombing, but on the decks of the barges they had all these hydrogen bottles lying right out there in the open. The shells from shore landed on the hydrogen bottles, and many of our men were badly burned by the exploding gas. A good friend of mine, Ed Bennett of Woodstock, Ontario, was badly injured, but in spite of this, he was the first one to get his tank on the beach, and was the very first to get over the sea wall and onto the promenade. Until the surrender, he was able to maintain good discipline among his men and continue to shoot the Germans all through the action. Ed should have received a Victoria Cross for what he did that day.

I was shot through the head that day, on my way out after our raid on the gun battery. Actually, it was a piece of shrapnel that went through the side of my head and knocked my eye out from the inside. The eye was hanging out on my cheek. I passed out, and when I came to I was making my way down over the cliff with the other boys. I couldn't remember what had happened or even how I got to the ladder. My theory is that I was plain shell-shocked. I just jumped into the sea and started to go. I must have had the idea of swimming back to England, 65 miles away, but fortunately, I was picked up by one of our boats shortly after.

Looking back on that whole fiasco today, I would have to say that Dieppe definitely earned a place in history. Churchill himself said that. Mountbatten said that if he had the same choice to make he would make it again, because it was something that had to be done.

Private J.S. Farrer of the Highland Light Infantry of Canada riding a captured German horse, France, June 20, 1944. (Photo by Ken Bell / Public Archives of Canada)

I think he was quite correct in saying that. We had a job to do, to go in there and do the best we possibly could. We failed through no fault of our own. The defences were far too fierce for us. However, I still maintain to this day that in spite of the massive snafu, Dieppe was very necessary in the overall scheme of things. Without Dieppe, we would not have won the war. The big regret is the knowledge that if we had had proper planning, Dieppe could have been successful.

Ed Bennett
Woodstock, Ontario

I BELIEVE that we did learn some lessons at Dieppe, but I think those lessons could have been learned without the loss of 3,000 or 4,000 men.

I have always believed that the decision to undertake the raid was a political move or, if you prefer, a political necessity. Our side, at that time, was at its lowest ebb. There were losses everywhere and something had to be done. Our Allies were starting to feel a sense of betrayal.

The Russians had been promised that there would be some action on the Western Front in the summer of 1942, to take some of the tremendous pressure off them. They had suffered huge losses in that first massive push into Russia by Hitler. They were totally unprepared for such a treacherous move from a country they felt was fighting alongside them.

The British had to get something started so it looks as though the raid on Dieppe was hurriedly brought forward as some kind of an answer.

Something that has been overlooked over the years in all the stories about Dieppe, are some of the units who took part in the operation. It was the Second Division that went in and so, naturally, the ones who are always mentioned are the infantry units — the Royal Regiment, the Essex Scottish, the South Saskatchewans, the Camerons and a few others. But in addition to all those, there were a great many Royal Canadian Engineers, quite a number of the Toronto Scottish Machine Gunners and other auxiliary units like the Medical Corps and the Provost who were involved. These units have rarely been given the credit for having served at Dieppe.

I think that certainly the Engineers and the Machine Gunners deserve as much credit and even more than the others, because they had to land with packs of explosives on their backs. It was their job to unload materials that enabled the tanks and troops to get over the sea wall. Unfortunately, getting over the wall was something that just couldn't happen because as soon as the doors of the landing craft were let down, the machine-gun fire was coming in and killing the troops as they were trying to scramble out and get to shore.

The landing craft I was in was hit as we were coming in about a quarter mile off shore. It didn't disable the craft so we just kept coming. I was shot in the eye at that point, and later, the eye completely closed up, but there was so much to do in a situation like that, you don't really notice these things. It wasn't until later in the action, around 11:00 in the morning, that I realized I was badly wounded and that my eye was gone. When there's so much excitement around you though, you just have a tendency to keep going.

I think that everyone who landed on that beach that day deserved credit for doing the best possible job that could be done. I don't believe in medals, but if there has to be such a thing, they should be awarded to anyone and everyone who was there.

No doubt Dieppe did teach the military planners a lot of lessons, but I think that those lessons could have been learned without such a great loss of life. It can be said, I suppose, that it served its purpose politically because it said to Stalin and the Russians, "Look, we've tried and it can't be done in 1942." They also learned that it couldn't be done in 1943. It wasn't until 1944 that they had the men and the equipment to be able to do it on D-Day.

PART 7

NAVY

The Battle of the Atlantic may have been the most crucial battle of the Second World War, because its purpose was to keep Britain from falling into Hitler's hands at the time when she was most vulnerable and unprepared. The Nazis had overrun Europe with frightening ease, and for a while, nothing seemed capable of standing up to and overcoming the power of their frightening and powerful war machine.

When Hitler turned his sights on Britain, the free world held its breath. Was it possible for England to survive? How could she? Her limited resources were used up and the Nazis had succeeded in closing off the supply lines from other countries. Would it simply be a case of starving Britain out of the war and forcing her to sue for peace?

A powerful force of German submarines patrolled the Atlantic waters surrounding Britain and, with apparent ease, they were sending to the bottom the ships of the merchant navy that tried to bring supplies to the embattled islands. It was a black period for the U.K. and the Allied nations, because, in the words of U.S. President Roosevelt, "If England should lose, all America will be living at the point of a gun."

The only hope was to somehow break the Nazi stranglehold on these supply routes, something that seemed at that time impossible. Allied ships were going down faster than new ones could be built. There were no miracle solutions. For the time being, the only thing to be done was to continue with the convoy system used during World War One. The theory behind convoys was that there was at least some safety in numbers.

Huge armadas of merchant and navy ships would depart together and head across the Atlantic for Britain, with the knowledge that while many would be sunk on the way across, at least some of their numbers would make it through. The job of the navy was to protect the merchant carriers as best they could, and to wage warfare with the wolf pack of subs that infested the waters below.

It was a chilling and, for a time, one-sided war that the enemy was winning hands down, but it was a war that the Allies had to win, because without that fragile lifeline to the outside world Britain could not survive. It was as simple as that.

Those ships carried food, fuel and munitions through waters that were literally infested with U-boats and surface raiders. The losses in men and ships were horrendous, especially in the merchant carriers.

The men aboard the merchant ships had no status in the war. Although they were frontline fighters, they were all civilians who laboured anonymously, never knowing from one moment to the next if their ship would be the next to be torpedoed. Those in a tanker's stokehold worked in the heat and confinement, knowing that if a torpedo struck, their chances were the worst of all. They were in the area of the ship at which torpedoes were aimed, and death by fire, explosion or scalding steam was what they could expect. If by some miracle they could escape from the hold, drowning in the frigid Atlantic was likely. Fewer than 50 percent of merchant crews ever survived the sinking of their ships. Even if they survived the sinking, they could not be picked up by other ships of the convoy who had orders to keep going at full speed to heighten the chances of their own survival.

In the early months of the Battle of the Atlantic, casualties among merchant seamen exceeded those of all British armed forces put together. When it was over and the figures were added up, 35,000 British merchant seamen including 1,000 Canadians had been lost. Added to this figure were the many thousands who were not British, the sailors from other countries that had already been defeated.

In spite of all this, Canadian merchant sailors were not, for some strange reason, being perceived as heroes in their own country. The common perception among their fellow countrymen was that they had chosen an easy path out of war service, that they chose the merchant navy in order to avoid military service. In the early stages of the war, merchant seamen were dying at a rate that was far out of proportion to their numbers and it could be classed almost as a "suicide job." Often, their pay was poor and some of the ships they sailed, especially in the early years, were little better than "tramps" with the most appalling of living conditions. Morale was at rock bottom and, not surprisingly, ships often could not sail in convoy because they could not find crews.

Proper credit has yet to be given to the men who manned the ships that kept Britain alive during those early years of the war.

Ted Watt
Victoria, British Columbia

I WAS ONE of those sailors often referred to as a retread. I served as an Able Seaman in World War One, and stayed on in the reserve navy when that war was over. Because of this experience, I was called back to action in 1940 while the Battle of Britain was on. They gave me a Lieutenant's commission this time, figuring, I suppose,

Ted Watt (Courtesy Ted Watt)

that an old dog could teach some of the young pups a few tricks. I was hoping for action at sea, but soon found that this was not to be.

I was assigned to a small group of officers and men in the Port of Halifax, whose unique duty it was to see that ships that went to sea were indeed worthy to go, and were, as the order ordained, "In all respects ready." Our job included inspecting the ships for explosives that might have been planted by enemy saboteurs and making sure that the ships had decent and humane conditions on board for the men who would crew them.

Our small group was called the Naval Control Service (NCS), and despite the fact that I had been in and out of the RCNVR since 1917, I had never heard of such a branch before. The officer in charge, I found out when I got to Halifax, was none other than Commander Dick Oland, with whom I had sailed for a while in the early twenties. Dick filled me in on the NCS during our first meeting.

Naval Control, he told me, was the fighting navy's co-ordinating organization which, at the outbreak of war, automatically took to directing merchant navy vessels to the ports where their cargoes were most urgently needed. NCS was the organization that set up the convoys for the passage of these ships through perilous waters.

Since Halifax was the major convoy assembly port in North America, the searching and verifying of all ships was a huge job for the Naval Control Service. The Germans had established a sophisticated sabotage system in the early years of World War One, whereby they would plant explosives in ships that were being loaded in American harbours before getting under way for Allied destinations.

To guard against this happening again, the Admiralty in London had asked Ottawa to search all merchant ships for possible explosive devices. That task fell to Naval Control Service, which was already overworked and suffering from a shortage of trained manpower. The best that the Drafting Office had been able to do in the way of a regular search party, was half-a-dozen Naval Reserve Able Seamen and one officer. I was to be that officer. Since this wasn't the "action at sea" job I had been hoping for, I was understandably disappointed.

I quickly pointed out to Dick Oland that I knew nothing whatever about anti-sabotage, and that my knowledge of merchant ships was limited to what I'd seen from the bridges of armed escorts, but my argument didn't work. He pointed out that none of the men under me were anti-sabotage specialists either, so we could all learn together.

And so it was that I set out along with my men to do the job as best we could. We soon found out how truly impossible the job of locating hidden explosives could be. The ships were fully loaded by the time we got aboard, and the task of locating a relatively small time bomb among all that cargo would be virtually impossible. Talk about your needle in a haystack! Also, with ten or so ships to be inspected each day, in that great harbour's widely separated berths, there simply wasn't time for much more than a checking of cargo plans and crew lists and, possibly, the opening up of an occasional hold for a spot check.

Providentially, as it turned out, the enemy had apparently decided that this form of sabotage left over from the first war wasn't worthwhile pursuing. We found no explosives and apparently there were none.

What we did find though, was that the truly explosive thing aboard all of these ships getting ready for convoy was the seamen's morale.

During the first few weeks I was there, I noticed that several ships were not ready to leave when the time came up for them to join a scheduled convoy. "Crew trouble" was usually the reason. This covered a wide range of complaints. Crews would go on sitdown strikes over wages, grub and lousy accommodation, or they would simply decide that they didn't want any more of the horror of life out there in the submarine zone. All of them knew just how many ships were going down, and it was demoralizing for them to hear the German propagandists rubbing it in on short wave radio. Instead of planting time bombs in the cargo, the Germans found it was easier and more effective to plant time bombs in the minds of men.

In the weeks that followed, I would see more and more vessels fail to hoist their identifying pennants at sailing time. Breakdowns of discipline, desertions, disabling industrial disputes and suspicious mechanical malfunctions left costly gaps in departing convoys. It was a very serious problem and one that was not easy to solve.

There was general agreement among our team that last minute delays and dropouts were basically attributable to the 50 percent loss of life which accompanied most convoy sinkings. Also, the obvious shortage of navy escort ships to reduce those losses didn't help seamen's morale either. One of the most important factors was the centuries-old, deeply resented exploitation of the man on the lower deck by greedy owners and unprincipled captains on what were called "hungry" ships.

I passed these thoughts from our small group's daily meetings to our Commander who thought that our findings were legitimate enough to transmit to the Director of Intelligence and Trade in Ottawa, Captain E.S. Brand.

The findings must have been what they were looking for, because from that point on events moved swiftly. The importance of Naval Control boarding parties increased. We were at first encouraged to submit more detailed accounts of what we were encountering among the crews and the conditions aboard ship. After a very short time, we moved from being encouraged to do this to being ordered to do it.

Two new boarding officers joined us, and the strength of the noncommissioned force was doubled, allowing for two parties instead of one. This, in turn, enabled more business-like searches and longer opportunities for intelligence gathering. "Crew trouble" — why it was happening, what could be done about it, and the serious effect it was having on the supply lines to Britain suddenly became a recognized, serious problem.

At government headquarters in Ottawa, a high level Committee on Questions of Discipline and Treatment of Merchant Seamen, chaired by the Under Secretary For External Affairs, Norman Robertson, was established.

On March 3, 1941, all officers of the Naval Control Service, including me, were brought together in Ottawa for the first time since war had been declared. This was followed by sessions with the Merchant Seamen's Committee. Out of all this came swift and drastic legislation for dealing with deliberate, incorrigible or misguided troublemakers, as well as a plan for bringing encouragement to those other merchant seamen whose dedication to winning the Battle of the Atlantic had remained unshaken.

Orders-in-Council were passed to permit the arrest and imprisonment of subversive agents and their followers without recourse to the civil courts. A civilian Director of Merchant Seamen was appointed to establish training schools and manning pools.

These new measures guaranteed replacements of crews where casualties or insubordination created gaps, and also guaranteed crews for the new fleet of merchantmen that were beginning to emerge from Canadian shipyards.

Along with this came a co-ordination of national effort by volunteer agencies concerned with the welfare of merchant seamen and other civilian combatants. It was also decided to immediately set up in all nine Canadian ports a boarding service like the one we operated in Halifax, as soon as the necessary officers and men could be trained. In addition, we were encouraged to conduct regular bull sessions with officers and men which discussed and analyzed what each man had noticed during his daily rounds. In Halifax, we found that these sessions had produced an amazing amount of valuable hands-on intelligence and viable solutions.

After that Ottawa meeting, things moved swiftly, which proved to all of us the sense of urgency that was felt by headquarters in Ottawa over the morale and efficiency of the merchant navy.

The word quickly spread that we were the trusted friends of the merchantmen, and if they had any problems we were the people to see.

Another plus for us was the co-ordination of the many voluntary agencies concerned with the seaman's welfare. The largest of these, the Red Cross and the Navy League, had been doing yeoman service supplying woollens, ditty bags, and other comforts for the merchant sailors. The problems came in the distribution, which the organizations had put into the hands of the ship's masters and chief stewards, some of whom were taking these comforts for themselves and selling them on the black market.

Although there were only isolated cases of this, most of the crews believed that they were constantly being shortchanged and robbed when it came to comforts. Our boarding parties were able to solve this potentially explosive problem by taking over the distribution of these gifts themselves, as part of their normal stay on board each ship. This extra bit of work paid off handsomely in terms of goodwill.

Things turned around dramatically. In the early days of our ship searches we were turning in only sporadic reports on crew trouble. Under the new system, our Boarding Officers were writing detailed reports.

The Royal Navy became very interested in what we had managed to do, and eventually, a system evolved whereby we exchanged information with our opposite numbers overseas. An extremely good relationship developed between our groups in Canada, the British Admiralty, and those in the British shipping world.

The Battle of the Atlantic continued to rage on — the worst years being 1942 and early 1943 — but eventually, it slowed down enough so that we knew we were winning — although there were enemy submarines and sinkings right up until war's end. In the latter years of the war though, enemy action at sea was but a pale shadow of what it had been at the beginning. Most of our merchants ships, and those vital supplies, were getting through to Britain and I like to think that our Naval Boarding Service played a large part in that.

Jack McClelland
Toronto, Ontario

I HAVE no doubt at all that my involvement in the war had a major effect on the rest of my life. The merciful thing about war is that for young people like myself at that time, there was a fun side to counteract the tragedy of it all. In the part of the navy where I was, we had a hell of a lot of fun. We used to say if we're not killed it's a great way to live.

Today, 50 years later, I am the first to admit that war is not fun and games, because now, if my son went off to battle, I would not be at all happy with that kind of philosophy. I feel now that war is terribly tragic, especially for those on the home front where you really feel the losses of those who are killed or maimed.

Or again, if you consider the cases of nations like England and the other European countries that were involved physically, it's a devastating thing to have whole populations decimated and the countryside destroyed. As one matures, one can only come to the conclusion that war is the greatest tragedy that can befall mankind. One always keeps hoping that there won't be another major conflict like the last one.

My own navy days were relatively happy. I went in as an officer. I was one of the fortunate people who, after having graduated from Royal Roads after four months of hard, concentrated training in everything having to do with the navy, was in terrific shape both mentally and physically to do battle. I remember one day before graduating I was in a class, and the Gunnery Officer teaching us said that he had joined the Navy in 1937 and he had been training ever since.

"Here it is the spring of 1942," he said, "and I've never been appointed to a ship."

In a loud stage whisper, I said, "God, I hope I can say that after five years."

Well, I was joking of course, but he was not one bit amused.

"Who said that?" he asked.

Nobody answered.

"You said that, McClelland," he said.

"Yes, sir," I admitted.

"Well, I'll promise you one thing," he fumed, "when you leave here you will go straight to a ship. Don't ever joke about that again."

That's what all of us wanted, of course, but he saw my feeble attempt at a joke as an indication that I wasn't taking the war or anything else seriously, which wasn't true. No sooner had we finished our training than we were all aboard ships, and I sure as hell found out that there was indeed a war on.

I joined a Banghor minesweeper, the *Chetibuctou*, which was an escort vessel engaged in accompanying vessels from Halifax up to

Quebec City. I joined her in Gaspé when she came in to refuel. The next morning about 2:00, I was standing on the bridge as Second Officer of the watch when there was a great explosion in front of us and we found out that one of the convoy ships had been torpedoed. It was a hell of an introduction for me to what war was all about. Before that night was over, I think seven of our ships went down. It was a wild night, and at one point a German submarine surfaced right out there beside us. We had expected our captain to ram it but he didn't. Instead, he made a big circle around it and then came back in again, to avoid the sub's gunfire I guess.

That was my introduction to the real war and to think that it was happening in the waters right off our own coast. I just couldn't believe it. It was like stepping out of the classroom right into the hell of war. We thought it was a pack of submarines but we found out later it was just one sub that was able to do all that damage. There was great loss of life in that encounter and it was one of Canada's big tragedies of the war.

I spent a few more months in that posting and then volunteered to go to Newfoundland in a class of boat called Fairmiles. That was a tremendous experience too. We were based in St. John's and I was eventually given command of one of these small boats. They were about a hundred feet long, made of wood and they did about 17 knots. They were sub chasers, but they were not very good sea boats.

There was a lot of enemy activity around Newfoundland. The enemy subs came in fairly close to get a look at the convoy traffic, because a lot of ships would put into St. John's to refuel or for repairs before rejoining the convoy.

Detection of enemy submarines was always very difficult, because you never knew what was enemy action and what was fish activity, but we certainly had enough real action down there to make it exciting.

After a while there, the opportunity came for me to volunteer to go overseas and join one of two new Canadian motor torpedo boat flotillas in the U.K. This appealed to most of us, so I was one of a group of friends who volunteered together, and we set sail for England just after Christmas, 1943.

Life in an MTB flotilla was very exciting. We worked only at night and we were sitting ducks for German aircraft, but we felt we were really doing something. To try and avoid these enemy planes we would always leave the English coast just before dark and would work at night, and then leave for home again just before the sun rose the next morning. So it meant all night work, but extremely exciting night work.

My boat was what they called a D Class MTB, and was about 112 feet long; it had everything. It had four 1,500 horsepower Rolls Royce Merlin engines which gave us 6,000 horsepower and although these boats were wooden, they could really move. They would barrel along at a top speed of 32 or 34 knots with a crew of 35 aboard, and when we went into action we needed and used that speed. We had four torpedo tubes, all the latest automatic guns, the latest radar, and we carried everything from depth charges to torpedoes. They were very sophisticated and very fast boats.

We operated initially out of Dartmouth over to the Cherbourg area of the French coast, and later in the war, moved up to Great Yarmouth and worked out of there when most of the fighting was near the coast of Belgium.

This was in the early part of 1945, and the Allies were very well organized by that time. I remember one night, in one of the most frightening actions we ever had, we were attacked by two Polish destroyers. Now these were Allied ships. They were on our side, but we had failed to give them proper identification when we first encountered them. I can tell you it was a terrifying moment for us.

I can't think of anything more frightening than having a tribal class ship, like the *Athabaskan* for example, trying to sink you with their four-inch guns. These were Polish ships, of course, but they were in the same class as the *Athabaskan* or the *Iroquois*. Here they were racing after you at full speed with guns blazing, and you're trying to get the hell out of the way. You're yelling at them but they can't hear you, and the Senior Officer of our flotilla is the only one who could possibly talk to them by way of radio.

You see, when we first saw these ships they just loomed out of the night hell-bent on sinking us before our Commanding Officer could even get through to them with our code on his radio. Of course, at a time like that you don't remember codes or anything else. You just do whatever you can to save your skin. The C.O. knew the names of these two Polish ships and he kept yelling into his radio at them, "For Christ's sake, stop firing! We're friendly!" Of course, they wouldn't pay any attention to this, and finally, a British flotilla of MTBS, perhaps three miles away at that point, called up and identified us, and finally the Poles called off the action, but not before killing a few people in one of our boats.

Even though we worked only at night on the MTBS, there was never any wasted time during the day. The day, of course, was when we did our sleeping and it seemed that most of the rest of the time was used in cleaning up the ship and getting it ready to go again. That is not to say that we didn't use any and every opportunity we could find to mix with, and find out more about, the opposite sex and also to do as much drinking as we possibly could.

I remember when our group first went over on the *Île de France*, there was this young kid who was a midshipman in our group. This kid was especially gutsy and he was always game for anything. I remember saying to him, just to quiet him down a bit, that I had had this dream that he was going to "buy it" on his first night out in a motor boat. It was really just an attempt to tame this guy down and make him see the serious aspect of war.

Well, the others in our group started to take this thing up, and they kidded the youngster interminably about not having much time left, and it really affected the poor kid. The awful part of it is that what I had kidded him about is exactly what happened. He went out on a British boat, as we all did after we arrived, and he was killed his first night, his only night, on an MTB.

My most memorable experience in all my navy years was when I first got command of my own MTB. I picked up my new boat in Loch Fine in Scotland. From there, we were to go into Glasgow, into the harbour of Grenoch, to get our torpedoes and our ammunition. We had empty torpedo tubes and not one bullet on board the ship.

We had a hell of a time trying to get into the harbour at Grenoch in thick fog. We had to go through all the patrol vessels to get there and I was brand new in command. I was terrified. When we finally got through the harbour entrance the sun came out and it was a beautiful day. Everything was just fine when suddenly I saw this big ship coming out from the other end, and it was the bloody *Queen Mary*.

Well, it had been pounded into us that every chance we could get, we should give our crew exercise with our guns and all the other things on board. So, I thought that this would be the perfect opportunity to make a dummy attack on the *Queen Mary*.

I called everyone to action stations and with the whole crew on the alert, we started heading for the bow of the big ship. At that point, the lights started to flash from the bridge of the *Queen Mary* and the couple of guns she had at the bow and the stern swung around and were pointing at us. I said to one of the crewmen,

"What are they trying to tell us?"

"Sir," he said, "I think they're trying to tell us to — off."

I suddenly realized that we'd better do just that, and so we headed down to our berth. When we got there, a Royal Naval commander was waiting for me and he said, "You've got to come with me."

I followed him up to a large room where a group of senior officers from civil defence — the army, the navy, and the air force — were all sitting around waiting for me. There wasn't a friendly face in the lot.

The person in charge was Sir Dudley Pond, the Admiral commanding the western approaches. I got in there just shaking, because I knew what an ass I had been. I had frightened everybody, I had alerted everybody, and even the air force had come out and scrambled because of this stupid dummy attack I had organized.

I went through about half an hour of listening to various senior officers recounting what had happened as a result of my exploit. Sir Dudley finally said, "Now this is a very serious charge. I think by now you must realize that you have incurred His Majesty's displeasure, which means being booted out of the Navy in disgrace."

With that he dismissed everybody except me and when we were alone he said, "Don't be nervous. There's nothing to be frightened about. Would you like a cigarette?"

He just started talking to me in the friendliest manner. He asked about the Canadian navy and all sorts of things like that and then he said, "You know, the *Queen Mary* must have made a very tempting target."

I said, "Oh yes, sir, a very tempting target."

"And you wanted to drill your crew?" he said.

"Yes, sir," I replied.

"You know," he said, "I would have been tempted myself. Now don't you worry yourself anymore. You'll never hear another word about it. I'm going to dismiss all the charges. Good luck."

As you can imagine, there was no more grateful man in the whole navy than me at that particular moment, and no greater man than Sir Dudley in my eyes.

I stayed with the MTBs right up to the end of the European war, and then I volunteered to go to the Far East for the war against Japan but that was over before I could get there.

What effect did the war have on me? I'm sure all of us who served have often pondered this question. I think, for one thing, that we certainly gained some maturity from the experience. I learned how to make decisions.

One of the other things I took away from the war was the realization of how brief life really is and that one should make the best use of the time given to them. You also come away from a war like the one I was involved in, fully convinced that there never should be another war.

War is all waste and it's all tragedy. It benefits nobody, and I often think that in a more enlightened world of the future, armed services on both sides will just refuse to fight and kill each other.

Frank Curry
Aylmer, Quebec

WHILE THE war clouds were forming over Europe during the late 1930s, I was doing my growing up in Winnipeg totally captivated and fascinated by what was going on "over there." My ear was constantly tuned in to the news on the radio and whatever else I could catch, every Hitler speech and every word spoken by the politicians and commentators. My father was convinced that a lot of posturing was going on and that there would be no war, but I felt a terrible sense of approaching doom. I knew in my heart that war was coming and when it did, I was going to be a part of it.

I spent the next five and-a-half years of my young life as an ordinary seaman on the North Atlantic and, believe me, there was nothing at all romantic about it. My particular job was operating the ASDIC equipment aboard tiny corvettes, trying to locate the German U-boats that were out there trailing and tracking our convoys. There were 125 other shipmates, all Canadian, and we all did the same thing — we tried to survive the grim and unbelievable cold of the North Atlantic under the most primitive of conditions.

The one thing I did that my shipmates didn't do was to keep a diary of those years, something that was strictly against the rules. I hadn't planned on doing it, but it so happened that the day before I boarded my first ship in Montreal, I spotted a five-year diary in a book store on St. Catharine's Street and I said to myself, "Why not?" All through the war I pursued it faithfully, even though at times it was an awful struggle to keep it going and keep it hidden. Diaries and picture taking were strictly forbidden but I decided to take my chances, because I felt it would be important, to me anyway, after the war was over. So, I just kept on and was never caught. It has surely helped me remember the true nature of war. My diary is now in the National Archives in Ottawa where anyone can have a look at it if they choose.

The thing that comes through most strongly as I go through it is the vast gulf that existed between the ordinary seamen and the officer class. This is an old story really, and it's one that probably goes back as long as men have been going to sea. The other ranks have always been pretty critical of officers who live in a totally different world than they do. I guess what bugged most of us was the knowledge that all of us, men and officers alike, were all in the same game, striving for the same goals. We were supposed to be a team, and it didn't make sense that some members of that team should ever be in a position where they could treat others as if they be-

*A Canadian Motor Torpedo Boat (MTB) in action in the English
Channel, May 1944. (Courtesy the National Archives of
Canada)*

longed to a lower class of humanity. You have to be careful not to
generalize about something like this, because there were some
officers who were terrific, not only as leaders but as human beings as
well. About the others, it *is* possible to generalize; the majority
wanted to maintain that strict division between "them and us."
Being at sea was tough enough without having that kind of extra
stress.

I remember the time I went aboard ship for my first posting.
After all the training and all the expectations of what it was going to
be like to be a *bona fide* member of the navy, it turned out to be the
major disappointment of my life up to that time. It was a shattering
experience. Right off we ran into the real thing. I found out, all too
soon, that being at sea was no picnic, especially if you happened to be

on a small ship. You realize the mastery that the ocean has over all craft, not just the small ones.

This was not a romantic business. Right away, we started to encounter all the elements of life on the ocean waves — sea sickness, roughness, and being crowded in together like sardines. It struck us right away that our small ship was like a small chip of wood bouncing around on a vast expanse of wild and unpredictable water.

The corvettes, on which I spent the whole war, were, in a sense, marvellous ships for the job they were given to do, which was escorting convoys. They could stay out for long periods of time. They were built simply as covers around engines and large oil tanks. The rest of the space — whatever was left over — was where they crammed in the crew. The only living area you could call your own was wherever you slung your hammock, and that could be any-where, alongside a pipe or a boiler or a walkway. There weren't such things as cabins or sleeping quarters.

The real value of corvettes was that they could stay out for up to three weeks at a time with the convoys. On the negative side, they were much too small and they took a terrible battering. But then, they were very, very seaworthy. They seemed to be able to with-stand anything and remain afloat. I've see them with their bridges ripped away, masts snapped off and practically nothing left but the hull, but they still would not sink. This was their greatest value. They weren't extra fast — 16 or 17 knots was about as fast as they could go — but it was fast enough for the job they had to do, protecting convoys and keeping the submarines away. They were very manoeuvreable and reliable, but the down side for the crew was that we were all jammed inside.

Life aboard the corvettes was really awful. They were always half under water, the mess decks would be covered with a foot of water with things floating around. I think most of us kept asking ourselves how nice boys like us ever ended up in such a horrible situation. We were the innocents just like all people caught up in war.

The pressure got to us all in some way. I soon began to dread leaving port; taking on yet another convoy; facing another solo ASDIC watch; two hours on, four hours off, day and night; solely responsible for safeguarding the ship, my 125 shipmates, and the whole wing of the convoy. It sounds self-serving to say that everyone depended on my ability to fulfill my role, but there was nothing conceited about being deadly tired and deathly ill, vomiting and retching into a bucket wedged against the ASDIC set, and going on, 24 hours a day, three or more weeks into eternity. On the grim night watches, fully clothed and wrapped in my high slung hammock for four short hours of respite before the next watch, I was often unable to sleep for fear of the dreaded thump on my hammock from the quartermaster, warning me that I was due back on watch in 15 minutes. And then it all would begin again. I would slide out of the hammock to the steel deck, always awash with sea water. I'd still be bone-tired and half sick, clutching at the stanchions as the ship plunged and rolled, and I'd glance at the weary off-watch sailors wedged, fully clothed as I had been, onto the lockers or in their hammocks, with their lifejackets wrapped around them. Stretching out every precious moment away from the ASDIC, I would finally venture outside, to climb the narrow steps to the bridge, holding on for dear life as the seas crashed over the fo'c's'le. Then, I would have to force open the door of the wheelhouse and feel my way to the ASDIC set, as the quartermaster, barely visible in the gloom, would be fighting the wheel to keep on course despite the plunges of our tiny ship. If I were a moment late I'd be greeted by a muttered curse from the man I was relieving, the same way I'd greet a late relief myself. There'd be no conversation before he scurried below to his few hours in the hammock, leaving me to my own two endless hours of intense and nerve-wracking ASDIC operation.

That's the way it was, day after day, week after week, year after year, for me and 100,000 others who served below deck in the navy. I think those five years were not wasted though. The experience made me conscious of an awful lot of things. I came out of the navy more determined than ever to be a strong person. Maybe I was before I joined, but it certainly cleared my vision of things. I knew what I had to do with my life and how to go about doing it.

Before the war I never thought I'd get to university, because all of us who came out of the Depression had very little chance for that.

When the opportunity to get an education came up, late in the war, it settled my whole thinking as to what was going to happen to me when the war ended. Five-and-a-half-years had been cut out of the prime of our lives and that's not an easy thing to make up. Not for me. Not for anyone.

Eleanor Sinclair
Toronto, Ontario

I WAS LIVING in Toronto when I joined the navy, and like all new recruits I was sent down to Cornwallis, Nova Scotia for my basic training. It was a huge base with something like 10,000 people at any

The departure of Women's Royal Canadian Naval Service recruits from St. John's, Newfoundland, August 29, 1943. (Photo by Second Lieutenant J.D. Mahoney / DND / National Archives of Canada)

one time. It was such a beautiful area to be in, very reminiscent of a holiday retreat, but it was there that we green recruits were taught the rudiments of life in the services.

When I decided to join up I didn't really know which branch of the service I wanted to be in. My sister had joined the air force right after she finished high school and in 1943 the war was dragging on, so I felt it was time to do something. The WRENs were the last women's group to be formed, and just about that time there was a lot of publicity in the newspapers about them — pictures and so on — so I saw one of these ads with a big picture of a WREN in full uniform. That sold me; I liked the hat.

It was the navy's second attempt at making a uniform for women. The first was really dowdy — made of heavy navy blue serge with a pork pie hat. No self-respecting woman would join up to wear anything like that, so I guess they figured they'd better smarten up. They brought out a smart blue uniform with these little round berets which were much nicer and also little tricorn hats to be worn on special occasions.

Anyway, one day after I decided I liked the WREN's hat and uniform, I saw Liz Monroe, a childhood friend from up the street, and told her that I had just come from joining the navy at the Automotive Building at the CNE and she said, "Oh, I'm joining too. Wait for me. Get them to hold your call 'til I come."

Strange to say, when my call came through in October, and I asked them if they could wait until my friend got her call, they agreed. Can you imagine any government department doing something like that today? A couple of months later her call came through, and we entered the navy together, and we stayed together for the rest of the war.

We took our basic training at Galt, Ontario, in what used to be an old reform school. We were there for quite a few months, practically freezing to death in the winter. It was pretty grim. We had about two months of basic training, which was a lot more than other people got but I think that was because they didn't have any other place for us to go. Then we were shipped off to Cornwallis. For most of us, this was the first time away from home, so it was really quite an event.

When we got to Cornwallis, we split up and started to get training in the occupations for which we had applied. Mine was the supply branch, which was divided into three categories: vittling, which had to do with all the food supplies; clothing, which I ended up in; and naval stores which had to do with mechanical supplies and motors and that sort of thing.

When that training ended we were posted out to different places. I was posted to stay on at Cornwallis. The wireless telegraphers went to places like Ottawa, Shelbourne, Halifax and all over.

I remember the time the first "real sailors" arrived at our base. We had mostly recruits at Cornwallis, but these new fellows had just come back from service off the coast of North Africa. They had been dive-bombed by German Stukkas which used to come right in screaming over the deck with their machine-guns rattling away, and I guess it must have been awful for the sailors who were spread out on deck like sitting ducks. One of them told me they used to be given whole glasses of rum to more or less knock themselves out.

We were very impressed by these sailors — they had actually been to sea! They had a certain look of sophistication about them, and it was easy to pick them out of a crowd. The ones who had been to sea

WREN *June Whiting flashes a winning smile as she first arrives in Britain from Canada in April, 1945. (Photo courtesy the National Archives of Canada)*

had their collars in faded, washed-out blue, while new recruits wore shiny navy blue, and any braid they wore was always sparkling white. You could tell the seasoned guys too by the angle of their hats and the way they tied their tally-bands. The correct navy way was to tie a little bow at the side, but these fellows would come back from service at sea with the ends hanging like rabbit ears and the knot tied in a way that only true sailors knew how to do. It was their badge of experience.

I was happy at Cornwallis and I was there the whole time, from February, 1944 until the war ended, and the time came to let people go. The navy had a system of "First in, first out," so those who had been in the longest were declared redundant at their stations and given their discharges.

Since I had been in a relatively short time, I was far down the list for release so they started sending me around to different places to fill in for those who had been discharged. First, I was sent to Sydney, Cape Breton, and then to Moncton, New Brunswick.

There, having worked in clothing supplies for two years, I was expected to work as a vittler, something I hadn't done, except for a few weeks training two years before. I was required to order all the food for the approximately 75 people there. I thought I'd have a nervous breakdown, because I knew virtually nothing about it. The two weeks there seemed more like two years but, thankfully, I don't think anyone starved to death.

I was glad, I can tell you, to get my next and final posting to Halifax, where I was finally discharged in March, 1946, ten months after the war was over. My friend Liz had been able to get out long before this on compassionate grounds, so I didn't much like those long extra months wandering around in those strange places alone. Liz and I had been together the whole time of the war, so I felt as if someone had cut my right arm off when she left.

I absolutely loved my time in the navy. I really did. You know, we have had reunions every three years since the war, but I didn't go to the early ones because I felt that the time had not really arrived to hold a reunion. I think a great spread of years should go by before anyone talks of reunion, because it takes people who are a lot older to really appreciate what reunions are all about. When the time is right, though, there is nothing as good as a get-together of contemporaries, sharing jokes and memories and ignoring wrinkles — yours and everybody else's.

For me, those war years were good and satisfying. Some of the friends I made at that time are still among my best friends.

Malcolm Knox
Pointe Claire, Quebec

I WAS A commander of one of those Navy Motor Torpedo Boats, better known, I guess, as MTBs, which did such a tremendous job of keeping the supply lines open to Britain in the latter part of the war, especially after 1943. There were two flotillas of these Canadian MTBs, the 65th and the 29th, which operated in the English Channel.

Offensively, our job was to stalk the convoy lanes of Holland, Belgium, and France to intercept German coastal convoys. Then, because the German E-Boats were doing exactly the same thing down the coast of England, we were to intercept these E-Boats as they were coming to attack the U.K. convoys coming down with supplies for England. Most of them were colliers loaded with supplies of coal. It took 25 of these ships every day just to keep London in coal so that the power plants could keep going. The Germans' purpose was to send these colliers to the bottom.

The Royal Navy had some MTBs that needed to be manned and there were many Canadians serving with the RN who had served with great courage and dash. So it was, that the Canadian navy decided to man these two flotillas and protect the shipping in the Channel. We were all Canadians. The direct Canadian participation in this was from 1943 to the war's end and, of course, before we came in, all of the coastal forces were an integral part of the Royal Navy and they were in operation from the beginning of the war, doing the same kind of work.

There were nine of our MTBs in each of these two flotillas and I think you might say we did a respectable job. The majority of our

C.O.s received DSCs and, in fact, one of them is as decorated as any Canadian. He came up with three Distinguished Service Crosses and two Mentions.

One of the biggest problems was trying to authenticate your results. You'd fire your torpedoes or get into a gun action, and of course you didn't linger around to count the results because the enemy was hot on your trail, especially if you were over on their coast. Your first purpose was to get in and strike them, and then get away safely to live for another day.

We were able to sink quite a few ships of varying sizes and types. There were some coastal craft, opposition E-Boats, and other defensive craft of the German navy. All in all, we managed to get rid of a pretty large number of their boats.

When I talk about their E-Boats, I'm talking about the German counterparts of our MTBs. If you were talking about American boats, the counterparts would be the PT-Boats. The three of them are in the same class. There were two types, one that ran 70 feet long and the others were 110 feet. The smaller ones were manned with 20 men and the bigger ones with about 35.

Before the war, we were just a bunch of Canadian kids from farms and small towns and cities across the country, most of whom would never expect to move in our lifetimes more than a couple of hundred miles from the places we were born. And yet here we were overseas, on boats in the English Channel shooting big guns and trying to send German ships to the bottom. It was strange. The really odd thing was that in the Canadian navy we had such a big proportion of boys from central Canada and the Prairies. Aboard my craft, for example, the bulk of them came from the Prairie provinces and they made wonderful sailors. I don't know why this should have been so, but when you look way back into their beginnings, their forefathers had had the courage and fortitude to set out to make a life in a new land and I guess these lads, their descendants, had some of that same determination and intestinal fortitude. Perhaps a little bit of that original salt water was still flowing in their veins.

Those of us in the coastal forces, although part of the larger navy, always looked at ourselves as a little bit separate. We weren't a large group and we fit into a somewhat smaller niche, so as a result of that, the lot of us always felt very close to each other. We worked together, we stayed together, we played together and we were very interdependent. In our line of work, it was necessary to have complete co-operation and understanding of one another so that we could survive. The thing is, too, that you remain buddies for ever. Years can pass without seeing one another, but when you do you can just pick up where you left off.

It was a fairly dangerous line of work and there were many close calls for all of us. You know, when you're sitting on top of 5,000 gallons of 100 octane gasoline, and when you get through with a gun fight and find that there are marks of tracer bullets that have passed into that area but didn't cause an explosion, you know that your number wasn't called. In battle we were on the edge of our seats all the time. As they say, there are no atheists in the foxholes, and to paraphrase that, there were no atheists in the MTBs either.

The one I was in charge of was 100 feet long, carried four torpedoes and was powered by four Packard engines that developed 5,000 horsepower. It had two automatic six-pounder guns, one fore and one aft, twin oerlicons, and two twin point-5 turrets plus four 303s dual mounting. They travelled in the vicinity of, supposedly, close to 40 miles an hour, but as time went on and they loaded us down with more equipment and more ammunition, it slowed us down a bit.

As you can imagine, there were no eight-hour days on the MTBs. We would leave just before sunset to reach the other coast of the channel under cover of darkness, and then we would try to get away from there with time enough so that the German air force didn't catch you in mid-channel after the sun came up. Back on the coast of England, we would start right in to get the craft ready for another outing when the sun went down again. We'd catch a little sleep before that, of course. That was our drill all the time, and the only days we weren't out was when there were engine repairs to do, or when the weather didn't permit. If the seas were so high that you couldn't have a stable base for a torpedo attack, there was no point in heading over.

In numbers of craft, the Canadian navy was the third-largest navy in the world at the end of the war, and it did a wonderful job in winning the Second World War. It's rather a shame that it has been allowed to deteriorate the way it has since that time.

Brigadier General R.T. Bennett (Bob)
Stittsville, Ontario

WAR WAS still a few years off when my time as a career officer began in 1935 at the Royal Military College of Canada. Though we were not to know it then, my class was the last to experience — endure might be a more appropriate word — the full four years of the old regime at RMC that ended with our graduation in June, 1939, just in time, so to speak, for the Second World War. Truthfully, I cannot say that our four years of training had prepared us for the realities of modern warfare.

Having majored in Chemical Engineering at RMC, with the intention of joining the Canadian Arsenal in Quebec as an explosives officer, I had gained acceptance into McGill University for the final year of my degree, and was posted to military headquarters in Montreal just prior to the declaration of war. The war forced me to put these educational ambitions on hold.

Though a very junior member of the officer corps, good luck pushed me aboard a Polish ship, the *Chrobry*, in Halifax, and we sailed out of there for "overseas" at noon on 23 December, 1939, along with soldiers of the West Nova Scotia Regiment of the First Canadian Division. Luck continued to be my guide, for I discovered that my table companions for the trip across would be the first group of Canadian war correspondents assigned to cover the war. Famous names they were too, or at the very least, would become. They were: Aby Coo of the *Winnipeg Free Press*, Andy O'Brien of the *Montreal*

Standard, Greg Clark of the *Toronto Star* and Sam Robertson of the *Canadian Press* who, later on, in 1942, lost his life when his ship became just another victim of the Nazi submarines. I can truly say that my education for life, and for war, began during that memorable crossing of the Atlantic.

We were on the water heading for England on the second day of our voyage, Christmas Eve, when Lieutenant Colonel John Bullock, who was also an Anglican priest and the only priest ever to command a regiment, conducted a Eucharist service, which was attended by members of all faiths. Barely was the service over when we pitched into the middle of a major hurricane. Although our ship survived in fine style, I can't say the same for a lot of the men, most of whom had never been to sea before.

Attendance at the dinner table was noticeably down. I made it to the dining room, but was not in the mood for eating. As the soup before me sloshed around with the ship's wild motion, I could feel the colour of my face change from healthy pink to deathly white, a change that did not escape the attention of my dinner companions.

As I rose rather unsteadily from the table, Greg Clark asked, "What's up, young Bennett?"

I replied I was just going to my cabin to lie down for a while.

"No one leaves my Christmas dinner," was Greg's reply. "Come with me."

Meekly, I obeyed his command, and to my dismay found that he was leading the way to the bar where he ordered two double champagne cocktails from Stefan, the Polish bartender.

"Coming up, Mr Greg," said Stefan and, as if by magic, they appeared before us.

In fear and trepidation, I followed Greg's next command of "Bottoms up," and down she went. So far so good. Then I noticed that Greg hadn't drunk his cocktail.

"When are you going to have yours, Greg?" I asked.

"That's not mine," he said. "That one's for you too. Bottoms up."

Again I followed orders, and to my utter amazement it stayed down and my stomach suddenly levelled out. That done, Greg led me back to our table and one of the most memorable Christmas dinners I've ever had.

Greg confessed afterwards that he had cured many others the same way.

Our destination, once across the Atlantic, was Aldershot, England, where we arrived at 7:00 in the morning of New Year's Day, 1940. The fog was so thick at North Camp station that you felt it could be eaten with a spoon. It was our welcome to Great Britain and one of the worst winters on record.

To match the weather, our life in barracks there was equally grim, cold and miserable until spring finally arrived, but my first English spring more than made up for the horrible winter and my memories of the damp and cold of the last few months were soon largely forgotten.

With the daffodils blooming and the bluebirds singing, it wasn't long before I was attached to a Canadian unit whose Commanding Officer was one of those who had been resurrected from the earlier war. He was a proud Scot whose favourite memory of World War One was having met the legendary Scottish entertainer, Harry Lauder, during the trench warfare period in France and Belgium when Harry was there to entertain the troops. When Lauder came to Aldershot that spring of 1940, the C.O. couldn't wait to have him in for lunch in the officer's quarters.

Without a doubt, when this living legend arrived, fully-kilted with sporran and black thorn cane, it created the same kind of attention and excitement as would a visit by the King and Queen.

During a truly entertaining lunch, when one of us commented favourably on the tartan tie he was wearing, Sir Harry said in his splendid accent, "Ye like it laddie? Then here it is."

With that he removed it from his neck, and handed it to a very embarrassed young subaltern with the words, "Ever since I've had a penny in my pocket laddie, when someone admires what I have, I give it to him. . . . with some exceptions, of course."

Sir Harry was undoubtedly a character of the first order, but characters are not restricted to the celebrity. That first year in

England, I was assigned a driver who would prove to be as much a character as any I ever met. Before he entered the army, John was a potato farmer from New Brunswick who was anything but the perfect model of a soldier. He was, though, a great and reliable driver, always amusing and very kind of heart, even though sometimes lacking in moral principles.

One could never describe John as having a head full of brains, but he more than made up for this by having more than a mouthful of teeth that would have created a nightmare for any dentist, if John would ever let a dentist get near him.

I tried, along with our outstanding dentist, Captain Ross Stewart, to inveigle John into the clinic, with no success, because John knew full well that I could not order him to do so. Because he rated the Dental Officer a step below any normal butcher, all my blandishments were repulsed with a knowing and triumphant grin, exposing his brown and gnarled choppers which looked as though they would interlock and close his gaping mouth forever.

One soft spring morning, with my thoughts a million miles away, John, from behind the wheel of the car, broke my reverie with, "Look sir. What do you think of this?"

He turned round, grinning his widest grin, to expose every crooked tooth in his maw but, lo and behold, the sun was glinting off the many planes of the whitest teeth I had ever seen. When I congratulated him on finally taking advantage of the dentist's offer he said, "No sir. This was none of the butcher's doing at all." He went on to explain, "You know that powder that the Barrack Stores issue to clean the toilets and tubs? Well, I used it this morning and it works like a charm. My gums are a little tender but you have to admit, the teeth are as white as snow."

They were. White as pearls, but still as crooked as a mountain path.

John was with me until late 1942 when I was sent back to Canada to attend the Staff College in Kingston. Upon returning to England ten months later, I received a promotion to the exalted rank of Lieutenant Colonel, making me at 25, the youngest of that rank in the Canadian Army. John was no longer at the same location but anyway, I was posted to serve for a while at the headquarters of our First Canadian Army under General Crerar whom I had known when he was the Commandant of Royal Military College while I was a cadet there.

While I was serving in England with Crerar, the famous General Montgomery returned triumphant from commanding his legendary Eighth Army in Africa, to assume his new responsibilities relevant to D-Day. Very shortly after his arrival, as was his wont, he assembled all senior officers for one of his famous "talks."

Immediately upon mounting the stage he voiced his well-known dictum, "There will be no smoking." This was followed by the injunction that there would be, "One minute for coughing. Then no one will cough again!" As this was late winter, the hacking that ensued was genuine and essential but such was the great man's influence that thereafter, although there were many suppressed convulsions, there was not one full-fledged, genuine cough.

Monty's successor at Eighth Army was his complete antithesis in physique and manner. Sir Oliver Leese was a great bear of a man, ebullient and always seemingly ready to burst out laughing which, when he did, came out in huge, honking sounds. He was nicknamed "the snorter" by the irreverent Canadians. Until he was transferred to Mountbatten's Supreme Command in Burma, he never seemed to tire of visiting "those colonial Canucks" and watching them play "their national sport of rounders." That's what he interpreted softball to be.

As the momentum of the war was gathering speed in March, 1944, and the unknown date of D-Day was approaching, a vacancy occurred in the fifth Canadian Armoured Division in Italy. I was delighted to be posted to fill that gap, and it was soon after that the spring offensive which cracked the vaunted Hitler Line erupted, and our tanks and troops were fanning out towards Rome bent on the liberation of the Eternal City. It was a time of hard battles and dreams of glory for an exhausted and weary Canadian army. The victory came, but not the expected public acclaim, because the greater event — the D-Day landings on June 6 — completely overshadowed everything else in the war. Glory is always a fickle mistress whose roving eye quickly finds ever greater glory.

It was during this time that John and I met again — on a dusty track in central Italy. There on the roadside leaning alongside a Salvation Army van, enjoying a fag in a most unmilitary position, was the unmistakably unkempt John. Our mutual surprise was only surpassed by our obvious delight at seeing each other again. He too had received a promotion, he told me, sheepishly displaying the two "hooks" of a Corporal. When I left for Canada, he said, he was a bit at loose ends until he discovered that the Auxiliary Services were looking for drivers for their teawagons. He figured this would be a good job for someone like himself who had a skill for making an extra dollar on the side. He figured he could do this by distributing such black market bounty as tea, chocolate bars, cigarettes and the like.

As though to prove his point, John pulled out several big rolls of Italian lira notes and showed them to me with pride. When I remonstrated that, surely, he couldn't have stooped to selling his merchandise to his own troops at inflated prices, he denied such actions with injured pride. "I couldn't do a thing like that sir. Never." Then he explained that as he slaked the soldier's thirst with mugs of hot Salvation Army tea, he would dry the dregs from the pot in the hot Italian sun, package the leaves in attractive tin foil wrappings and flog them to the poor peasants. As I say, John had a strange sense of morality.

He had another scheme going too, he told me. At that time, you could get vacuum-packed tins containing 50 cigarettes. John said he had unlimited supplies of these Salvation Army gifts for distribution to the troops. He'd open them up, take out the cigarettes, fill the empty space with sand to provide weight and then cut off about a half inch from each cigarette before giving them to the soldiers who didn't seem to notice or care that these free cigarettes from Sally Ann were shorter than usual. The short butts he would sell to peasants, packaging them back in the cans with the sand in such a way that they could only see the bottoms and had no way of knowing how long (or how short) the cigarettes were.

Fortunately for John, he was never very long in any one place because, as the troops rapidly advanced upwards toward Rome, he advanced just as rapidly, out of the reach of the angry peasants.

Good thing for him too. I'm told that the Italian peasantry had special methods for dealing with con men who lacked a conscience.

That was my last encounter with John, but I have little doubt that somewhere in that vast expanse of New Brunswick there is an old veteran of the Second World War figuring out new ways of turning a dishonest buck.

I've often pondered the fact that when old soldiers get together they can regale each other for hours with stories from their years at war. The interesting thing about this is, that I can never recall hearing any that were not humorous, entertaining or, at the very least, amusing. The sad or unpleasant are long forgotten or suppressed in the farthest reaches of memory. It must be some form of defensive mechanism that protects one from the dark and evil of mankind.

William N. Anderson
Toronto, Ontario

EVERY YEAR when Remembrance Day rolls around, I go back almost half a century to my days in the Second World War.

Many people will recall a tiny freighter called the SS *Bayanu* which operated before the war started. She carried bananas between the West Indies (as they were called then), and the rest of the world. I never knew her in those halcyon days but I got to know her intimately in November, 1943.

November 11, 1943 was one of the nearly 19 days she took to cross from Halifax, Nova Scotia, to Avonmouth in England. My recollection of the trip is mostly of the company provided by ten nursing sisters who were part of the entire troop complement of 90 officers. It was a trip of endless bridge games, five meals a day, and the coatless comfort of a sea voyage to Europe via the Azores.

On that particular morning, we watched two biplanes take to the air, drift off to the east, and then return to their aircraft carrier below. The first cruised over the carrier and I waited to see her turn to the wind. This done, she landed, braked and cleared the deck for her wingmate coming in behind. The pilot of the second plane made his pass and circled. The aircraft carrier corrected her heading to meet the seas, and the pilot lined up the tiny deck in preparation for his landing. He made his approach and in the split-second before his touchdown, his bow went down in a wave trough and the ship's stern came up directly into his flight path and he hit it head-on. The plane fell back into the sea like a broken toy.

As we watched in horror, helpless and spell-bound, the carrier captain ordered full power and drove the ship away as fast as he could before the depth charge, which had jarred loose from the wrecked plane's belly, reached its exploding depth. When the explosion did come, the resultant column of water threw the aircraft and the hapless pilot skyward. It was the end for the pilot and his machine.

In little more than an instant, our idyllic cruise to Europe became a real and frightening experience.

Travellers aboard this noble ship, and there are many of us still around from those days, will remember the craggy, bald skipper for his British sailor demeanour and his bright, all-seeing eyes. The ten nursing sisters in our group will recall that those bright eyes never missed an obvious charm, and some that were not so obvious.

His cabin was very much the model of the ship shape quarters of a wartime carrier. The desk, chair and bunk were made of well-polished teak, and the desk top was immaculate, with just one ornament to complement the blotting pad and pencil. This was a sterling silver cigarette box engraved with the ship's name. It was a beautiful piece, and just as an aside to the story, I saw this artifact once again, many, many years after the war ended and the *Bayano* was just a memory.

I was taking a noon hour walk on Toronto's Bloor Street, and I slipped inside The Olde Gold Shoppe to do a little browsing. This was about twenty years after the war. To my astonishment, there it was — the captain's cigarette box tucked away in a dark corner of the store. It was the same box all right, with SS *Bayano* engraved into the surface.

The clerk told me that it would be a beautiful piece once they removed the engraving.

"No thanks," I said, "Just wrap it up the way it is." For 35 dollars I

walked out with my precious wartime memory, although I do remember thinking at the time that thirty-five dollars was quite a lot to
pay for an old cigarette box, even if it was sterling silver.

The funny thing is, that within a week of first seeing that box in
the store and buying it, I started bumping into people who had
made that crossing in the *Bayano* with me — four of them in all.
That's more than I have ever met anywhere since the war ended.
Other people too, who crossed the ocean during those years on that
same old ship keep popping up all the time.

PART 8

HOLIDAYS AND LEAVES

Bill Warshick
St. Catharines, Ontario

ON THE LAST day of December, 1944, I was in Boulogne getting
ready to cross the Channel the next day with the first batch of troops
to get leave from the Continent. This leave came about as the result
of a promise that General Montgomery made shortly after D-Day.
He said that things were going so well in the Normandy operations
that some of our troops would be able to take a New Year's leave in
the U.K., and the first to get that leave would be those who landed
on D-Day. That included several British divisions and two
Canadian.

Now this was a big deal, as you might imagine; the very first
troops to go on leave from the Continent to the U.K. was kind of a
signal to the world that we could start breathing a little easier, and
that the war must be winding down.

Well, we sure didn't expect a reception like that awaiting us at the
Oosterwijk railway station. The place was alive with scores of news-
men and photographers, and the official photographers were men
from my own outfit, the Signals.

The train arrived in London's Victoria station about 7 P.M. on
New Year's Day. To keep Monty's promise, every passenger train in
the U.K. had been stopped to ensure that our train had a clear path
all the way.

The station was packed to the rafters with cheering people, and

311

*When these soldiers were granted a rotation leave in December,
1944, the war was winding down and would, in fact, be over in
less than five months. Their moustaches were just added treats
for their wives! (Courtesy the National Archives of Canada)*

we were the stars of the moment. We received the kind of treatment
normally reserved for the Royal Family. A couple of majors from
Canadian Military Headquarters in London were there to carry our
bags to wherever we wanted to go. They got off easy on that one
though, because all we wanted was food, and we let them go when
we reached the nearest buffet.

That sort of started a trend for the war weary troops of Europe.
Thereafter, a trainload of personnel came back on leave every day.
It was lovely to get a respite in dear old Blimey but oh my, it was hard
to go back to the front after that.

Jack MacBeth
Victoria, British Columbia

THAT WAR, like all wars, was fought mainly by the young people of the world, by youngsters really, under the direction of others who were only slightly older. Controlling the natural exuberance and fun-seeking nature of youth, and redirecting it to the serious business of war, was no easy task for those who found themselves "in charge."

Aside from the main conflict — the war with Hitler — there existed in all the services other small wars between youth and authority. It was a constant search for ways to beat the system and not get caught doing it. I was part of that small war too. For example, come back with me to December 31, 1943.

Canadians call it New Year's Eve and the Scots call it Hogmanay, but whatever you choose to call it, it's a night for celebration. That particular New Year's Eve, I, along with all the other members of Royal Canadian Naval Beach "W" Commando, began celebrating early at our training base at Loch Long in Scotland, which was called HMS Armadillo.

There were 84 of us there, 72 men and 12 officers, and most of us had been given a two-day leave for a holiday present. Well, by 8:00 that night the smart ones had caught the last ferry over the Clyde to Greenock and were on their way to a big night on the town in Glasgow.

Two others, who were not quite so smart, Sub-Lieutenant Forrest Angus of the RCNVR and one other young lieutenant, me, stayed behind enjoying ourselves at the wardroom bar. There, we were joined by a young British sub-lieutenant, George Mortimore, who was attached to one of the Royal Navy commando groups who were also training there.

By about 10 P.M. the three of us were all getting pretty tired of each other's company, so we decided that the time had come to head for Glasgow too. The only question was how? There were no more ferries, which we called "duty drifters," to take us across the river, and if you couldn't get across the Clyde, you simply couldn't get to good old Glasgow town. At that point, someone came up with an absolutely brilliant idea. Why not "borrow" one of the LCMs, those small landing craft that we regularly used for commando assault exercises? There they were, anchored just offshore, practically begging us to use one of their number as personal taxi. After all, we were the perfect crew. Mortimore had been a cox'n aboard such a craft in the Mediterranean, Angus knew all about diesel engines and I was a specialist navigator. What an ideal crew!

It was raining steadily, and a cold winter wind was whistling down from the surrounding highlands as our adventurous trio quietly stole down to the rocky beach a few hundred yards from the Officer's Mess. On the shoreline, as if waiting just for us, we found a dory to take us out to the nearest LCM.

In no time at all, Angus had the engine going, Mortimore was at the wheel, the mooring line was slipped and off we chugged. On the way across the Clyde, good souls that we were, we stopped alongside a couple of anchored merchant ships and took aboard some additional passengers who were absolutely elated at this unexpected but splendid opportunity to go ashore and see the New Year in. One of these fine fellows was good enough to present the LCM crew with a bottle of fine Scotch whisky in appreciation of our kindness. It was a gift we heartily welcomed but definitely did not need.

What happened ashore that night in Glasgow will remain forever blurred in our collective minds, but two days later, when our sorry-looking trio returned to the Armadillo base, there came the rude awakening. All three of us were promptly arrested and charged with participating "in the unlawful sailing of His Majesty's Landing Craft (Mechanized) No. 998."

At the subsequent disciplinary court, Sub-Lieutenants Angus and Mortimore pleaded not guilty and were defended by "prisoner's friends," which is military lingo for navy lawyers. I chose to plead guilty and throw myself on the mercy of the court, using as a defence the argument that, instead of being censured for their actions, all three officers should be commended "for their eagerness and enterprise in using their own time to advance their experience and expertise" in the handling of a landing craft.

The British court did not think that was very funny. As punishment, I was docked six months' seniority with a severe reprimand and a caution. In addition to all of this, I was "required on board" (i.e., no leave) for a period of two weeks. On the other hand, with their navy lawyers, Angus and Mortimore were acquitted.

Oh well. It seemed like a good idea at the time.

Les Hollington
Toronto, Ontario

IT SOMETIMES goes unremembered, or maybe it wasn't even known at all, that not all Canadian troops were stationed over in the battle zones of Europe during the Second World War. I, for one, spent most of the war in India and my experiences would be totally different than those of the boys who did their fighting on the continent. It was a different kind of war. We had all the nasty things of the European war, but we also had scorching heat and sand to contend with, not to mention long periods of absolute boredom and the feeling that you had been detached from everything you were familiar with and had been sent to the end of the earth.

At one point, I was involved in a very nasty accident that almost ended my life. We were a motorcycle corps out on patrol that day, speeding along pretty fast, when all of a sudden everything went black. When I woke up in hospital, I learned that I had been involved in a head-on crash and got busted up pretty badly. A young friend named Mostyn Williams can probably be credited with saving my life. He stayed behind with me while the rest of our group had to carry on. I'll always be grateful to him for that. Despite some pretty serious injuries, I was out of the hospital and back on my motorcycle inside of three weeks.

In December, 1942, our group was feeling pretty bushed. We had had no leave for a long time, but at long last we were assured that we would get some soon. There were five of us reporting back to H.Q. Eastern Army (later renamed 14th Army) at Blackmore, outside Calcutta, after detachment to another unit. Because of this and other detachments, we were the last without leave in our parent unit since leaving Blighty in 1941. Now at last it would be granted. You can imagine how we were looking forward to that holiday, but only death and taxes are certainties in this world. There was to be a small delay, we were told. Our names were posted and we had to report to H.Q. 15 Corps at Chittagong right away. What a rotten turn of events.

After some delays, we arrived at Chittagong, where we met the C.O. who seemed to know all about us and told us that he sympathized with our plight and that he was granting us our overdue leave plus travelling time right away.

Well now! That's more like it. We were on track again and all we had to do was make up our minds about how we would like to spend this much-looked-forward-to leave. Lovely Kashmir, with its beautiful climate, lakes, houseboats and much else, was very hard to resist but this fortnight would include Christmas, and as Canadians, we thought we should have something that offered a bit of snow. So where do you find snow in India? Darjeeling, of course, with its 8,000 feet and more of elevation. The possibilities of a white Christmas looked pretty good.

We had lots of the usual train and boat passes to get there, but being members of the Royal Signals and veterans of many detachments with a lot of consequent travelling, we knew our way around pretty well. Scorning the passes, we hitchhiked a ride with the RAF from Chittagong to Dumdum, the airfield for Calcutta, thus saving ourselves two days. We did a bit of shopping there, so that our clothes would look new and clean, and besides, we were tired of the look of battle green. We were to find out later though, that the tropics had taken their toll on our strength, and we would have been better off in the cooler climes with our warmer army clothing.

The long train ride north from Calcutta was only fairly interesting, but on reaching the terminus at Silygury and transferring to the wonderful, unique, Darjeeling Highland Railway, we all felt that we

Les Hollington (left) *and Mostyn Williams pose after Williams picked up Hollington after a motorcycle crash. (Courtesy Les Hollington)*

were truly beginning a memorable Christmas with absolutely new experiences, in total contrast to what we had been through.

This fantastic British-built railway and rolling stock climbs 8,000 feet in less than 40 miles, which is a world record for the kind of smooth rails we were travelling on. It accomplishes this by many loops and spirals and by zig-zagging up the steep slopes of the Himalayas. It's not without consequences though, as many of the passengers suffered from motion sickness, especially on the downward run. Also one's ears tended to "pop."

Arriving at Darjeeling, hemmed in by the loveliest and highest mountains in the world, we were met by girl porters, good looking and very strong. They just grabbed hold of our bags, and strode off as it were nothing, leaving us to struggle after them up the steep slopes to the home where we were to spend Christmas.

Leaflets dropped by air, on Japanese occupied Burma

ဗြိတိသျှအစိုးရ၏ကြေငြာချက်

Declaration by the Secretary of State for Burma

H.M.G. appreciate the difficulties of the situation facing the
civilian population of Burma
while it is temporarily overrun
by the Japanese. The British
and their Allies well understand
that some pretence of co-operation
with the enemy in civil matters
may be necessary to safeguard
the lives of citizens. Britain will
return to Burma; when she does
it will be in no spirit of vengeance
against those civilians who have
been forced by events beyond
their control to conceal for a time
their loyalty to the cause of the
United Nations provided they
have not deliberately assisted the
enemy's war effort or taken part
in injuring or persecuting British
or Allied prisoners or interned
civilians or minority communities
of British or Allied nationals.

A leaflet dropped over Japanese-occupied Burma, found in December, 1942. (Courtesy Les Hollington)

The lady of the house was a Norwegian whose husband was English and the flag of Norway fluttered on the flagpole, but as it turned out, we all enjoyed a wonderful English-style Christmas with them, complete with all the trimmings. It was the same in all the other homes they took us to visit, which were complete with traditional decorations and many children, who made us realize how much we had missed our own.

Private clubs are a main ingredient of all white settlements in India and Burma, and this place high in the Himalayas was no exception. The Gymkhana Club had tennis, other outdoor sports and roller skating, which suited me just fine, and a lovely ballroom with a well-sprung floor. I was in heaven! I had been a dancing fiend for years and was more than pleased with the high quality of the dancing and the equally high standard of the music.

One of my dancing partners was a delightful woman in her twenties from Eastbourne, Sussex. She had been in India for years and her husband was manager of a nearby tea plantation. He was in the forces, of course, but at the moment he was home on leave. They, like a lot of the other people there, had come to the dance on horseback, which was the only way to travel, except of course by foot, which wasn't really practical as they lived many miles and 1,300 feet higher up the mountain. They invited us to visit them and we gladly jumped at the invitation.

Well, it was easier to accept, as we found out, than to get there. We walked and we crawled and we slid our way to their place, but it was worth it. We were waited on by many servants, fed and wined and dined in the most sumptuous manner, and treated to some wonderful tennis. This was followed by music, both recorded and live, from the lady of the house, who played well on a small grand piano.

One can only begin to imagine the treat all of this was for a group of culture and pleasure-starved soldiers who had been living more like animals than human beings since our arrival in this part of the world. However, it was wartime and one also learns to live for the moment. Too soon we would be back where the war demanded, and all of this would be like a dream. In fact, as I look back, almost 50 years later, it seems more like a dream than ever. But I can assure you it wasn't a dream. It was the real thing — the only good thing I can remember about that whole time in India.

John Hider
Brantford, Ontario

NOTHING brings back the days of the Second World War for me more than music; not the monuments, not the movies, not the marches by the veterans. When I hear the songs that were popular at that time, the places and the people are all with me again. When I hear the first few notes or the first few words of a piece like Glen Miller's "In the Mood," for example, it's just as if someone turned on a videotape. All of the sights and sounds of the war are there before my eyes.

As the war was in its closing stages, I had the good fortune to spend some of those months of 1945 at the King's expense not far from Victoria, British Columbia. Since we were waiting to join a newly-built ship, we had little to do, and in the meantime, we were based at H.M.C.S. *Naden*. Thanks to many of the lovely Victoria girls, my other navy pals and I were frequently able to dance our feet down to our ankles at the Empress Gardens. The song, "There, I've Said It Again," was high among the top ten. Whenever I hear it, Victoria, the Empress Gardens and those lovely girls are with me once more.

I have to laugh now at the puritanical British Columbia government of the time which didn't allow any alcoholic beverages to be served, but they knew, and everybody else knew that under each table was an extra shelf where the bottles could be hidden in a brown paper bag or in the purses carried by the girls. The only visible form of beverage was the array of soft drinks on the table tops. I must admit though, that I cannot recall anybody ever being caught. Actually, when I think about it, there was not an awful lot of drinking being done, because those lovely girls were more interested in being twirled around the floor from first to last dance, and there were lots of us willing and ready Fred Astaires.

Unfortunately, that lovely spell of the war had to come to an end as V-J Day occurred, and the war itself came to an end. It was the end of the ships and the end of a way of life for a lot of young fellows like myself for whom the navy had been everything for quite a while.

M. Janega
Westport, Ontario

I CAME over to Canada from Czecholovakia the year before the war broke out. My father had a job at the steel plant in Sydney, Cape Breton, and before long I was working too, as a mechanic. The Depression was still on, but before the year was up, I was better off than I could ever have been back home in Europe. I had my very first pair of skates and my very first bicycle, and, thanks to my parents, a better home to live in than ever before.

I was madly in love with my new country by the time the war started, and I couldn't wait to get into the fight against Hitler. I enrolled at flying school out at the Sydney airport, which wasn't much more than a large field with a few buildings and small planes, but it was doing a good job of turning out airmen under the British Commonwealth Training Plan. It was there I took my first training with the air force as a student pilot, and in 1942 I was sent overseas.

For the next two years, life was very exciting as the war heated up and it was just one mission after another, it seemed, with hardly a day off. So, you can imagine how thrilled I was one day in Scotland in 1944, to find myself in possession of that rarity, a four-day pass. This meant that I could do anything I wanted to do for a period of 96 hours.

There were many things that I had dreamed of doing if ever the opportunity presented itself, and some of those dreams were pretty exotic, but a four-day pass wouldn't even get me started on those. I don't know why, but I had a sudden yearning to see London. I had been to London a few times on short visits but I never saw enough of this great city to satisfy me, so, I decided, London it would be.

Off I went on the Flying Scotsman, return train ticket in my back pocket, and enough money to have some fun in London before making my way back to Edinburgh.

After checking into one of the many cheap rooming houses in the city, I was given a pillow and two blankets and assigned a fourth floor room that, by the way, didn't have windows. That didn't matter. Before long I was sound asleep and I stayed solidly that way until the following morning.

When I came down to the lobby, to return my pillow and blankets and have some breakfast, everyone seemed surprised to see me. I was supposed to be dead, they said. There had been a bad air raid in the district the night before, and the rooming house suffered severe damage. A lot of people had been killed in our building and up to this point they had assumed that I was one of the victims. I just snored my way through the whole thing and never even heard a sound. The building was very badly damaged, especially up on the fourth floor where my room was, and so, they hadn't been expecting to see me anymore. I didn't mention that in the air force I had become quite accustomed to loud noises.

The thing that most concerned me at this point was finding a Catholic church. Sunday morning, after all, was Mass time.

After crossing over several bridges and tramping through miles of streets, I finally spotted one. There was the cross and there was the steeple.

The only problem was that the church, a very large one to be sure, was surrounded by barricades which made it very difficult to get inside. But I was determined. Barricades were not going to deter me from my Sunday morning meeting with God. Wearing my very best blues and my air force wings, I jumped over the barricades and bounded up the steps to the church.

It was a relief to find that the doors were open and I could just walk in. Yes, it was a church like any other church I knew despite its immense size. The altar was exactly where I expected it to be, as were the pulpit and pews. No doubt about it. This was a Catholic church.

Walking down the centre aisle, I stopped, genuflected and slipped into a pew. Kneeling on the bare floor, I averted my eyes and devoutly began to pray. Very shortly, I could hear footsteps coming up the aisle and stopping beside my pew. I looked up and gazed into the eyes of a tall, grey-haired man who was smiling at me. He put his arm around my shoulder and in a very kindly voice he whispered, "It's a Roman Catholic church you want, isn't it, son?"

I replied in the affirmative, and he said, "I thought so. This is an Anglican church, my son, but you are perfectly welcome to worship here if you wish."

"How did you know I was Catholic?" I asked.

"That wasn't a bit hard," he said, "Catholics have an uneasy look about them in strange churches. You had the look."

He laughed at that and so did I. Then he told me that it would be perfectly all right to finish my prayers and that the Lord would listen.

"When you're all finished, come see me at the back and I will show you around."

Sure enough, when I was all through there he was waiting for me. Speaking in whispers, he asked me to go along with him and to tread as gently as possible, being sure to make no noise at all. I thought that this must be a very special kind of holy place where even the sound of the human voice would somehow desecrate the sanctity of it all.

"It's your first time here, I gather," said the man in black.

"Yes it is, sir," I replied.

"Well then," he said, "let's go up these stairs and I'll show you around."

As we walked, we kept talking quietly about where I was stationed and what my job was and so on. And then I became aware that I could hear my own voice coming out of the air right back at me. My voice and that of my tall, grey-haired companion.

"Don't be alarmed," he said, "What you're hearing is the famous

St. Paul's echo." Until that moment I didn't realize that the little Catholic church I was searching for was the famed St. Paul's Cathedral.

When I got over the shock of all this, my companion led me under the pulpit, halfway to the altar, to a side door which was partially jammed opened because of bomb damage. As we slipped through to the outside, he asked me to look up at the large tree which was just in back of the church.

My heart missed a beat when I saw what was hanging in the branches. There, dangling only by a parachute cord was a huge German block buster bomb, and above it to the right, another smaller one of two or three hundred pounds, also hanging by a few cords. It was then I realized the necessity for soft speech and quiet footsteps. Even the slightest noise held the possibility of setting those things off. I said to myself, "It must have been another Slovak Catholic who made those cords just so I could go on for another while saying my prayers." At that point I started praying again, that these bombs would be disarmed successfully without the loss of human life.

Later, after I left London for my return trip to the base at Edinburgh, I heard that a German expert had been brought in from one of the prison camps and both bombs had been safely defused. I also heard that not long before I had chanced upon St. Paul's, a children's hospital just across the street had been destroyed by bombs. It's extremely hard to understand war and, for that matter, those who wage it.

PART 9
LOVE AND WAR

Eileen Topham
Brighton, Ontario

WE HAD been married only a few weeks when my husband Bill was
called away to service in the RCAF. After six months of training, he
was posted to the Bombing and Gunnery School at Dafoe, Saskatchewan. This small station was located about midway between the two
small towns of Dafoe and Watson. Each of them was 12 miles from
our station. It was a remote and lonely location, but the school was
put there because of the open space and the proximity to Quill Lake
— an alkali body of water that was ideal for bombing and gunnery
practice for the students.

Bill and the other airmen never knew when they might be posted
overseas, so many of the wives, me included, followed their husbands to this isolated base in order to be with them as long as
possible. It was no picnic.

The station had no accommodation whatsoever for families, with
the result that a collection of old granaries, garages and shacks
started to appear from out of nowhere directly across the road from
the station gate. These were soon joined by a couple of grocery
stores, a drug store and a restaurant. Boomtown, Saskatchewan, was
on the move and by the time I arrived, there were about 150 shanties
and a population of 400 wholly made up of young couples and
children.

As husbands were posted out to other locations or overseas,
families moved on, and the shanties were rented that same day to

someone else on the long waiting list. As always happens in situations of severe shortage, rents rose to exorbitant levels until finally the Wartime Prices and Trade Board stepped in and reduced them by an average of forty-five percent.

I couldn't quite believe it when I first saw that little shack that was to be our new abode. It was a converted grain barn measuring 12 by 16 feet with a partition straight down the middle. One half was kitchen, dining room and living room and the other half housed a double bed and a chest of drawers. That was it.

In the living area there was an old cook stove, a couch and a drop leaf table with chairs. There was no electricity or water or inside plumbing of any kind. The biffy was outdoors, and all garbage had to be burned or buried. Water had to be purchased at five cents a pail from a local farmer whose truck came around twice a week. In between, we collected rain water or melted snow in the winter. For those who like to keep statistics, it takes one big laundry boiler filled with snow to make a half-pail of water. All water, of course, had to be heated on the wood stove and the laundry had to be done by hand. I was a city girl learning about the other side of service life the hard way.

How we would have managed without the local farmers I don't know. Every day, unpasteurized milk, butter and eggs were delivered to our door and in the summertime, because there was no refrigeration, these dairy products had to be kept in a hole that was dug out under the floor.

The shack had only one door to the outside and by anyone's minimum standards, it was a fire trap. To make matters worse, there were only a couple of small windows, one of them in the bedroom. As a precaution, we kept an axe in the bedroom in case we ever had to chop our way to the outside.

The first winter was a bit grim. Several times my face was frost bitten when the temperature dropped to minus 52°F. It was no wonder then that any fruit and vegetables had to be wrapped up in blankets or coats to keep them from freezing.

When the farmer delivered the milk in wintertime in his horse-drawn sleigh, he would be all wrapped up in a buffalo coat and fur hat and his eyebrows would be white with frost.

The second winter was a bit better as the landlord in his generosity came around and added a second layer of boards to the floor.

Many times I would stay up all night reading by the Aladdin lamp with my feet in the oven while my husband was on night shift. I wasn't alone though. All the other wives were in the same boat and we learned together to take everything in stride. For example, no one had room to entertain very much so we had what we called "progressive dinners" — appetizers at one house, main course at another, and dessert at still another, with everyone, by the way, carrying their own cutlery around with them.

Sometimes the wives were allowed on the station to have a shower or to attend a social function. Another treat was to have a friend with a car drive a group of us to Watson for a shopping spree but that didn't happen too often, because gasoline was strictly rationed.

Looking back, I realize now that we had more fun and comradeship there than at any other place. The elements and the hardships made it difficult to live, but all of these things combined provided an impetus for real friendships, especially among the wives.

One had to be young and in love to make such an adjustment, but all in all, it was one of the happiest times of my life.

Olga Rains
Hyde Park, Ontario

WHEN THE war ended there were thousands of girls like me — those who fell in love with soldiers from another land — who now had to make some decisions about their futures. There were two possibilities of course. One was that the foreign soldier might choose to stay in the country of his wife's birth, which didn't happen too often, and the other was that the new wife would follow her husband to his homeland. That was the road that most took — myself included.

"C" Company of the Highland Light Infantry getting off a barge in Dalfsen, Holland, April 13, 1945. (Photo by Lieutenant D.I. Grant / DND / Public Archives of Canada)

I've always been very proud to call myself a war bride, and so are all the other girls I know who came here at the end of the Second World War. We think of ourselves as a very special group of women who had to suffer a lot to earn the title. All of us had to endure great hardships during the worst war that mankind has ever experienced.

The Dutch people like me, probably suffered as much or even more than the people of any of the other countries because we were invaded early on, and we were subjected to five years of direct oppression and harassment by the German army. That was a horrible period for the Dutch as the Nazis turned their country into what was, more or less, a giant prison camp for all the people of Holland. When the Canadians came and we were finally liberated, there wasn't a person in the whole of Holland who wasn't grateful and madly in love with all things Canadian. The Canadians were our saviours.

The war ended on May 5, 1945, and it was towards the end of that month that I met the man who would later become my husband. It was at the Maple Leaf Club, an organization that was set up by the Canadian army for the entertainment of their troops. The boys could bring in a girl and there would be dances and shows, food and all kinds of other activities for entertainment. The club was in a small town about 15 kilometres from Amsterdam.

I was very young and very innocent and so too, I might add, was this young Canadian soldier who came over to ask me for a dance. He was just as shy as I was, so, when he kept asking me for the next dance and the next, I was delighted. We were both nineteen years old and I can tell you that before the evening was over we were madly in love with each other.

He walked me home when the dance was over and my parents invited him in. We spent the rest of that evening talking and getting to know all about each other. We did this in spite of the fact that he couldn't speak Dutch and the only English I had was the little bit I learned in high school. We managed though, and anyway, I guess love has a language of its own. Before he left that night, he asked my parents if he could come calling the next day.

From that time on we were dating every day and falling more and more in love. I really didn't want to fall in love, because I knew that very soon his regiment would be going back to Canada and I would be left behind with a broken heart. But he kept coming back and I kept going out with him every day despite the warning signals my heart was sending out.

Then, sure enough, the word came through that his regiment would be going home to Canada in three weeks time. I just felt so horrible. I had gone through so many hard experiences in the war, including the loss of several members of my family, that I didn't think I could face one more. He came rushing over to my house in as much distress as I was and said, "We are getting engaged right now and I don't want any arguments. I am also going to apply for a transfer to another regiment so that I can stay here longer and I won't have to go back now without you. I'm also applying to the army for permission to get married."

Talk about getting swept off my feet! One moment I'm all depressed about losing him, and the next thing I know we're engaged and talking about marriage. We had only known each other for three weeks.

My parents, although they liked him very much, thought that this was all happening too quickly and I have to admit that I had a lot of concerns myself, but not enough to say no. My parents thought that maybe he should go back to Canada for a while — six months or so —and then if he felt the same way, and if I did too, he could come back and we could get married then. But no. He didn't want that and I didn't want that. We were in love and we were going to get married. That's all there was to it.

He was able to stay on for a while in Holland with another regiment. We had our engagement period and we were married in December, 1945. Two weeks later, he was shipped back to Canada with his regiment, but I had to wait another seven months before I could join him over there.

That was a very, very difficult time for us but that's the way things were at the time. The soldiers went home first and their brides had to wait for transportation. Some had to wait even longer than I did, some for periods up to a year or more.

When I did arrive over in Canada, finally, my husband and I had a short period of time to get to know each other all over again. This man I was meeting here didn't even look the same as the soldier I had married over there. That one wore a uniform. This one wore a suit. That one lived in an army barracks. This one told me he now had a regular job and he had found an apartment for us to live in. These were all changes that took some getting used to for both of us. This was real life. He had to go to work every morning. From now on there would be no dancing every night. From romance to reality in one short lesson.

I fell in love with the beauty of Canada right away, living as we were in Sault Ste. Marie, Ontario. It's very lovely there, but also very cold in the winter. I hadn't experienced anything quite like that before, 35 and 40 degrees below zero, but you get used to it after a while.

That's the way life was at the beginning: getting used to things; getting used to living with the unfamiliar, including the unfamiliar language and the unfamiliar people. I worried about everything, including, most of all, "Will people over here like me?"

I'm sure it was just as hard for those who were meeting me for the first time too, including my new in-laws.

I came over on a boat that was carrying 500 war brides. The trip across took over two-and-a- half weeks and I was never so glad about anything, before or since, than to walk down that gangplank and put my feet on Canadian soil. I said to myself, "This is it. This is my new beginning. Our new beginning."

I remember the first meal I made for my husband. When he came home from work and sat down to this one-pot dinner of sauerkraut and potatoes and little bits of bacon all mixed together, I could see he was confused by it all. All the things he was used to at a Canadian dinner table were not there. There were no different dishes to sample, just this one pot of something he wasn't used to at all. There were none of the things that his mother used to make. By the same token, I couldn't find in the stores any of the things I liked and remembered from Holland. In time, though, those things sorted themselves out, as I learned to think and cook Canadian.

I cried a lot the first few months I was here. I'd sneak away all by myself and the tears would flow like a river. I'd be lonesome for those parents I had left behind and I would think I would never see them again. I knew they were lonesome for me too. I felt sorry for everybody — for them, for me, for my husband who was trying everything to please me, and also for his parents who were trying so hard to understand what this new daughter-in-law from Europe was all about.

It was a difficult period for everybody but I knew that it would work out all right in the end. I knew that I just had to try a lot harder. There was never a point when I thought it was not going to work and that I should take myself back where I came from. I used to literally grab hold of my own shoulders and shake myself in times of depression and say, "Come on! You wanted this, so get going and get at it!"

What helped me most through that first winter, was the arrival of another war bride from Holland. We were able to get together immediately and more or less cling to each other through the toughest early months. We could cry on each other's shoulders. One day she'd be down in spirits and I'd lift her up. The next day it would be me who'd be down and she'd do the lifting. We'd spend a lot of time together during those long hours when our husbands were away at work.

Once that first winter was past, things got better, and gradually I came to accept that Canada was my new home. Today, I love it very much and I love my life here.

You never forget your past either. I still feel very deeply for Holland and the Dutch people but I wouldn't want to go back to live there. I have maintained contact with many other Dutch war brides across Canada, mostly by mail or an occasional visit at Christmas or something like that but the feeling is more like families getting together rather than a yearning for home. I think everybody likes to stay in touch with their roots. I even wrote a book about my life and the other war brides called "We Became Canadians." I saved all their letters over the years, and I had so much other good material that I felt it should all go into a book.

We held a convention of war brides in April, 1991, and it was a wonderful experience to meet so many others who came to this country the same way that I did, and who went through the same kinds of experiences no matter where they lived in Canada. Some of them are already widows and feeling very lonesome. Seeing other war brides who are in the same position as themselves gives them a new lease on life. Some have gone back to their different countries for visits over the years, but that's all they did — visit. Canada is where their hearts are.

Aili T. Brown
Lindsay, Ontario

MY FIANCÉ, John William Newman, a flying officer with the RCAF, was being posted overseas so, like a lot of young couples in the same situation at that time, we decided to get married before he left. It wasn't too long after the wedding ceremony that he received another notice telling him that the previous order had been rescinded and that he was being sent, instead, to Transport Command, flying to points overseas out of Dorval, Quebec, close to Montreal.

John was a pilot, and the other members of his crew along with their wives and families, also lived in and around the same area, so anytime John and his men were sent out on one of these overseas trips, the lot of us got together so we could worry in a group.

It was a nerve-wracking time for us when they were away. We never even knew where they were going or the length of time they would be away. All of that was top secret and our husbands couldn't even give us a clue. A trip to Egypt and back could take three days while one to Scotland could take six weeks. It all depended on how they could make their way back. You see, they were delivering Canadian planes to overseas locations, leaving them there and then coming back for another assignment. This was what Transport Command was all about.

When our son was born a year later, I didn't even know which country his father was in. That time John returned by way of the Cape of Good Hope. He had been away six weeks and returned when our son was ten days old. Trips could be refused but that was something that these men did not want to do, unless it was a real emergency. Our son arrived almost three weeks early so John didn't even have a chance to make any arrangements to be there.

After the baby's birth I became ill with septicaemia, so my husband and I decided that since he was away so much it would be better if I returned to live with my parents for a while. This was shortly after the new miracle drug penicillin had been discovered so I was lucky. My doctor gave credit to penicillin for saving my life, but even so, the recovery was long and complicated.

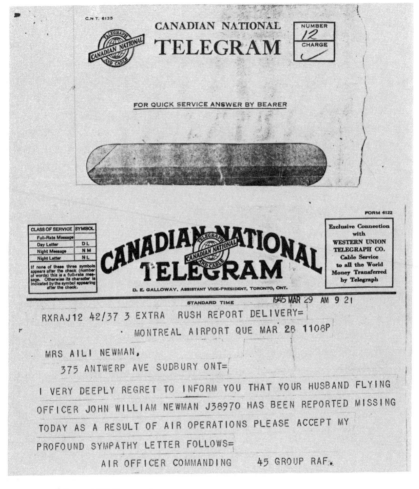

(Courtesy Mrs. Aili Brown)

Things were looking up, however. The war was almost over, and pilots had been told that if they had any civilian jobs to go to they could ask for a discharge. My husband had been offered such a job, so his discharge was set for April 1, 1945.

THE SECRETARY,
DEPARTMENT OF NATIONAL DEFENCE FOR AIR.
OTTAWA, ONTARIO.

REF. YOUR
DATED

R E G I S T E R E D   M A I L

ROYAL CANADIAN AIR FORCE
OTTAWA, Canada, 8th September, 1945.

Mrs. J.W. Newman.

375 Antwerp Avenue,
Sudbury, Ontario.

Dear Mrs. Newman:

It is with deep regret that, in view of the lapse of time and the absence of any further information concerning your husband, Flying Officer John William Newman, since he was reported missing, it is now proposed to take action to presume his death for official purposes.

Will you please confirm by letter that you have not received any further evidence or news concerning him. The presumption of death will proceed after hearing from you, and on completion you will receive official notification by registered letter from the Chief of the Air Staff.

May I extend to you and the members of your family my sincere sympathy in this time of great anxiety.

Yours sincerely,

R.C.A.F. Casualty Officer,
for Chief of the Air Staff.

R.C.A.F. G. 32B
500M-3-43 (3112-3199)
H.Q. 885-G-32B

(Courtesy Mrs. Aili Brown)

Towards the end of March, he received a call from his commanding officer. He was to deliver one more aircraft overseas and he couldn't refuse. His regular crew wasn't available so that meant he would be flying with strangers. He didn't like that and neither did I.

The doctor insisted that I was far too ill for him to leave, and said he would write a letter to the air force headquarters saying so, but my husband worried that it might cloud his honourable discharge.

"Anyway," he said, "It will be my last trip, so I really feel I should go."

Well, it was his last trip. On March 28, 1945, I received that fateful telegram, "Missing. Presumed Dead." Nothing was ever found, only a Mae West life preserver and mail bags presumed to have come from the aircraft.

As I heard the story later, contact had been made with the plane at Prestwick, Scotland, and landing flares had been placed on the runway to guide it in, but it never came. The aircraft just "disappeared."

Much has been written about veterans; those who returned and resumed their lives, those who were killed or injured, those who had been prisoners-of-war, their war brides, even their VLA benefits. But nothing has ever been written about those of us who went through the hell of not knowing, and whose husband, son or father, is one of those who has no known grave.

People like us whose loved ones were "Missing" didn't fit into any veterans group, and because I had moved away from where we were stationed, no padre ever came to call on me.

When the time allotted by the air force for the holding of the veteran's belongings ran out, they were returned to the next-of-kin. In my case, they arrived just in time for Christmas. Perfect timing!

It was very hard not to be bitter. After all, was that last trip he was asked to make really necessary? I can't believe that it was, what with him due to receive his discharge in just a few days. On top of that, everyone knew that the war was about to end and that the Germans would surrender shortly. It was ironic that he should die then, after having survived most of the war.

At that time, widows received a pension of $60 a month while a child received $15. If she remarried, she was paid a year's pension in one lump sum.

When the Queen came to Canada in 1959, to open the Seaway, one of her other duties was to unveil a monument on Green Island across from the city hall in Ottawa. It was dedicated to the memory of those who had died in the air force and had no known grave. Because my husband's name is on that monument, I was invited to the ceremony. Everyone I spoke to that day agreed that the ceremony, for them, took the place of the funeral they had never had the opportunity to attend.

It was devastating therefore, to read afterwards that the monument had been defaced, the doors of the memorial chamber ripped off, the names smeared with crayons and tomatoes and dead fish. Garbage and excrement floated around in the reflecting pool.

After it was repaired, the beautiful bronze globe showing the countries of the world was painted black.

I found this poem at the time. It was written by 11-year-old Mary Esther Wheatley for her father William B. Wheatley. With her permission I will quote it here because it seems so appropriate.

To My Father
They say my daddy died. He did not die.
Why just tonight I heard him fly
above my roof.
Is that not proof
that he's alive and breathing where
the world is safe and free from care?

They say he "folded wings at sea,"
but Daddy would have wanted me
to doubt those things.
You can't fold wings
that for a lifetime have been spread
to fly above a first child's head!

Tonight when all the world is still
I'll lean upon my window sill
and listen for you, Daddy Bill,
and though the whole world fails to note
a fast-approaching Flying Boat
with ghostly motors in its throat,
I'll hear it come and I shall be
proud — proud that you flew east to me
on wings that no one else can see!

Is it any wonder then, that those of us who received one of those dreaded telegrams, morbid as it may seem, actually envy people who can attend a funeral? Those people don't have to go through the rest of their lives looking at faces, wondering, hoping.

Anonymous

FOR ME, the war meant almost six years of living apart from my husband. It meant raising three children on my own, with all that that entails, from feeding and nurturing them to being the disciplinarian in the family. It was six years of being head of the family and assuming total responsibility for three other humans in addition to myself. It may have been a long six years for other women in my position, but for me, those years sped by all too quickly. They were the happiest years of my life. Let me explain.

I was married in 1935, the dead centre of that awful depression. It was a terrible time for the world, but really, it offered nothing that was new to me. Poverty was the normal state of affairs in Glace Bay, Nova Scotia.

I was eleven years old in 1929, when the Great Depression started, but in our family, and in those other families around us, nobody even noticed. We lived in a coal-mining town where having nothing was the norm. We kids didn't dream impossible dreams of fancy cars and exotic vacations like today's young people do. We dreamed of a world where there was always plenty of food, where you could eat whatever you wanted, whenever you wanted. We dreamed about oranges and apples and dinner tables piled high with hot, steaming food. I remember Santa Claus coming to our school one day and asking me what I wanted for Christmas. I couldn't think of anything I wanted except food. "A pound of sausages," I said, "all for myself."

Girls married young; after all, a girl married off was one less mouth to feed. I walked down the aisle with Bobbie at the age of 17, already three months "in the family way." That was okay at that time, just so long as you legitimized it all with marriage vows before the baby arrived. I remember one girl in town getting married one day and becoming a mother the next. That, too, was all right. "God bless you, my child," said the priest to the 15-year-old bride. The next day he said it again to her offspring.

My husband beat me up the night we were married, and he did it every Saturday night for the next four years. When he wasn't blackening my eyes or knocking my teeth out he was getting me pregnant. By the time the war started and we had been married four years, I had three kids, no teeth, and the skin around my eyes had acquired a permanently discoloured look. He had pulled chunks of my hair out so many times I looked like a dog with mange. I was 21-years-old and looked more like 40.

Bobbie joined the army the first day they started recruiting, and he was overseas with the First Division by Christmas, 1939. I prayed that he would get his just rewards quickly, and suffer at least as much pain as he had caused me.

His troop ship hadn't pulled away from Halifax harbour before I started my program of renovations. The government was sending me money regularly, so, by doing a bit of scrimping I soon had a better set of teeth than the ones Bobbie had knocked out of my gums and halfway down my throat. I had my hair cut and styled in the latest fashion, bought makeup and perfume and a few half-decent clothes to wear. I couldn't do any of this when my dear Bobbie was home because, if he saw me wearing a nice dress that some friend had given me out of pity, he'd accuse me of sneaking around looking for other men. Then he'd beat me.

Make-up of any kind, even if I ever had any, was out of the question before he went to the army. There was one time, for example, when a girlfriend came over while Bobby was out getting drunk — something he did every day — and she made up my face. I looked in the mirror and started to cry. I realized I was actually kind of pretty, except, of course, when I opened my mouth, because the teeth were gone by this time. Well, just at that moment Bobbie staggered in the door and when he saw me he flew into another one of his drunken rages. He grabbed hold of my hair with one hand and with the other he started rubbing the lipstick and rouge off my face with a towel. He practically tore off the skin, he was so rough. My girlfriend was screaming at him, the kids were crying and so was I, and he was calling me a whore and everything else he could think of. He finally dropped me down on the floor, grabbed hold of my friend, and literally threw her out the door.

You might wonder why I continued to stay. Well, that's a good question, but the truth is, I had no where else to go. I had three small children and nobody who could take them off my hands even for a short while. My parents hadn't enough to feed themselves and my sisters and brothers who were still at home. Also, now that I was the mother of three, there was no way in the world they could find space for us in their miner's shack. As the saying goes — I had made my bed and now I must lie in it.

Well, he was gone across the ocean now and I didn't have to lie in it anymore and, by God, I was going to make the most of it! Sure as hell, I was going to make up for lost time.

There was an air force base near our town, and there were young guys there from all over the country and all over the world. They used to have regular dances and young women were always welcome. I had one of my young sisters living with me by this time, and there was never any problem for me in having a night on the town. I had a built-in baby sitter. My girl friend and I became regulars at the air force dances and at all the other affairs around town. We soon found out about other shindigs at army or navy bases in nearby cities and towns like Sydney and New Waterford. Pretty soon we were on the go every night of the week, and since I had no man in the forces I wanted to be loyal to, I didn't lack for the kind of loving I had always wanted but never got.

Sure, the neighbours talked and my reputation really bottomed out, but I didn't give a damn. I'd rather be called a party girl than a floor mop, which is all I was before Bobbie went away.

I had a ball for the whole six years he was gone. I knew he'd find out, if and when he survived the war, but I didn't care. I enjoyed every minute of his absence and every new love affair. He didn't write any letters to me and I didn't write any to him. Every week the papers would be full of news about local boys who were killed in action but his name never came up on the lists. I didn't want that bastard back and if it took a war to get him out of my life permanently, well, so be it.

The problem was, though, that the war didn't do it. He came home in August, three months after the action in Europe ended. He came home drunk and full of knowledge about how I had spent the six years of his absence. It didn't matter to him that he had been doing the same sort of thing himself over there.

He tore into the house, and immediately grabbed hold of me, swearing and kicking and choking me. He threw me on the floor and delivered a kick to my face. My denture flew out across the room and he pounced on it, picking it up and jamming it into the coal-burning kitchen range. He gave me several more kicks for good measure and I was soon, mercifully unconscious.

When I came to he was busy stuffing all my dresses and blouses in the stove too. Then he went out in the backyard and soon had a bonfire blazing with every shoe or coat or jacket that I owned. I was left with nothing but the blood-stained dress I had on.

The next week, on the Monday, he went back to his job in the mines. On Tuesday, he was killed in an underground accident. On Wednesday, in that same kitchen stove, I burned his uniform and every other reminder of him that I could find. I burned his boots and his greatcoat in the backyard. The next day, they buried his body with military honours in our local cemetery. They tell me it was a nice ceremony. I couldn't attend because I had nothing to wear.

Bobbie probably doesn't know it, but his army benefits made a new woman of me. I went back to school and took some secretarial and business courses. Eventually, I started a nice little business of my own and gained back my war-tattered reputation. My kids all finished their schooling and one became a Registered Nurse, another a school teacher, and the other became a doctor. They don't remember all that much about their father, and I'm not about to tell them much. When they ask, I just say, "Your father would be so proud of you if he were alive today."

Dorothy Harrison
Mississauga, Ontario

IT WAS the Second World War that brought me to this beautiful
country and I've been living here, with gratitude, since 1944.

I was born and raised in England, and September 1939 found me,
at age 18, living in Baker Street in London.

An aspiring actress, I had just returned from a few months with
the Oxford Repertory company, but was anxious to do something
more useful, so I signed an application to join the W.A.A.F. As the
weeks passed through the winter, I started to assume that my
qualifications for the air force must have been useless or insuffi-
cient, for I was not called.

Meanwhile, my family and I were experiencing London during
the Blitz, often using the air raid shelter in the basement of our
apartment building. It all seemed so unreal, until the night a bomb
fell in the street between our building and Madame Tussaud's
Museum next door. Clouds of dust rose, but we were grateful to
be merely shocked and not hurt. When the "all clear" sounded, I
vividly remember visiting friends whose apartment was a shambles,
and looking out of their windows, I noticed that Tussaud's too was
damaged and a macabre row of waxwork heads was exposed to
view.

Fortunately, our apartment was untouched, but we were notified
by the management that we must evacuate within 30 minutes as
there were several unexploded bombs in Baker Street and Maryle-
bone Road. Our destination then became a concert hall further
down Baker Street where we gathered to discuss whatever plans we
could make. My brother, stepfather and I were dressed, but Mother
had made her departure in a nightdress and gown, bringing along a
small suitcase which held some butter, an orange and her corset.
When we had all finished laughing, my stepfather, who worked in
the War Office and was in uniform, and I decided to return to our
building, to get some suitable clothing for Mother.

By this time, the area was cordoned off but the police finally
agreed to let us enter the building at our own risk. Those wonder-

ful, brave men who worked to defuse and remove unexploded bombs were already at work. God bless them. We Londoners owed them so very much.

I believe it was in May, 1940 that I returned home from a day's work at the film studios — theatrical work was sporadic but I took what I could get — and was told by my mother that a Flight Lieutenant Kerby from Canada had phoned me. As it turned out, he was a friend of my cousin who had settled in Toronto, and she had given him my address.

Hal Kerby, as it turned out, had recently arrived in England and was stationed with an Army Co-operation Squadron, something I learned when we went out for dinner the following evening. Hal was a thoroughly delightful young man and a divine dancer, with a great sense of humour. He told me he had learned to fly when he was 15, and had had to wait until he was 16 to obtain his pilot's licence. He was 23 years old in 1940 when I met him. From that time on, whenever he had leave, he would phone and we would share theatre-going, sightseeing, walks in the park, and, always, dancing.

Meanwhile, having not heard from the w.a.a.f., I joined n.a.a.f.i. (Navy, Army Air Force Institutes). My initial training was at Wellington Barracks and finally in Surrey, where I boarded until my training was complete. After that, I was posted to Cranwell Air Force Station in Lincolnshire, as an Assistant-Manageress to one of the canteens there.

When I reported to the Manageress, she was initially stiff and somewhat leery of this untried newcomer. She was a much older lady. However, I was anxious to learn and willing to work hard, and once she saw that, we soon became good friends. She finally allowed me to serve in the canteen one night.

One of my first customers was a young Cockney lad who came up and asked me for "a cup of Rosie Lee and a wad!" I think he wanted to throw me for a loop, but I figured out that what he wanted was a cup of tea and a rock bun. A short time later he returned for another and I said, "So you like the rock buns?" Leaning towards me in a conspiratorial fashion he said, in his gorgeous Cockney accent, "Not bad, Miss, but would you tell the baker to stand a bit closer when he's throwing the raisins in!" Well, I just loved this and all of the other banter that became a daily experience when the canteen opened.

Some months later I was transferred to another canteen at Cranwell, where I became manageress. Well-versed by this time in all the other facets of running a canteen, my only new chore to learn was "balancing" the safe every night. Mostly it worked but there were those nights when a few pence would elude me and I would wonder, "Why ever did I join?"

This new canteen was further from my sleeping quarters, and as Cranwell was large, it entailed a fair amount of walking. I can recall one overcast morning with low clouds, as I walked to the canteen. Obviously, all flying had been scrubbed, and it was remarkably and unusually quiet. Suddenly, a plane appeared, coming towards me, very low, and then there was machine-gun fire, which startled me into a fast sprint toward the canteen door. It was an enemy plane and all I could think of was, "He's really shooting at me," and he must have been, because I was the only person around. That was scary.

I often think of how great a bunch those N.A.A.F.I. girls were. They came from all walks of life, worked extremely hard, and endured all the vicissitudes of wartime Britain with great good humour. One cook at the canteen came in to the office one day to ask me something, and I noticed for the first time that she wore a wedding ring. When I asked about this she said, "No, I'm not married. I just wear this to keep the flies away." It wasn't hard to figure out what she meant by that.

My only war wound came later, when I was working at a night fighter station. A new barrel of beer had just been placed in position and a helpful sergeant had offered to bung it for me. He raised the wooden mallet, but the head came off and hit me in the forehead, occasioning a trip to the M.O. and a couple of stitches. My one and only wound in "the Battle of the Barrel."

Late in 1942, I left Lincolnshire and returned to London, where I had a job at Drury Lane, checking Concert Party reviews.

One evening when I was out with an American, I met Hal Kerby

again. I hadn't seen him for several months. We lunched the following day, and I soon learned that our original attraction for each
other had not lessened. So, as neither of us was committed to anyone
else, we became engaged. He was due to take a course at the Royal
Air Force Staff College which, on completion, would have put him
into the position of "flying a desk," something he didn't want to do.
Instead of that, he opted for a bombing course.

We were married on January 16, 1943 at St. Marks, in London,
honeymooned a couple of days at Claridges Hotel, and spent a week
in Edinburgh. Upon our return to London, we moved into a flat in
Shepherd's Bush. Hal, who was by then a Wing Commander, left
shortly after for his bombing course at Stratford-on-Avon, and I
returned to my job at Drury Lane.

Hal completed his course and was given three months to form
Squadron 432 RCAF, in Number 6 Group Bomber Command, at
Skipton-on-Swale in Yorkshire. He had it ready in half that time so
that he was able to notify me, in a mere six weeks, that he wanted me
to join him there.

We boarded at a farmhouse not far from the airfield and I
became used to a much different life. I was given the title of
"Comforts Officer" and a small office at the airfield, from which I
dispensed pyjamas, socks, sweaters and so on from the Red Cross
and the many generously donated parcels from Canadians. The
officers' Mess also became a second home to me, and I soon came to
feel all these dear young Canadians were part of my extended
family.

Hal was an extremely popular Commanding Officer who put
himself on "Ops" — flying to battle with his men — more often than
regulations allowed. He was delighted when I confirmed early in
July that I was pregnant, and he immediately sat down and com-
posed a cable to his parents back in Canada, to the effect that "New
Kerby stock will be issued in March of 1944."

On the evening of July 29, 1943, the planes took off for a raid which
I later learned was on the city of Hamburg, and Hal, in his Wellington bomber, was with them.

When Hal was off on a mission at night, my habit was to wake up early and count the number of planes returning to base. Then I would wait for the sound of Hal's car pulling up outside our farm-house, and the sound of the car door being slammed. On the morning of July 30, after counting the planes coming home and waiting for Hal's car door to slam, I heard instead the sound of three doors slamming. I knew immediately what to expect. The acting C.O., along with the adjutant and the padre, told me that Hal's plane was missing and offered what comfort they could.

Sadly, I left the 432 Squadron and all my wonderful friends there, returning to London and a job at Drury Lane. It was three months before the Red Cross were able to confirm to me that Hal was buried outside of Hamburg. Only one crew member of his plane had survived and he was taken as a prisoner-of-war.

The RCAF people were wonderful. They offered me a passage to Canada, which had to be taken before the sixth month of my pregnancy. Because I knew how dreadful had been the loss of their only child, I felt it might be a comfort to Mr. and Mrs. Kerby if I travelled to Canada and had our child in Toronto, to which they agreed. Accordingly, I bade farewell to family and to London.

The ship docked in Halifax on December 10, and once again, the care and the courtesy of the RCAF was apparent, as they shepherded me through all the formalities, and saw that I was ready for the train ride to Toronto. On that trip I never tired of looking through the window at the snow-covered countryside, particularly at night when lights could sometimes be glimpsed. At least, I thought, I am free of the blackouts.

My father-in-law met me at Union Station, and we took to each other right away. We drove to his home and my initial, emotional meeting with Mother Kerby.

Hal's son was born at Toronto General Hospital on March 19, 1944, and is still a comfort to me.

Life does go on, and for me that meant another marriage to another fine Canadian and four more Canadian children. It was the war and the tragedy of war that brought me to Canada in the first place, but it was my choice to remain here and to do so with gratitude.

PART 10

P.O.W.

Perhaps the most controversial decision taken by Mackenzie King's wartime government in Ottawa, was to relocate all Japanese who were living on Canada's west coast. The move was sparked by the Japanese bombing of Pearl Harbour on December 7, 1941, an action that immediately brought the United States into the war. In both Canada and the United States, anyone with Oriental features was a person under suspicion, who couldn't be trusted, whose sympathies must naturally fall in the direction of the homeland of their ancestors.

A state of near-panic and hysteria erupted. If the Japanese had already reaped such destruction on one American base, what would be their next target? Would it be San Francisco on the shores of the Pacific Ocean or would it be Vancouver, a little further up the same coast? Both cities had large populations of Japanese who had lived and worked there for years.

In the climate of war, people in these cities and other coastal areas became totally paranoid about their Oriental neighbours and saw them as potential saboteurs and as enemies in their midst. An immediate clamour was raised to get rid of the Japanese.

It was a time when cooler heads were needed but not found. Japanese communities up and down the West Coast became targets. Japanese property was seized and held in trust while the people were shipped off to holding camps, where they would remain until the war was over.

The sweep-up of the Japanese was complete. It made no difference that many of them were native-born Canadians. To the police and the politicians it was enough that they looked Japanese. They had and deserved no rights.

Nobody in authority worried about such small details. Off they were shipped to makeshift communities in the middle of British Columbia, or California.
   Helen Sakon, who has made her home in northern Ontario ever since those unhappy days, was born in Canada but lived out the war in a camp for aliens, because her parents were born in Japan.

Helen Sakon
Kapuskasing, Ontario

AT THE time of Pearl Harbour, I had been married for some time to a man who worked in the bush for a lumber company. We considered ourselves ordinary working-class Canadians. We lived in a small company-owned house, had one small baby, with another on the way, very few luxuries, and no knowledge of world politics whatsoever. We had hopes and dreams, the same as those enjoyed by any young couple, and we looked forward to a happy life together. That's what it was like for us when Pearl Harbour was bombed — the start of a four-year nightmare for us.

I think it was on the second or third day after Pearl Harbour that we were all ordered to leave our homes on Vancouver Island and go to Vancouver on the mainland. My husband and I had no idea what this was all about. We really didn't. The authorities just came to our door and told us to take everything we owned and get onto the boat to the mainland. This was an order which applied to all Japanese families, so there was a great deal of confusion and crying as we all hurried to pack and get things down to the dock.

I considered myself Canadian, and why not? I was born in Vancouver. I couldn't understand what was going on at all. My husband was born in Japan, but he also considered himself Canadian. He'd lived on Vancouver Island a long, long time and would have become a citizen except for the fact that in the years leading up to the war, it was very hard for Japanese in British Columbia to become naturalized. There was a lot of prejudice.

Exactly one week after Pearl Harbour we were in Vancouver where nobody, including the government, knew what to do with us.

We were frightened, but so were ordinary Canadians who lived on the coast. They were worried about invasion, I suppose, and Japanese submarines, which were said to be operating off the coast. Anybody who looked Japanese became an immediate suspect.

Anti-Japanese propaganda filled the newspapers, and the average west coast Canadian was being educated to fear "the enemy in their midst." As far as they were concerned, I suppose, every Japanese they saw was out to murder them. It was so bad that any Oriental was afraid to venture out on the streets.

To show it was doing something, I guess, the government passed all kinds of orders-in-council. One of these said that anyone born in Japan would be sent to road camps away from the coast. My husband was sent to one in the Rockies, a place called Lampier, while I was left behind with our three-month-old baby. We were herded with thousands of other Japanese into the Pacific National Exhibition grounds, where each family was given a space barely big enough to spread a mattress.

Families who came from Vancouver Island were put into buildings where they show cattle during the Fair. I remember it was all concrete and very unpleasant, especially with me having a small baby and expecting another. Those who had parents living in Vancouver could stay in their family homes, but even though my parents had a house, I chose to stay in the barns at Hastings Park because I wanted to be there when my husband came back from the road gang.

By this time, they had a system for families living in the park to be shipped out first to the ghost towns and camps in the interior of British Columbia. Our baby was due in October, so I wanted all of that moving around to be over and done with so as to be settled before the baby came.

In the meantime, they began evicting Japanese families from their homes in Vancouver. My mothers and brothers and sisters received their orders to get out by a certain date. It was such a mixed-up time. I heard that my husband was shifted from the road gang to a place in the interior called New Denver, where he was put to work building places for Japanese families.

It was the churches in Canada who first interceded in all this madness. They raised quite a big fuss about families being broken up and separated, and it was also the churches that had a lot to do with having the men brought back from the work parties and reunited with their wives and children in these settlements.

It was a good thing I was so busy with the baby during that period, as it kept my mind off these other troubles. They took our cameras and our radios, and they kept searching for guns, which nobody had anyway.

This was the second search they made, because even before we were allowed into Hastings Park, we had to go through a process where we registered all our belongings with something called the Custodian of Alien Property. We were told that all our property would be there for us when the war was over.

It wasn't, of course. While we were in the camp, we received a letter from the Custodian that said my mother's house had been sold, and that they would hold the proceeds of the sale for us until after the war. It had been sold all right, but for a fraction of its worth. They never asked if they could sell it — they just did. There were so many things that were done and even today I can't understand why. I keep telling myself it was wartime, and war brings on irrational behaviour, especially as there was so much propaganda plastered around Vancouver.

That town was full of posters warning against spies, and there were caricatures of sinister-looking Japanese faces. Emperor Hirohito of Japan was depicted as a monster trying to scoop up Canada in his hands.

I must say, though, that the RCMP, who were in charge of looking after us, treated us kindly. First, we had to register and get a number. Mine was 02371, and that number had to be on everything we owned. We were at a place called Lemon Creek and we had to report to the RCMP once a month. In those ghost towns and camps every resident was expected to do this.

There were 2,000 of us there in these little pre-fab houses at Lemon Creek, and if there was less than four in a family, your house had to be shared with another family. We had an older couple and their daughter with us. It was only one big room and a wall down the middle, with us on one side and them on the other. There was an outhouse in the yard, and there was a pump where we all went for our water. Often there would be a quarter-inch of ice on the floor in the morning, as the wood stove we had would go out while we slept. We lived there from 1942 to 1946.

We were the last ones to leave when the war ended. We were given the choice of going to Japan or staying in Canada — east of the Rockies. They wouldn't permit us to go back to the West Coast because, we were told, the people there didn't want us. Then stories began that the people in eastern Canada didn't want us either, and that if we went there we would get awful treatment. We decided then to go to northern Ontario, where we found that people opened their hearts and couldn't have been nicer to us.

While we were in that camp for all those years, I decided that I had no choice but to make the best of it. I was busy with the children, and my husband worked in the bush, as he had done before we were incarcerated. He wasn't paid much, but it was enough to get by on. The camp was in the Slocan Valley, which is very beautiful and we grew very fond of it. They told us, however, that we couldn't stay there after the war, so we had better start making other plans.

Many chose to go to Japan, terribly disillusioned and bitter because of the way they were treated in a country they had come to love before the war interrupted their lives. They didn't stay there, though. Most came back to Canada because they found they weren't Japanese anymore. They couldn't stand the style of life there anymore. It seemed so completely foreign to them. They found they were now Canadians, no longer Japanese. That was especially true for those children who were born here.

In my case, having been born and brought up here, but being treated like the enemy, I suppose I could feel very bitter. But what good would that do? When the madness of war was over, we were able to rebuild our lives in a lovely community in another part of the country. To dwell on those things would only bring more unhappiness.

Bill Ostlund
Regina, Saskatchewan

I ENLISTED in the RCAF in November, 1941, anxious, like everybody else, to get over there and be part of it but it wasn't as easy as all that. For the next several months, it was all training right here in Canada — in Toronto, more training in Winnipeg, and finally, a gunnery course in McDonald, Manitoba.

Then, instead of instant action, it was more training at Stormy Downs in Wales and in England at the Operational Training Unit (OTU) at Gayden, Warwickshire. That was the way it went until August, 1943, when I finally received a posting to Middleton St. George and Squadron 428, known as the Ghost Squadron. Nobody could ever say we weren't well-trained.

After that, I was posted to 429 Squadron and a new pilot, Flight Lieutenant Stephens of Toronto. We made two successful trips to Berlin, but on September 6, 1944, on what was to be our final bombing trip, our plane was set on fire over Leipzig, Germany. On orders from the pilot to abandon plane, I grabbed my parachute and rotated my tail gunner's turret to the escape hatch position, but in doing so I lost my oxygen mask. I passed out soon after I jumped, as we were at 25,000 feet. Still on the way down, I came to and landed on a frozen summer fallow field with a broken ankle and several bad cuts. I lay there for three hours, until I was spotted by a German guard who approached me with his gun. I willingly raised my hands and when he saw that I couldn't walk, he returned to a farmhouse about a quarter of a mile away and brought back a wheelbarrow to haul me back. From there I was taken to Berlin, along with some other air force crews who had been shot down in the same vicinity the night before. Some of these guys were in pretty bad shape, broken bones, some badly burned and another who died before he made it to the Berlin hospital. I learned later that I was the only member of our Bomber crew to escape.

At the Berlin hospital my ankle was set and placed in a cast, and after about a week I, along with the other prisoners, was taken away to the Interrogation camp near Frankfurt where I spent three miserable days being slapped around and questioned. Then it was on to a holding camp in Frankfurt, where I joined several more Canadian air force POWs. We were loaded into a boxcar destined for another camp in Lithuania. Half of us in the boxcar were POWs, and the others were German guards who delighted in making life for us as miserable as possible. They wouldn't even let us out of the boxcar to relieve ourselves whenever the train stopped, so you can imagine what that car was like after we'd been in there for a week. In fact, when we did get to Lithuania, I was hospitalized for another week. While I was in there with the broken ankle and other things I had picked up aboard the train, I wasn't allowed to have a cane or a stick to support myself, so I ended up having to be carried from one place to another, usually by one of the other patients who was in slightly better shape than I was.

Life in a prison camp is completely foreign to anything one has ever experienced before. First of all, there is the loss of freedom and the knowledge that your life is hemmed in by barbed wire, guards, and guard dogs. There is never enough of anything, including soap, clothing, water, and food. Thanks to the Red Cross, the food situation was not too bad unless the parcels got held up by train wrecks or heavy Allied bombing attacks. When we had to get by on German rations we had to make do on a couple of slices of heavy dark bread once a day, and a small bit of horse meat. Along with this we'd get some contaminated sauerkraut that had been sitting in a container left right out in the open so that it was usually full of worms. We didn't throw it away though. We'd just boil it an extra long time and close our eyes as we ate. The Red Cross was our true salvation.

In a POW camp, the smallest amount of space around one's person becomes terribly important and privacy totally disappears. On arrival at any camp, the first thing you hear from the German guards is the only phrase they know in English, "For you the war is over," after which, in a dazed and bewildered condition, the prisoner goes through endless interrogation. They use all the tricks in the books in their attempt to extract information of some military importance. It isn't until they are sure that you have nothing of value to impart that you are finally released into the general population of the camp, where one's prime purpose in life is just to survive as best one can.

You learn to obey all of the rules, at least to give the appearance of obedience, and you learn to cope with the endless boredom. Also you learn to hope, and to enjoy the smallest of pleasures, like a small piece of chocolate from somebody else's parcel from home. You learn to share your little pleasures with others, including your own parcels from home, and even your personal mail. Mail of any kind, not just parcels, was always eagerly anticipated — even other people's mail. Letters were often passed around and shared. It was amazing how much a letter from someone you didn't know, written to someone else, could be enjoyed. I guess it was kind of a confirmation that the life we used to know was still going on, even though we were no longer part of it. Some of those letters were sad. Some were optimistic, and some were just plain hilarious, mainly because those who had written them had no real conception of what life in a prisoner-of-war camp was really like, and also because some of the things they wrote were unintentionally funny. Here are a few examples:

Dear Son,

The first contingent of repatriated POWs arrived home today, terribly maimed. Hope you'll be with the next lot.
　　(POWs judged by German doctors to be medically unfit for further military duty, and therefore no longer a threat, were sent back to their home countries in regular prisoner exchanges.)

Dear Son,

I am so glad you have met such a nice set of boys. I do hope the Germans keep you there.

Dear Son,

The German POWs over here are issued flannels to play tennis in. Are you?

Dear Son,

Hope you are working. It will keep your mind off the war.

Dear Son,

You have done something in this war that I never done in the last.

Dear Son,

I wasn't home when word arrived that you were missing and that you will agree was a blessing.

Dear Son,

I am enclosing a Postal Order so that you can buy yourself some chocolate.

Dear Son,

Joe is in Stalag Vɪɪ B. I hope you can pop around and see him soon.

Dear Son,

We had a real old-fashioned Xmas. Plenty of blancmange, jelly and crackers, a Xmas tree, Xmas pudding and turkey. I hope you enjoyed yourself too.

From some of the letters, one got the idea that the writers felt we had been the winners of a holiday prize in a game of chance. We kept a regular list of the best ones and added to it daily after the mail was distributed.

I've got a grandmother in Germany. Have you met her?

How are your mother and father? I haven't seen them lately.

Are the German girls good dancers?

Hope you are having a good time but I expect it's a little boring on the inside looking out.

Can you buy beer over there or is it all wine?

I was so glad you were shot down before flying became dangerous.

Have you seen the latest film, "Stage Door Canteen"?

I wrote you last week. Nothing came of it, so here I am again.

Letters from wives could sometimes be very innocent and naïve, and they could often be devastating.

Darling,

I've just had a baby, but don't worry. The father is an American officer and he will be sending you cigs every week.

Darling,

I hope you are behaving yourself at the dances and not drinking too much.

In a letter from a girlfriend:

My sympathy is with all you boys. This is really why I am writing.

Sweetheart,

Last week I took your mother to the movies and a Canadian soldier tried to get off with her.

Darling,

Please write more often as I adore the way you print.

Dear John,
You were missing a month so I got married.

Darling,
What would you like in your first parcel?

Darling,
I hope you are still true to me.

Darling,
Be home soon, won't you?

Darling,
I hope you haven't transferred your affections.

Darling,
In your May letter you asked for slippers. What colour would you like?

Darling,
The sandals you asked for are hard to get, so I am sending you ration coupons to get your own.

One POW received a roll-neck sweater in a Red Cross parcel, so he wrote to the donor whose name was inside to thank her. Here's the reply he received from her:

I'm sorry to hear you received the pullover. It was meant for someone on active service.

Nobody will ever be able to imagine how much laughter those writers unwittingly gave to the boys behind the barbed wire, where laughter was a precious commodity. I think if they knew how much we were cheered by the unintentional humour, they wouldn't be offended that their letters were passed around.

One POW got this letter from an ex-girlfriend, and I think you'll agree it's pretty amazing:

You'll be surprised to hear I'm getting married on November 30, but you can look forward to our happy reunion when you come home. It will be too bad if my husband doesn't agree, because I'm going to see you anyhow. If he's away we'll stay at my home, but if he's home we'll go to Mother's. I can go on holidays and not tell him why. We'll give the family five dollars cash to keep their mouths shut.

As you can see, mail was often the high point of our lives. There were other things to do too, of course. Some of the guys spent a lot of their time painting or learning to paint with materials supplied by the Red Cross. Some tried their hand at writing, and just about everybody was secretly planning a way to escape. A few actually did make it, but not very many. The camps I was in were always surrounded by barbed wire, sometimes electrified, and were patrolled by guards and vicious dogs. One or two made it out by concealing themselves in service vehicles that passed out the front gates, but the way they inspected anything that went though the gates, those few escapes were miraculous. A few tunnels were successful, but most were discovered before they were finished. That didn't deter the inmates from starting a new one right away.

One early morning in January, 1945, we were told that the Russians were approaching our camp from the east, so the Germans lined us all up and started us on a road march in the opposite direction. Our destination was to be another camp near Bremen, Germany, but it was slow going in the middle of winter; it was very cold. It was impossible to make much more than a few miles a day. The first night we were herded inside an old church and I'll never forget how cold that was, with no blankets or anything else to cover us up.

That's the way it was during the whole week we were on that

march. The only thing that was good about it, was the fact that the guards who were with us were older men, and they didn't like the experience any more than we did. When we finally arrived in Bremen, and what we thought was the end of our ordeal, we were put out on the road again towards another camp. This time they allowed us to sleep in the straw stacks at farms along the way, although one night, one of our fellows was shot by one of the guards for wandering too far from his assigned space. Luckily, the shot only got him in the leg, but that didn't excuse the guard in our books, because he knew that the guy was just wandering around and not trying to escape.

In the meantime, my commission came through, so that my next trip was by passenger train rather than boxcar, and this took us through Berlin to Sagan, Germany, a camp made famous by the movie *The Great Escape*. On it went — to camps in Fallinbostel and Lubeck, until May 2, 1945 when we were liberated by the British army. I will never in my life forget that day. It all happened without a fight. The German soldiers joined in with the prisoners and cheered the British troops as they came through. They were as happy as we were that it was all over. Some of our fellows managed to scrounge some booze with raids on local wine cellars, and we just had ourselves one wonderful time. I got my hands on a German army truck, and you can imagine how wonderful it was for me and the other prisoners who piled into it to drive into the centre of Lubeck in triumph.

Very soon we were flown back to good old England where we were greeted with good food, showers, new uniforms and some welcome backpay. It wasn't long before I was on a boat to Canada, along with a lot of other POWs.

Got my discharge, got me a job and a wife, and I'm still going strong. On April 1, 1991, I celebrated my 78th birthday.

In 1944, 76 Allied officers crawled through a narrow 340-foot tunnel in a bid to escape imprisonment in a Nazi prisoner-of-war camp. That tunnel, and the mass bid for freedom which become the basis for a famous Hollywood movie, **The Great Escape,** *was designed by camp inmate Wally Floody, a* *captured fighter pilot from Toronto. Wally Floody was a tall, dark, amiable man who survived the war, was successful in business, popular with all who knew him and modest about the part he played in one of the best-known escapades of the Second World War. I met Wally several times, and whenever he could be persuaded to talk about himself and the war, he always made it clear that he never considered himself any kind of hero.*

Wally Floody
Toronto, Ontario

I JOINED THE RCAF in 1940 and it wasn't long after, that I, like a lot of other Canadian boys my age, was flying Spitfires in Europe. In fact, it was a Spitfire I was flying when I got shot down over northern France in the fall of 1941. I was able to parachute out of my plane, but was almost immediately captured when I hit the ground. I landed in a little village in front of a small house and, in a way, it was kind of humourous. Here was this strange man dropping out of the sky, and you'd expect the people to be frightened or even hysterical, but that's not what happened at all.

A little old lady opened the door of her small home and came out with a bottle of cognac in one hand and a glass in the other, and poured me a welcoming drink. By this time, I knew I'd had it anyway because I could see the German soldiers all over the place, and before I had properly swallowed the cognac they were closing in on me. I handed the glass back to the lady and thanked her in my high school French. She just smiled, filled up the glass again and passed it back to me. I swallowed that one pretty fast, I can tell you, because by that time the Germans had a firm grip on me and were leading me off in the direction of one of their armoured trucks. I ended up at prison camp Stalag Luft 3 in what is now part of Poland.

I wasn't too worried or upset by any of this, because in the first place, I was delighted to be alive and, after a few days at Stalag Luft 3, I started to get into the same routine as all the other guys who had been there much longer.

I had always accepted the doctrine that if ever I should be captured by the enemy it was my duty to try to escape, so before long I was involved in a plan to build a tunnel. The other guys in on this plan found out that before the war I had been a miner in Timmins and Kirkland Lake in northern Ontario, so they just figured that naturally, I would know all there is to know about digging underground. Before I knew what was happening, they made me supervisor of the whole operation.

Most of the other men were English, and for some strange reason these Brits laboured under the impression that anyone who is a miner must therefore be an engineer. I tried to explain that there was a big difference between a barefaced miner and a mining engineer, but they just couldn't see to get that through their heads. Anyway, Wally Floody, hardrock miner, ended up as supervisor and boss of the project, whether he liked it or not.

Now the plan we eventually came up with was to dig three tunnels code-named Tom, Dick, and Harry, so that if the guards found one, we'd still have two others left. If they found two we'd still have one. We figured the odds on them finding all three were pretty remote.

It turned out to be an immense mining operation involving literally hundreds of camp inmates.

The biggest problem of all, of course, was in the area of security. Then came the problem of getting rid of the sand as the tunnels went forward. After that, we had to make plans for what we'd have to do if we did get out — the passports, the papers, the uniforms, the civilian code, the compasses; all of this had to be done by other prisoners. We had to find these people places to work at these jobs and make sure of tight security while they were working.

Also, as you can well appreciate, none of this could be put on paper because you couldn't take the chance that the Germans would find it during one of their searches. All of our discussions and planning had to be done in the open air so the Germans couldn't overhear us, and each person, including me, was only allowed to talk about his own specific little part in what was a very large operation.

Everything down to the smallest detail was planned by a committee of the best brains in the camp, and it still amazes me how well those plans progressed. Even the date of the breakthrough and the spot where that would happen was known.

The date for the mass escape of 200 men was set for the night of March 25, 1944.

As it turned out, there were only 76 men who actually made their way through the tunnel to the outside that night, and to my mind, there were two reasons for this smaller number.

First, I think was that our engineering had been rather amateurish. They had given me a figure of 340 feet to the trees beyond the fences, but we found out by sad experience that 340 feet took us to a point that was 20 feet short of the trees. What this meant was that people emerging from the tunnel had to be much slower and more careful, because with no cover from the trees they were right out in the open and had, therefore, to watch the guards very carefully.

The second reason for the lower number of escapees, was that right in the middle of our operation there was a big bombing raid nearby and all the lights at the camp, including those in our tunnel, went out. That will give you an idea though, how sophisticated our operation had become. Imagine — electricity lights! However, when the bombs put our tunnel into darkness we had it loaded with men who had never been down in a hole in their lives before, and they became terrified. We had a severe epidemic of claustrophobia. You couldn't blame them, but the result was that there was no way we could get them to move at all in that total and frightening darkness. That slowed everything down completely.

The ironic part of all this is that I wasn't even there the night of the escape, because the German guards had discovered and destroyed one of my tunnels a few weeks previously, and about 20 of us who were suspected of being involved were transferred immediately out to another prison camp a few miles away. Naturally I felt devastated by this turn of events, but, as it turned out later, I was among the fortunate.

Of the 76 men who emerged from the tunnel to "freedom" that night, 18 were recaptured, 50 were executed and just three made it back to England. The other five were returned to the prison population.

I spent four years in those dreary camps, but I often think that the experience I had in building those tunnels had a profound effect on the rest of my life. I guess the biggest plus, as I look back on it, is that digging those tunnels gave us a sense of purpose. You had a sense that there was something that had to be done, and everybody there was doing it together.

When the war was over I felt that after those years in Stalag Luft, I was exhilarated that I'd made it, and I knew that nothing in my life could ever be any worse. I felt that everything was going to be upwards and onwards from then on. In my opinion it has been.

Wally Floody died in 1989 at age of 71.

There are two names that bring about instant recall of the Second World War for anyone who was alive at that time. Their voices offered us constant reassurance that all was not lost, even at the worst of times, and that there would be better days tomorrow. One of these voices belonged to a world leader and the other to a popular singer of the day. One of these voices shouted out defiance, "We will fight them on the beaches!" and the other told us that sometime soon "There'll be bluebirds over the white cliffs of Dover," and that, "The lights of London" will shine again.

Winston Churchill and Vera Lynn played vastly different roles in winning the war, but in our hearts it all amounted to the same thing. They both had the same message — we couldn't and we wouldn't lose. "Winnie" and Vera symbolized our hopes and our dreams and both became icons of the victory that surely would come. They were one with all of us on the Allied side, regardless of nationality.

I cried along with millions of others when Churchill died. For many of us, he was the greatest man of the twentieth century. I travelled to England to visit his grave shortly after he died. Standing bare-headed, on a typically English misty day, I bowed my head and said a belated thank you to the man who had given us the resolve to continue and to win.

Vera Lynn was no less a hero for me and millions of others. There was something about the sound of her voice which told us that we could never be

*defeated, no matter how badly things were going at the moment, even, for
example, during the worst days of the Battle of Britain. They may have us
down for a bit, Vera's songs would say, but we'll come out all right in the end.
That was her message, just when it was most needed.*

*After the war I met and talked with Vera Lynn on several occasions, and I
was pleased that she was just the way I hoped she would be. I never met
"Winnie" but I did meet his grandson and namesake, Winston S. Churchill. It is with those two interviews I would like to close off this book of wartime
memories.*

Vera Lynn
London, England

WHEN THE war first broke out I was in my very early twenties, and I
had been broadcasting regularly with various bands and on various
programs. Almost immediately after the declaration of war I started
to get a lot of letters from listeners requesting certain songs for their
loved ones who had already gone into the forces. There were so
many of these letters, that I suggested to the BBC that I do a special
program that would handle these requests. It started for me just as
simply as that — a request program from home where I would tell
them little bits of news — that we were okay in London, telling them
about their wives, about their new babies and just chatty little things
that I would intersperse with the songs they requested. It was
basically a program to entertain the boys who were away from
home. It seemed to fill a spot that needed to be filled at that time,
and it just went on from there.

They wanted to hear the same songs over and over again: "We'll
Meet Again," "The White Cliffs of Dover," "Yours" and many
others. These were all songs that I had the good fortune to have
associated with me. I was always very careful about the songs I
chose. I'd study the lyrics very carefully. The ones I would choose to
do were always lyrically, very optimistic, and they all spoke of
loyalty, love and better days ahead.

I suppose when one has a certain style of song, one looks for certain patterns, especially in the lyrics. I know I did. I wanted songs that would speak to the servicemen and give them the messages that their wives and sweethearts were unable to deliver directly. I was a go-between, really.

Looking back on those days, I was very fortunate to have had the opportunity to play a role in boosting wartime morale, and to have reached the hearts of so many people, not just the serving members of the armed forces, but also the families they left behind. It is a great joy to me now, so many years after the war, to think that they've stayed so loyal. I've been to Canada many times since then, and wherever I perform, the audience is made up, in large part, of those men and women who became familiar with me during the war.

Their loyalty is not just to me but to the memories of those times when we all went through a great deal together. We did experience it all together, because I wanted to be where they were — near the battle lines, in their camps, in the hospitals or wherever they were. I knew their loneliness and I knew the fears they were experiencing, and I felt that if I could do anything to alleviate those fears, that was a way for me to serve my country during those dangerous times.

When I first started singing to them, I was engaged to be married, so I could appreciate what it would be like to be separated, and in some cases, the separation would be forever.

I was constantly travelling around, and when the raids came along at night we would just pause for a little while to let people go out to the shelters if they wished, and then we would just carry on with the show afterward.

Because I lived outside on the edges of London, I used to have to stay overnight in the theatre sometimes, and try to find a safe little spot to curl up and go to sleep until the All Clear was sounded. It was often quite an adventure, especially if the bombing started while I was driving home in my little Austin Ten. The sirens would go and the bombs would start falling, and I would never be sure which way to turn or where to go. You could never be quite sure if you were driving away from the bombs or right into them. However, it would never occur to you to quit because everyone in Britain was going through the same kind of thing. My job just happened to be the boosting of morale. Other people had equally important jobs.

I always seemed to be getting caught in the middle of air raids no matter where I would be — in the centre of the city, in the suburbs or in another town altogether. Sometimes, I used to think that the very act of me stepping into my Austin was the signal for them to start bombing. I'd be driving along and then the raid would start and I'd always have to make a decision — should I just keep going or should I stop the car and wait for the bombs to start falling on me, or should I get out of the car and roll myself up in something in the gutter?

I remember driving home one night through a thick fog and there were no lights, of course, in blacked-out Britain. Cars weren't allowed to have their lights on and, in fact, there were no lights anywhere. Right in the middle of all this, while I was going over top of a funny little bridge, the sirens started to go and the bombs started falling. It was a most uncomfortable scene. I couldn't see where to go or what to do, so I just kept going until I reached home. I just prayed that I would be all right. What else could I do?

I also spent a lot of time going around visiting the boys in hospitals. That was hard, because some of them would be horribly wounded — the kinds of wounds that if they survived at all, they would suffer from for the rest of their lives. Most of them were just youngsters who would, in normal times, just be starting to live their adult lives, dating girls, beginning new jobs and things like that. To say that I found it very depressing is just too minor an explanation. It was heart-breaking really, because one felt so useless. There was I going out thinking I was doing something by singing to them but, in the end, what could I really do?

There was a certain something in those days that we don't seem to have anymore. Nobody was fighting for themselves like they do today in modern life. There was this feeling that everybody was working and fighting for the common good. I always had the feeling at that time, that everybody seemed to sincerely care about what was happening to everybody else, whether it was out in the fighting areas or whether it was at home. Each and every person seemed as though they just couldn't do enough for the other person.

I remember doing a concert in Canada a few years ago and there were, surprisingly, quite a lot of young people there. A group of them came up to me after the show and several of them were in tears. They said that they had been so moved by the songs, and it had had a great effect on them just to be sitting there with all those older people who were in effect reliving such an important part of their lives. They said that they could understand for the first time what it must have been like for those who had gone through that war. Music seems to be the key that unlocks the memory box. Many young people today seem to sense that there was something very special about those years of the Second World War, when so many were truly united in a common cause.

It's always a joy for me to come over to Canada and recreate those days of so long ago. The men who served over there always come up to me and say hello, and tell me that they saw me in such and such a place and remind me of certain things that have been buried away in my mind for such a long time. They gave me as much joy as I gave them. Memories are so precious.

Winston S. Churchill
(Grandson of "Winnie")
London, England

I THINK one could make a case that had it not been for my grandfather, Britain would have had to negotiate peace with Hitler, which would have been the thin edge of the wedge leading to ultimate surrender by the Allies. There would have been no D-Day and no liberation of Europe, because it would have been quite impossible to mount the Normandy invasion of a million or more men from Canada or the United States and other countries. The swastika could now be flying over the houses of Parliament, Westminster and over all the capitals of Europe. Even now, I shudder to think of the horror of such a scenario.

My grandfather stood firm against any negotiated peace settlement with the Nazis. He had nothing but disdain for them, and had absolutely no trust in anything they had to say. Their whole history was one of broken promises, so that even though there were other men of influence who wanted to negotiate peace when things were going very badly for us, he refused to consider it at all.

There was a magical quality about him, the very sound of his voice and that bulldog look of his face gave heart to the cause all over again, when people on the Allied side were feeling at their very lowest. We would win that war. We had to win. He had a tremendous inner confidence. He just knew that we could stand firm on our island, provided we had the spirit, and he was convinced that we had.

Just to give an example of that spirit, in the summer of 1940, within a month of my grandfather becoming prime minister, Hitler was preparing his invasion forces. They were massing in the Channel ports facing Britain, large numbers of landing craft and ships of all kinds, along with an invasion army, all of which Hitler called Operation Sea Lion. This was in June, and at that time my mother was six months pregnant with me. My father was away, and so she was living with my grandparents at 10 Downing Street.

One evening as they were dining — my grandfather, my grandmother and my mother — there occurred a long and unaccustomed silence in the middle of the meal. My grandfather looked up and turned to both my grandmother and my mother and said,

"If the Germans come, I'm counting on each of you to take at least one with you before you go."

My mother said, "But Papa, I don't have a gun and I wouldn't know how to use it if I did have one."

"Ah, but my dear," grandfather replied, "you can use a carving knife," brandishing his fist high as if he were holding one.

The fact is that if you have that sort of determination, that if every man and woman in the country is going to take one German invader with him before they surrender, it makes the country unconquerable.

That was the kind of spirit with which he inspired people. You know, the truth is, that *he* was unconquerable. His spirit was unconquerable. Mother often told me that even in the darkest days of the war, he would be there shouting out defiance at Hitler, sometimes to a completely empty room.

The strange thing is that he never gave himself the credit that everyone else believed he deserved. Even at the end of the war he once remarked, "I've never accepted what so many people have kindly said — that I won the war. It was the British nation dwelling around the globe, in countries like Canada and Australia and New Zealand, that had the lion's heart. I just had the good fortune to be called upon to give the roar."

Well, there's no doubt that he was the lion's roar and the bull-dog's heart, too.

I wasn't born until 1940, the year of the Battle of Britain, so for those early memories I go mainly on the things that my mother told me, but I was so interested in wanting to know all about him that sometimes I have the feeling that I can remember everything from the day I was born. My earliest actual memory of him, and this surprises a lot of people, was the time that he scoured the shops of London to find a second-hand model railroad set for me. There were no toy shops operating at that time during the war, so he would go searching out these second-hand places and pawn shops trying to find a set of trains for me for my second birthday. He eventually found one, and I can still recall him getting down on the floor on his knees with me setting up the track. When he saw that there were two little clockwork locomotives, his overdeveloped sense of mischief got the better of him. He said, "Winston, why don't you wind one up and I'll wind the other up, and we'll put them back to back and set them off in opposite directions so that we can have a crash."

He was full of that kind of fun. He was a real grandfather in every sense of the word, despite the tremendous responsibilities he was carrying as leader of the country and the free world.

My principal memories of him are of the years immediately following the war. He had been unceremoniously dismissed from office during the very hour of victory by the British electorate. I remember my grandmother saying to him, "Perhaps my dear, it's really a blessing in disguise." He wasn't having any of that. He said, "If it is, it's certainly disguised very effectively." I think my grandmother was very probably right, because he had put his all into defeating Hitler and winning that war. It was a long six-year slog for him. He was, after all, already sixty-five and had qualified to draw the old age pension before he even became prime minister. It gave him a breathing space and a chance to retreat to his country home at Chartwell in Kent to write his famous war memoirs.

That's where I really got to know him well. My parents' marriage, like so many wartime marriages, hadn't survived the war. My father put it very well when he said that it was a marriage made and broken by Hitler. My parents married within six weeks of the start of the war, and within three weeks of their meeting. With him in North Africa and then being parachuted into Yugoslavia to fight with the partisans and Marshal Tito in the hills of Bosnia, their marriage didn't have a chance to blossom.

As a result, I spent much more time with my grandparents than I would otherwise have done. As far as I was concerned, my grandfather was not an ex-prime minister or Leader of the Opposition, he was the local bricklayer. For two hours each afternoon, he took a break from his writings to go down to the gardens where he was in the middle of constructing an absolutely huge brick wall around his kitchen garden. He was the bricklayer, and I was the brickee's mate. We spent many a happy hour together there. He was a wonderful man.

Heritage

I picked up a paper,
'Twas just yesterday,
And I read of the war,
Of the blood and the fray;
And I saw in the corner
An item which said,
"Private John Simpson
Of this city, dead.

"Killed in action," it added,
"No relative known;
Age: twenty years,

An orphan, alone.''
I passed it by quickly
With only a glance:
Another ship's lost
From a convoy to France!

But when I had finished
My look at the news,
Back I lay in my chair
And my mind came to muse
On the heritage left
To this country by those
Who had given their lives
In the service they chose.

If they gave their lives
To save your way of life,
Are you doing enough
To keep freedom's sharp knife
Poised ready to cut
Any bonds that betray
The freedoms at home
Bought by death far away?

Let's face it: this country,
Now grown to be free,
By freedom alone
Finds its own destiny.
Check foreign control;
Work for peace as in war;
Seek deep in your vastness
For riches of ore;

Push northward your frontier;
Drill oft for your oil;

With care choose your crops;
Keep a vigorous soil;
But, above all, be sure
You leave to your heirs
A country where freedoms,
Once yours, are still theirs.

W. Ralph Moxley